D0231530

YOUNGER BROTHER,
YOUNGER SON

BY THE SAME AUTHOR

The Prince, the Showgirl and Me

COLIN CLARK

Younger Brother, Younger Son

A MEMOIR

HarperCollins*Publishers*

HarperCollins*Publishers*
77–85 Fulham Palace Road,
Hammersmith, London W6 8JB

Published by HarperCollins*Publishers* 1997

Copyright © Colin Clark 1997

The author asserts the moral right to be
identified as the author of this work

A catalogue record for this book is
available from the British Library

ISBN 0 00 255799 1

Set in Bembo by
Rowland Phototypesetting Ltd, Bury St Edmunds, Suffolk

Printed and bound in Great Britain by
Caledonian International Book Manufacturing Ltd, Glasgow

All rights reserved. No part of this publication may be
reproduced, stored in a retrieval system, or transmitted,
in any form or by any means, electronic, mechanical,
photocopying, recording or otherwise, without the prior
permission of the publishers.

TO CHRISTOPHER

Contents

Illustrations

My father in the library at Portland Place in 1934. (*Hulton Deutsch*)
My mother, drawn by my father during their honeymoon in 1925.
My twin sister Colette and me in 1934. (*Hulton Deutsch*)
Colette and me with our parents at Portland Place in 1934. (*Hulton Deutsch*)
Henry Moore's pencil sketch of me when I was ill in bed at the age of nine.
Studio portrait of myself in 1943, aged eleven. (*Douglas Glass*)
A picnic at Eton.
With Vivien Leigh at the Oliviers' Buckinghamshire home Notley Abbey in 1947.
Gabriel Pascal on the lido with Jean Simmons during the 1947 Venice Film Festival (photograph by the author).
Vivien Leigh at Notley Abbey in 1950 with the actress Linda Christian, wife of Tyrone Power (photograph by the author).
My first plane, the de Havilland Tiger Moth.
With my MG TD in 1952.
Saltwood, 1954. Sir Colin Anderson poses as a Henry Moore sculpture.
A typical house party at Saltwood in 1956 (photograph by Cecil Beaton).
Paço da Gloria.
Peter Pitt-Milward on his Lippizaner at Paço da Gloria.
One of Margot Fonteyn's many first-night parties in the Crush Bar at Covent Garden.
At Saltwood village church with the ushers for my first wedding, 29 April 1961.
Violette and me with my father on our wedding day. (*Alpha/S&G*)
Photographed at Saltwood in 1962 by Janet Stone.
With my father in 1963.
My father on the battlements of Saltwood Castle in 1969.
Going over the script of the *Pioneers of Modern Painting* film on Manet with my father at the Clos de Lilas in Paris, 1970.
Filming at Windsor Castle with Alistair Cooke and Prince Charles in 1976.

A sketch by Graham Sutherland for his 1970 portrait of my father.
The Lola T70 Mark III B.
My father at Saltwood in 1978. (*Camera Press*)
Alan and me posing at Saltwood, 1984.
With Alan at the Sotheby's sale of our father's estate in 1984. (*Topham*)
Alan at Saltwood with his Rolls-Royce Silver Ghost. (*Times Newspapers Ltd*)
In the house at Hammersmith. (*Evening Standard*)
Helena and our son Christopher, 1988. (*Woodner-Shaw Collection*)
In Portugal with Helena, 1990.

Introduction

I HAVE ALWAYS LOVED HEROES. And heroines.

I am irresistibly drawn to those great men and women who stamp their personality on the events of their time. I do not mind if they are friendly or ferocious, successful or doomed. I only ask that they should be larger than life, unfettered by all those little foibles and failings which drag most of us down.

It takes great courage to be a hero. A human being has to be extraordinarily brave to insist on going their own way, especially if they know that very few will follow. Most people, including me, lose their nerve long before anyone has even noticed that they were trying to rebel. That is why the great characters in Shakespeare's plays never lose their appeal.

Who could forget Richard III, especially when played by Laurence Olivier? 'I am not' – and he could pause for as long as he liked, while the audience held its breath – 'in the giving vein today.' Who could resist the passion of Cleopatra, or the iron determination of Lady Macbeth? 'Unsex me here, and fill me from the crown to the toe, top full of direst cruelty.'

That is how I was taught history, and I revelled in it. It was of little importance whether the stories were accurate or not. What mattered was the people. What did they feel? What did they say? What did they do?

This point of view has now become unfashionable with historians. They prefer to see the past as a pattern of inevitable social change. If we admit the existence of heroes, we have to accept the uncomfortable fact that some men and women are quite simply better than we are. In an age when equality is considered all-important, this is an unpopular idea.

My first memory of being in the presence of a truly great personality was at a poetry reading in an American servicemen's club in

London. This is not normally the sort of occasion at which you would expect to encounter heroism, but it was in 1941, and the Blitz was at its height. Edith Sitwell was on the stage, six feet tall, with a Plantagenet nose and a long black cloak down to the floor.

'Still falls the rain,' she bellowed, as a large number of German bombs started to fall all round us. 'Still falls the rain.' A little man with a tin hat stuck his head round the door and blew a whistle. Edith glared at him. 'Still falls the rain.' I can't recall the rest of the poem, but the audience was so transfixed by the personality of that great poetess that not one of us dared to move.

Since then I have met a large number of great men and women, and I must admit that I have enjoyed their company enormously. I recognise them immediately for what they are, and I always admire them without reserve. For this reason, I suppose, we usually get on together rather well. I do not flatter them – a great person does not need that – but nor do I feel driven to push my ego under their noses, as so many people do.

Sometimes my encounters with great people have been very brief.

In 1960 I was going down in a crowded elevator in the United Nations building in New York when the doors opened and Eleanor Roosevelt got in. One is not supposed to talk in American elevators. 'Good morning, everyone,' said Mrs Roosevelt, beaming. 'Good morning, Mrs Roosevelt,' said the whole elevator, as one man. I am sure we all felt better for the rest of the week. On another occasion, in the early seventies, I was in Paris and I was asked to lunch by a very handsome film director friend of mine. 'I want you to meet my lover,' he said, and we went to a beautiful house in the Bois de Boulogne. There, waiting for us, was Grace Kelly, no longer young but still incredibly good-looking. What a great lady she was. Many years before I had gone over from Eton to watch her brother win the Diamond Sculls at Henley Regatta. Now I could see the same strength and determination in her, but combined with a sort of serenity, which is very rare.

Greatness does not come with physical beauty, of course, although in many cases – and Grace Kelly was an example – it can lead to it. Greatness comes from inside. Every now and then, someone is born with an extra spark that makes them able to achieve much more than a normal person can. They may wait all their lives for an opportunity to show the world what they can do, or they may blaze away, like Mozart or the singer Michael Jackson, almost from the day they are born.

The first television documentary that I worked on was with Sir Thomas Beecham. Although Beecham was a rather flashy conductor, the amount of music in his head was prodigious. At the same time, he was witty and articulate and wise. He was the sort of great man who is not afraid to show off every now and then. The writer Norman Mailer was the same. I met him in New York in the winter of 1962, and he had the reputation of being an *enfant terrible*. Mailer and I spent the evening discussing show business and philosophy, and finally we came to the decision that if it snowed that night we would get drunk. The skyscrapers of Manhattan hidden under a blanket of snow are a rare and beautiful sight, and it was almost as if Mailer's power with words conjured up a snowfall for the occasion. We ended up very drunk indeed.

Greatness does not necessarily attract fame. As with the minor parts in Shakespeare's plays, one can find extraordinary qualities in very humble surroundings. I have been to only one Spanish bullfight. The cruelty was matched only by the inefficiency, and I hated it. One bull leapt over the barrier and rushed round the spectators' corridor, forcing everyone there to jump into the ring as fast as they could, or even faster. Just below my seat there stood a grizzled old man with a black waistcoat and a black hat. He was a bull-herder, and had clearly spent most of his life out in the fields. When the young bull charged him he did not run. He simply put his hand up, looked the bull in the eye and shook his head. 'Not me!' The bull slid to a halt. It snorted, swung round and charged someone else. That absolute confidence in what you can do is the sort of greatness which I envy very much indeed.

My father was also a great man. He was wise. He was brave. He knew what he was doing. He never wasted his time talking nonsense, as many of us are so often tempted to do. He listened, and he learned. He gave considered and usually correct replies to important questions. He balanced the evidence and took momentous decisions with a clear head. You could absolutely count on him to be fair. And he also possessed, of course, a marvellous understanding of the arts. If my father had one foot of clay, if he was perhaps too fond of a good dinner with an intelligent and beautiful lady, well, who could blame him for that? He was human. Great men and women must be human. 'Essere umano.' Nothing is more important than that.

All of us have our eccentricities, our little foibles which we would prefer that the world should not see. It seems to me quite natural that men and women who rise above the crowd might have failings on a larger scale than normal people do. For the most part these flaws are unimportant in comparison to what they achieve. I am not talking about wickedness, or cruelty, or ruthlessness. But greatness is in no way diminished, as so many people seem to think, by the inability to resist a pretty figure, of either sex.

Bearing this in mind, I think that my brother is a great man, too. He would like to become Prime Minister of Great Britain, and who knows, he might make a very good one. He would certainly be a breath of fresh air. The fact that he has not yet achieved his ambition does not in any way detract from his greatness. He is bold, far-sighted and compassionate, and he is very intelligent indeed. He has an uncanny ability to see into the mind, and even into the heart, of his audience on the tiniest piece of evidence imaginable, and yet he very rarely takes advantage of his exceptional brain. He has also managed to come to terms with his eccentricities, which is more than most of us can do. If he sometimes appears to be a maverick, that is only because he has become impatient with the conventional way.

I grew up in the shadow of these two formidable characters – my father so remote, and my brother so involving – but I did not feel that their size made me small. I did not resent the fact that they obviously possessed gifts that I could never even aspire to. I would have liked a little love from my father, as what son would not, and perhaps rather fewer surprises from my brother, but I admired them both enormously, and I still do. Any stories which I tell about either of them, and there are quite a few, are told with deep affection, and not with malice.

The same is true when I talk about my 'love life'. I look back on all my relationships with great joy, even if those relationships did not always go well for everyone involved. This book is not a 'kiss and tell'. My aim is to show that it is possible to lead a rich and varied life even if you are not great and not that clever. With a little wit and a moderate education, it is possible to avoid the obvious, the humdrum, and all those petty little squabbles and concerns that so easily drag us down.

I must confess that I started from a privileged position. My parents had money and rank. They sent me to Eton, the best school in England, if not the world, and introduced me to their influential circle of friends. At the time I found this very claustrophobic, but I admit that it was a great help. It certainly got me my first job in 1956, on the film *The Prince and the Showgirl* with Laurence Olivier and Marilyn Monroe. But in order to keep that job I had to be myself, and I hope I have been myself ever since.

I have had to ignore a great many conventions. Conventions don't help when you are flying a single-seater jet plane in a storm, or when you are trying to start a brand new television station in New York. I realise that most people live by conventions, so I suppose that I have trodden on a lot of toes, and I am afraid that this book will tread on a few more.

But, looking back, there is not much which I would change.

Younger Brother, Younger Son

I

THE FAMILY

WHEN MY FATHER DIED IN 1983, I experienced the most enormous sense of relief. It was not that I wished him any harm, but for the first time I felt that I would not have to struggle for approval on any terms but my own. My father was seventy-nine years old, and all he wanted was a peaceful death. I had revered him deeply, but he and I did not have very much in common, and when he was gone I suddenly realised that it had always been so.

I had made over a hundred films on the arts, twenty of them with my father, but we could never have discussed the merits of a painting together. That would have seemed impertinent. He had taught me the language, but I was not allowed to use it in front of him. All my life I had seen him amuse and educate people, but I had never quite dared to join in. He was courteous and cautious towards me in a way which, even though I was his son, I was never quite able to change. He had given his children a good education, but even this seemed more by accident than design. He never explained why he sent his sons to Eton. He himself had been to Winchester, and he had hated British public-school life. Although he certainly did not think of himself as conventional or upper class, he tried to take my twin sister Colette out of Cheltenham Ladies' College to send her to a fashionable finishing school in Ascot, and was heartily surprised when she insisted on staying at Cheltenham and became head girl.

My father was the only child of a long line of Scots. By nature he was reserved, detached and independent. He always had a very high brow: his dark hair did not start to grow until high up on his head, and then it was smoothed back without a wrinkle (when I once saw him with his hair swept forward after swimming, I hardly recognised him). I never saw him lose his temper, and although he had many affairs, I never saw him show real love except to my mother. He normally only revealed his emotions in front of works of art – which have the convenient quality of not being able to answer back – and he hated any sort of emotional intimacy. He had never had it from his parents, and he simply could not cope with it in adult life.

His greatest loves were painting and sculpture, but he was almost equally involved with theatre, opera, ballet, music, architecture, and anything else that he considered art. Although he always described his own father as a philistine, he had clearly inherited some of his taste. My grandfather liked huge paintings of highland cattle and stags at bay, but he also admired an exhibition by 'this chap Corrutt' (Corot) so much that he bought the lot.

My father's earliest passion – at the age of eight; he had been extremely precocious – was for the Japanese prints which had had such an influence on Picasso and Matisse. He fell in love with Cézanne while he was still at school. When he was sixteen he bought two of Cézanne's notebooks (for £3 per page), and spent the rest of his life giving the pages away as Christmas presents. He also loved books, and when he bought Saltwood Castle in 1955 he turned the great hall into a library. By 1960 it contained over ten thousand volumes. He did not often read novels, but he could quote whole passages from the most famous of them. His knowledge, especially of the arts, was what might be called encyclopaedic. When someone once asked him how many researchers he employed on the *Civilisation* television series which he made for the BBC in 1967, he simply did not know what they were talking about.

The walls of our houses were covered with the most beautiful paintings – Renoirs, Cézannes, a Turner seascape, a small Giovanni Bellini *Madonna and Child*. Among these masterpieces were many works by contemporary artists – Henry Moore, Graham Sutherland, John Piper, Victor Pasmore and many more. At the same time my father was interested in Gothic ivories, Renaissance bronzes and Egyptian and Greek statuettes. With his collection, just as with his lady friends, you could never pin down which his favourite really was. His incredible range of knowledge and taste meant that some pure scholars of art history looked down on him as a lightweight. Actually he wrote many books of great scholarship – on Leonardo, Rembrandt, Piero della Francesca and the nude, for example – but he could not resist a wider audience, and his success as a broadcaster made his colleagues even more jealous than before.

For some reason my father always denied that he could draw himself. When I found a beautiful, sensitive pencil sketch of my mother as a young woman, done when they were on their honeymoon, I showed it to him as a surprise, holding my hand over the bottom left-hand corner.

'Well, well,' he puffed, embarrassed, I suppose, by even the faintest twinge of real emotion. 'It's Jane. I don't remember having anyone draw her at that date.'

'You drew it, Papa,' I said.

'Me? Oh no. Quite out of the question. I can't draw. It's not by me.'

'Well, you signed it, Papa,' I said, removing my hand.

He glared furiously at the little 'KC 1926'. 'Humph,' he said, and walked off.

When my father died, my brother Alan found a large stack of similar drawings hidden among his papers. Not for nothing had he won the school art prize at Winchester two years running.

What my father enjoyed most was to write. No matter where he was, he would balance a pad on his knee, take out his fountain pen and put all his thoughts on paper. His words seemed to flow onto the page. As a child, I couldn't understand why he didn't dictate them. Now I find myself sitting exactly as he did, pad, knee and all. I also realise how difficult it is to express oneself. My father took immense pains to choose each word for the right effect, and the results were dramatically different from most of the art historical lectures which had preceded him.

And he certainly knew he was clever. When I was about twelve, I read him out a really difficult quiz from the newspaper. He got all the answers right.

'It says here you should be on *Brains Trust*, Dad.' (We were still allowed to call them Mum and Dad in those days.)

'I am,' he said, and went on with his breakfast.

One of the few things that my father was not, was religious. He wrote many beautiful and inspiring things in his books, but the fact is that he did not believe in a god. If he was at his happiest in front of a great Renaissance altarpiece, it was because he was involved with the creative process, and not the Creator. Raphael meant much more to him than the Virgin Mary.

And, wise though he may have been, he was not a philosopher. Profound thoughts about the meaning of life made him very nervous, and it was with the greatest reluctance that he included the 'credo' at the end of his book on civilisation. 'The failure of Marxism,' he wrote as his final conclusion, 'has left us with no alternative to heroic materialism, and that isn't enough.' He did not want to think any more deeply about the human condition than that.

So rarefied was my father's upbringing – he wrote that he had never kissed anyone as a child, including his mother – that I don't think he realised there were other human beings on the planet until he was about twenty-eight years old. His parents, his schooling, his wife and first child, and even his beloved art had all just flowed by like interesting scenery. He was an aesthete to his fingertips, totally uninvolved in the humdrum details of daily life. But then, in 1932, just before my twin sister and I were born, my father discovered women.

There is no doubt that this is a very pleasant discovery at any age, but in my father's case it rather went to his head. He had always had a great eye for beauty: in his autobiography he describes holding 'beauty contests' at the age of eight among the fashionable ladies who stayed with his parents at their grand country-house parties. Now, to my mother's intense dismay, he started to chase, and often catch, every beautiful lady he met. The fact that he could become Director of the National Gallery and Chairman of the Arts Council and the Independent Broadcasting Association, and write so many books, while all those love affairs were going on shows evidence of a very powerful mind.

Only at the very end of his life did it become too much for him. 'I can no longer go for a walk on my own,' he groaned. 'I start thinking about all those ladies.'

The trouble was that he combined these passions with the strange detachment of his childhood, and he never really seemed to mind which of his beautiful ladies was with him at any given time. They were like his paintings: he could get equal pleasure from his Renoir *Baigneuse Blonde* or his Turner *Storm at Sea*. But he hated to hurt the ladies' feelings, and this often meant writing half a dozen intimate letters every night to keep them all happy; he was a writer, after all, so this was not too hard to do.

As can be imagined, my mother was not at all happy with this state of affairs, and she used to chastise him dreadfully. He would often repent, but he could not resist, and so the whole cycle would start up again. Contemporary thinking would have it that my mother should have left him at once, to start 'her own life', but I am not so sure. They shared many periods of great contentment throughout their fifty years of marriage, and on the day she died they had spent a happy afternoon together, holding hands and discussing the Florentine artists of the *quattrocento*.

From about 1970 onwards, there was a constant refrain from people I met: 'Oh, you're Sir Kenneth Clark's son? Do tell him how much we enjoyed his *Civilisation* series. It really changed the way we look at art, you know.' Yes, I did know, and it had been a great achievement, but I never quite understood why I was meant to get so much pleasure from such remarks. My father did not enjoy flattery, or even praise, so I could not pass it on. Gradually, I came to realise that if he had been a good father, it was by example. He was very wise. He was very calm. I never ever saw him lose his temper. He spoke four languages fluently and without affectation, and he never used his intellectual powers to make one feel inadequate. But he was remote. It would never have occurred to him to ask about my childhood concerns. Was I happy at school? Had I passed my exams? Did I love him? The truth was that he didn't really care. All this had a depressing effect on me. It was clear that I could never hope to follow in my father's footsteps, and frankly, I did not want to.

Although my father did not encourage intimacy, even from his own children, as I grew up I began to know him better. Very rarely, driven by desperation, I would seek his help (he was my father, after all). I would go into his study looking as forlorn as possible.

'Excuse me, Papa,' I would say. 'I've got this rather serious problem. I wonder if I could explain it to you.'

Papa would look up from his writing, and peer at me over his half-glasses, his sense of duty battling with his fear that some embarrassing revelation was on the way.

'You see, Papa, it's like this . . .' and I would outline my situation in the blackest possible light.

My father would listen carefully, and then think for a while. 'Yes, Col, that is bad,' he would say. 'That's very bad.'

And he would go back to the writing pad on his knee, and take up his pen again.

Occasionally my mother would have got wind of my predicament, and would come sweeping in. She was practical on these occasions, and could see immediately how the problem could be solved.

'Colin needs a cheque, K' – she always called him 'K' – 'Or would you rather have cash? Get your chequebook, K, and give Colin what he needs. It isn't that much.'

I would not, of course, have described the problem in financial terms, but most young people's problems can be eased by an injection of cash.

Although my father was clever enough to know what I was getting at, he would have hoped fervently to avoid the subject of money. 'But, but, but . . .' he would say.

'K, give Colin a cheque.'

'Yes, dear. Yes, dear. Oh dear, how much was it you needed?' Fluster fluster. 'A hundred pounds? Oh dear. Well, I'll ask the secretary to prepare . . .'

'Now, K.'

'Oh, all right, all right. Here it is.'

Triumph for my mama. Gloom for my papa. Agony for me. It would be at least six months before desperation drove me to do that again.

My father had an old-fashioned attitude to money. He was often generous with works of art, but rather mean with pound notes. He hated to equate art with money, and he never really caught up with the way in which art prices had soared. When he thought he needed to sell a painting to pay for some work at Saltwood (he had plenty of stocks and shares, but to sell them would have meant spending cash), he took a Cézanne portrait into a grand London art dealer in Bond Street and accepted the first offer they made him. I couldn't bear it. I bluffed the dealer into letting me have the picture for a day, took it straight round the corner to the Lefevre Gallery and got an offer of exactly double. But when I gave my father twice the money he had expected, he was furious, and suspected some sort of trick. On another occasion he gave Henry Moore an oil sketch for Cézanne's *Baigneuses*. When the Inland Revenue sent him a letter about Gift Tax, he simply exploded and refused to pay. Luckily, the tax office had second thoughts about the two men they were dealing with and dropped the demand.

My mother's background was quite different from my father's. She had been born in Dublin as Elizabeth Martin, the eldest of five children. Her mother was a doctor, and had been the first woman to be a member of the Irish College of Surgeons. I remember her as a flame-haired old lady of whom the whole family was very much in awe. My mother's father was Scottish, and we thought of him as a bit of a coward. At some indeterminate date he had taken off for Durban in South Africa, and there he remained for the rest of his life. So 'Granny Martin' was deemed to be responsible for most of my mother's character, while Grandpa Martin was never mentioned as having contributed to her genes in any way. He did, however, father four sons as well as a daughter. My mother's brothers were called Kenneth, Alan, Colin and Russell, and I only mention their names because they so closely mirror those of my own family. Kenneth, of course, was just a coincidence, and so, we boys were always told, were Colin and Alan. For some reason it was very important to my mother that we did not think that we had been named after our uncles.

If my mother considered herself Irish, her brothers were definitely Scots, like their father. Uncle Kenneth went to New Zealand, where he raised a large, friendly family. His children would some-

9

times come over to visit us, and filled our houses with cries of 'Aunty Betty,' which set my mother's teeth on edge dreadfully. (Although she had been christened Elizabeth, she was always known as Jane.) I would say that my mother's brothers, nephews and nieces were the only people in the whole world with whom she did not get emotionally involved. Uncle Alan settled in South Africa, as his father had done, and Uncle Colin joined my father's family firm, J. & P. Coats Cotton, and lived his life in Glasgow. Only Uncle Russell still survives, a gentle, peaceful Scottish doctor of ninety-five. He lives quietly outside Edinburgh with his loving Scottish doctor wife, who is herself ninety-three. When I went to their fiftieth wedding anniversary, Uncle Russell was wearing the same double-breasted blue suit that he had worn on his wedding day. Not only had his figure not changed over the years, but he had kept that suit in the cupboard all that time in case of just such an eventuality. You can't get more Scottish than that.

My mother persuaded her parents to send her to Oxford University, where she met my father, and enjoyed great success with the young men. She had even become engaged to one of them. He had asked my father to keep an eye on her while he had gone abroad and, of course, he had lost her. But he did not seem to mind, and remained a staunch friend for fifty years.

My mother was very unlike her brothers. Her incredible emotional drive meant that she spent money with abandon. My (Scottish) father would wring his hands, convinced he was going to go bankrupt any minute, but he always gave in to her. They lived the most sumptuously comfortable life together for over fifty years. When he died in 1983, my father left over £17 million in his will (not to me!), so I suppose my mother was right.

My mother's emotional life was far more draining than her spending habits. All her relationships were imbued with drama. Everyone was either an ally or an enemy, and those who upset her became monsters of legendary proportions. She was said to have had love affairs during the war with several of the more distinguished of my father's friends – including the composer William Walton and Henry Moore – but I can't imagine how she found the time. A love affair implies moments of tranquillity as well as passion. It also implies a certain deception, of which she seemed to be incapable. In fact it was the way in which she always wore her heart on her sleeve which made her so sympathetic. In 1974 I went to a grand dinner party at the Metropolitan Museum in New York where I met Carlo Pedretti, the great Leonardo scholar, and his wife. Pedretti, who had been my father's pupil many years before, asked politely after his health. 'And how is Jane?' asked Mrs Pedretti, and they both burst into tears.

Most of us only get emotionally involved with a very few people – our parents, our siblings, our husbands and wives, our children and so on. Those whose job it is to care for people in distress, like doctors and nurses, have to make great efforts to remain detached, even when their patients are dying. If they cannot do this, they can find themselves unable to do their jobs efficiently.

My mother did not just get emotionally involved with people in distress. She got emotionally involved with everyone she ever met. Everyone. People in society; people in the street; her children; her husband's mistresses; her domestic servants; her dressmaker; her dentist – the list was endless. For my mother they all carried the same emotional weight – which is to say about a ton. She didn't seem to possess the sort of filter mechanism which most of us need to keep sane, and this made her extremely vulnerable. She had to pluck up all her courage just to come downstairs in the morning. Anyone she met could plunge her into turmoil.

'Oh, K,' she would suddenly say in the street, 'look at that fat man getting on the bus. He nearly fell over the step. Really, people that fat shouldn't be allowed on buses. You must go over and tell the bus driver to go slowly. He might fall off.'

'Yes, dear, you're right, dear.' My father rather liked to play the henpecked husband. He had learned to let it all go over his head, but I was never able to do this. 'For goodness sake, Mama,' I would say, time and time again, 'don't take it on.' It was pointless. She could never resist. She simply did not know the meaning of the word 'detached'.

Christmas was a mixed blessing. My mother felt that she had to give a present to everybody she had ever met, and this taxed her emotions dreadfully, to say nothing of my father's bank account.

By the time Christmas Day actually arrived, she was always in a state of total collapse. The gloom this caused was relieved by two regular guests, who amused my father enormously. Maurice Bowra and John Sparrow had been his fellow students at Oxford, and were now heads of colleges, Wadham and All Souls respectively. They were both confirmed bachelors, and at the university they were famous mock enemies, although in fact they were the oldest of friends. The whole holiday became an intellectual battle of wits of the sort that my father loved and normally could not indulge in. After dinner, they would get out the *Oxford Dictionary of Quotations* and challenge each other to remember which author wrote what, and when.

'*Varium et mutabile semper femina,*' Maurice would bellow.

'*La donna è mobile* – Woman is always fickle. How true,' Sparrow would reply, and I would wait for him to say '*Rigoletto*' – 'Virgil, *The Aeneid*, 25 BC.'

'While pensive Poets painful vigils keep, sleepless themselves, to give their readers sleep.'

'Alexander Pope, *The Dunciad*, 1742.'

'The great religious art of the world is deeply involved with the female principle.'

'Goodness, what nonsense. Who can have said that?'

We all looked at Sparrow, who was now holding the book.

'Kenneth Clark,' he read out, with great disapproval.

My mother's passions were unpredictable but intense. She was completely convinced that our father was the most important man in the whole world, and always made it clear to us children that he was the only person who really mattered. None of us could, or even should, dream of attempting to measure up to him. For one of us to try to achieve something was almost an insult. Alan write a book? K had written seven books. Colin make a film? K had made ten films. The very idea was ridiculous. (This is something which Alan has inherited. When I told him in 1995 that I was going to publish the diary of my time working on *The Prince and the Showgirl*, he dismissed the whole thing out of hand, writing to me: 'Regarding your book – "And Now the Quiet One Speaks" – nothing sold!')

My mother's attitude towards my father was naive and rather touching, but it did not stop her from screaming at him about his other women. We could hear her giving him hell every night, through our bedroom walls, but he never answered back, and the next morning it would be as if nothing had happened. She, though, could not escape her feelings, and quite early in their marriage she had started to use the anaesthetic of alcohol. She had always liked cocktails, but when she realised that my father was being unfaithful, she became rather hysterical, and needed something stronger. She soon found a Harley Street doctor called Bedford Russell who suited her perfectly. Bedford Russell had discovered that spraying the nasal passages with a mixture of morphine and cocaine had a very welcome calming effect on the nerves of his rich female patients. My mother wasn't neurotic, but she certainly needed calming. Bedford Russell gave her what she called her 'puffer' – a glass nasal spray filled with some narcotic solution – and from then on whenever she felt hysteria coming on, she would dash upstairs to her bathroom. 'Puff, puff, puff' we would hear as she squirted the liquid all over her sinuses, and when she reappeared she would be in a beautiful haze. It didn't seem to do her any harm, and when Bedford Russell died, and alcohol became the only tranquilliser available, its effects were much worse.

As a rule, my mother did not get quite so emotionally involved with foreigners, so she was at her best abroad. Of course there is something very relaxing about staying in a five-star hotel, but also she could not get at quite so much booze to knock herself out in the evenings. If she could stay sober for dinner, she would eat more and feel better, and often enjoy herself as well. In 1945, as soon as the Second World War had ended, the whole family started to go abroad for the school holidays. We twice went to stay with 'Mr Five Per Cent', the oil millionaire Calouste Gulbenkian, in Portugal, and then, as soon as it was possible, we went to Italy.

Both my parents enjoyed going round museums. They would plunge into them with glee, as soon after opening time as possible. My brother Alan was not and never has been an aesthete. He refused to join in, and went exploring on his own. But Colette and I were too young to escape. The Uffizi, the Brera, the Academia – we soon knew them all like the backs of our hands, and we dreaded them.

My father liked to go from masterpiece to masterpiece, giving us a little mini-lecture in front of each. Even in those days he would sometimes be recognised, and a small crowd would collect and go round with us. My mother wanted to look at every single picture. It was as if she was afraid that she would hurt their feelings if she left some out.

'No, K, you haven't looked at this one,' she would cry.

Grimly my father would retrace his steps.

'That's the wrong attribution,' he would snap, and on he would go.

When we were in Venice, we would be allowed to go out to the Lido for a swim in the afternoons, but if we were in Florence there would be no such relief. After a quick lunch we would be off again, perhaps with a visit to a famous church altarpiece thrown in to break the monotony. Occasionally we stayed with my father's great mentor Bernard Berenson, who lived in the hills above the town. Berenson was immensely old, and wore a hat and scarf even in the summer. His mistress Nicky Mariano, who was Colette's and my godmother, always gave us a huge welcome, but Berenson's house was cold and unfriendly – like a museum itself. In the evening I used to enjoy wandering round the great library. The books were mostly in German and Italian, but I got a lot of pleasure from a little section devoted to pictures of nude ladies in provocative poses which obviously had very little connection with art. But such diversions were rare.* All through our childhood, one thing was made perfectly clear by every grown-up we met: 'You can never be, will never be, and should not even attempt to be as clever as your father.' We three children all reacted to this in different ways. Alan decided that he would rebel. As someone once said, 'Alan Clark

---

* I had a similar sort of pleasure when we were staying with the writer Nancy Mitford outside Paris. I had climbed out of my bedroom window onto the roof, the way boys will, and when I peeped over the parapet I saw Miss Mitford sunbathing naked on a ledge below me. She had the most wonderful body – the first really handsome female I had ever seen in that state – and I have never forgotten it.

can't see an applecart without wanting to kick it over.' Even if he wanted to eat the apples.

My twin sister Colette, on the other hand, accepted my father's influence with admiration and pleasure. She did not get on well with my mother, but she has stuck all her life to my mother's principle that Kenneth Clark was the wisest man on earth, and she has led a very successful life on those terms.

As for me, I only wanted to escape. I was proud of my family, but they cast too deep a shadow. I wanted to be left to my own devices. Brains aren't everything. My father and Alan both had more than me, but I didn't envy them a bit. There is an enormous happiness to be found in not wanting to be the best, or have the most, or shout the loudest.

I was once having dinner with a famous millionaire in Hollywood when one of the guests, who was anxious to please him, told his wife that she looked very nice.

'Nice?!' she screamed with rage. 'How dare you tell me I look nice? Tell me I look fantastic, elegant and dramatic. Don't tell me I look nice!'

I just wanted to be nice. I didn't want to be admired, or feared, or even loved. I suppose I would have liked to have been elegant, but nice would do.

~~~~

II

BEING DIFFERENT

IT HAD ALL STARTED ON 9 October 1932.

Emerald Cunard was giving one of her famous cocktail parties, and on this occasion the guest of honour was the brilliant young art historian Kenneth Clark, whose wife was due to have her second baby that very night.

Lady Cunard, widow of the shipping magnate, had a sumptuous apartment in Mayfair which was much more attractive than the maternity clinic round the corner, but Kenneth Clark did keep in touch by telephone. Finally the news came through. 'It's twins,' my father announced to the assembled company.

'Boys or girls?' they cried.

'One of each.'

'That always means different fathers,' said a gloomy Sir Thomas Dewar, of Scotch whisky fame.

Sometimes my father would ascribe that quotation to different people, but it became a very popular story in the family, and I was often told it as I grew up. I never quite knew why.

Actually, my parents were very proud of their achievement. Their son Alan had been born four years earlier, and in those happy pre-ultrasound-testing days, they had only been expecting one more. In the rush of pride and excitement that followed the arrival of twins, they committed one of their very rare breaches of good taste and named us Colin and Colette. We lived in a grand Regency house in Portland Place in London, and were immediately provided with an army of nannies and maids. We would often be paraded for the sake of visitors, dressed in identical white mink tippets in a vast double pram.

All this had a dramatic effect, of course, on our brother Alan. Until now he had been the adored and spoiled son of a spoiled couple. Suddenly he found that he was pushed out of the spotlight completely, permanently ignored in favour of 'the twins'. No little boy likes that. From then on, he had to stamp and yell if he wanted attention. If he felt a little ill he had to pretend he was dying; if he scratched his leg he had to say it had been cut off. He had to develop his powers of persuasion, and his charm, to a very high degree. It is not hard to see how the birth of the twins was to influence Alan's life for ever.

The effect on my parents was less obvious. They needed more servants, of course, and a country house, but their social life was, if anything, enhanced. The American writer Edith Wharton had recently become a great friend and was made one of my godmothers. Nicky Mariano, the mistress of art historian Bernard Berenson, was the other, and my godfathers were Sir Owen Morshead, Keeper of the Royal Library at Windsor Castle, and the composer William Walton.

In 1934 my father was appointed Keeper of the King's Pictures. The following year he was made Director of the National Gallery, and the year after that he was given a knighthood for his services to the arts. To my parents, their three children were yet another example of their success and good fortune.

Children are natural conservatives. They all believe that the way they are brought up is the norm, and like to assume that they are more or less the same as everyone else. And they don't like change. This is why so many of our childhood habits stay with us all our lives. When Alan's son was seven years old, he was horrified to find that I had a bath in the mornings. In the comfortable confines of an English nursery, it had never occurred to him that there was anyone who didn't have their bath at night. Twenty-five years later, I can see the same characteristics in my ten-year-old son. And why not? He doesn't want to know that at any given moment there are five hundred million children in the world, most of whom are being brought up completely differently to him. His assumption that he is the norm is essential to his security.

My brother and sister and I did not have this luxury. It was always impressed on us that we were different from everyone else. This was certainly not because we were 'upper class' in the conventional English sense – my parents had a horror of the nobility. Like many intellectuals, they considered the landed gentry to be boors and philistines. They didn't like the middle classes any better. 'How dreadfully bourgeois' was one of their favourite ways of dismissing something. We children had no idea what bourgeois meant, and were most perplexed when we discovered that there was actually a perfume called 'Bourgeois' – for ladies, we presumed, who wanted to smell middle class. My parents had to approve of the lower classes, since it was they, after all, who did all the work, and from whose ranks their servants were drawn. But one must never behave like them. 'Common' was even worse than 'bourgeois'. It was common to wipe your nose with the back of your hand; it was common to like milk chocolate; it was common to enjoy waltzes by Johann Strauss.

No one could say that our parents were common. Our father was different because he was so clever; our mother was different because she had so much 'taste'; our grand London house was different, even from other grand houses, because it contained so much art. So we children had to be different too. We hardly ever saw our parents during the daytime, and if they came to the nursery to say goodnight, they would often be in full evening dress – white tie and tails with decorations for my father, long Schiaparelli gowns for my mother. We were not even allowed in the main house except on special occasions. We lived in a smaller building tacked on to the back, and connected by a green baize door. We had a nanny and a maid, and we even had our own cook (my parents' chef would never have dreamed of cooking for the children). So we thought of ourselves as different, even from our parents. Alan was boisterous, Colette was serious and quiet, and Colin was nervous and difficult, but at least we weren't bourgeois or common!

None of our parents' friends seemed to have children of their own, so I suppose our parents did not know what other children were like. They never realised that the world is simply brimming over with boisterous, serious, nervous and difficult youngsters who are all different, and all 'common' too. I didn't like being 'different'. Somehow I felt that if I didn't have to be 'different', life would be less of a problem. I wanted to be able to relax. I actually wanted to be 'common', and I still do.

Once, on holiday in Italy, I paid a visit to Assisi. Assisi is not only the birthplace of St Francis, but also a very attractive town, and it is filled with tourists all year round. I was talking to a Franciscan friar in the little square one morning as the first coachloads of foreigners pulled in.

'Don't you ever feel overwhelmed by all these strangers?' I asked.

'If you look at them all together,' he said, 'they are rather daunting. But if you look at each one individually, you will find they are very beautiful.'

What a Franciscan thought — and with a few exceptions, I have found it to be true.

My sister and I did not go to school — any school — until just before our eighth birthday, so we did not have any friends apart from each other. There was only one other little boy with whom I was sometimes allowed to play. Arthur was the son of the gardener at our home in the country, Upton House in Gloucestershire. He was 'common' all right. He taught me how to cock a snook and run away, and he let me read the weekly comic-strip papers, the *Beano* and the *Dandy*, which I am glad to see have hardly changed to this day. Arthur and I used to climb the apple trees that leant over the walls and try to pee on people coming up the drive. This did not present too much of a danger to our visitors, given the size of our bladders and the difficulty of aiming off for wind, but one day we did score a direct hit on the local farmer, and he made the most terrible stink (literally): 'Goodness me, how common.' I could see that my father was having difficulty in suppressing a guffaw, but my mother was horrified. Poor Arthur was banned for ever, but I continued to envy him. His family must have been dreadfully poor — I remember that at Christmas his parents couldn't afford to give him presents, so they stuffed his stocking with potatoes — but at least he had those comics.

It wasn't just our parents who were different; all their friends were different too. They really were. They were artists and composers, and writers and scholars, and actors and musicians. They were the new intellectual élite of England. They all came from that glorious generation which had been too young to fight in the trenches of the First World War. Now that all the dusty prejudices of the nineteenth century had been swept away, these talented young men and women found themselves with a clear field in front of them, and they proceeded to take a fresh look at the arts.

Actually, in matters of taste my parents were surprisingly old-fashioned. Their houses were decorated in the style of the Ashmolean Museum in Oxford, where my father started his career as Keeper of the Department of Fine Art. But due to his scholarship and wealth, and my mother's love of society, they now found themselves at the centre of London's artistic world, modern as well as traditional.

Alan, Colette and I took our separation from our parents' lives for granted, at least until the Second World War began in 1939. Then, as the governesses and the servants vanished, we simply had to be included. When the war started, my sister and I were eight and Alan was twelve – too old to start forging strong parental bonds. The first test of our new relationship came during the Blitz, when the Germans were sending planes over London every night and trying to bomb Britain into submission. We were living in a small (but beautiful and 'different') house at the top of Hampstead Hill, called Capo di Monte. Our mother's lady's maid, Miss Leach, was the only servant who had remained with us, and she had grown very stout and become the cook. Every night, all of us – my mother, my father, Alan, Colette, myself and Miss Leach – had to take refuge in the dining room inside a low metal box with wire sides called a Morrison shelter. This was a sore test of everyone's patience. Soon after I had dozed off in my cool, comfortable little bed upstairs, the sirens would start to wail, and all the lights would go out. I would be shaken awake, and we would all squeeze into the shelter, like sardines. My poor father was responsible for keeping the National Gallery going and a great deal else besides (he was Director of the Film Division and later Controller, Home Publicity at the

Ministry of Information). He desperately needed his sleep, and I am afraid I didn't help. Like many little boys I was restless, and found it very hard to get back to sleep. 'Stop fidgeting!' my father would bark. He was normally such a mild man that this would have an electrifying effect. No one dared move a muscle, and it was often over an hour before sheer exhaustion caused us all to pass out. I won't say that my father actually loathed me on those occasions, but it certainly did not create an ideal early relationship between him and his younger son.

One of the great 'credos' of the smart set in the 1930s had been that relatives were a bore. Somehow it was thought that, although the upper classes had a network of brothers and sisters and uncles and aunts, and the working classes bred like rabbits, intellectuals should be unique. My father had been an only child, of course, so he had few relatives, and my mother had put as much space as possible between her four brothers and herself. One result of this was that my parents could not find anyone with whom to dump their children in the holidays. We could be sent away to boarding schools in term-time, but in the holidays there was nothing to do but to take us along. This proved to be a serious problem for my mother and father, not least because they did not really know us at all well.

For the summer holidays my parents would take us to a place called Portmeirion on the coast of Wales. Portmeirion was about as dotty and 'different' as you can get. It was a fake Mediterranean village built out of cement by an architect called Clough Williams-Ellis, complete with a fake yacht in a fake harbour. The advantage for our father was that it was very near the Manod, the mountain under which the paintings of the National Gallery had been stored, and he was able to escape there every day, away from the horrors of family life.

Portmeirion should have been a children's paradise, but it wasn't. There were very few other children there, for a start. There was a boy called Hugh who is now the premier marquis of England, and who we called 'the Pink Peer' because he had such a rosy face. I am sure he was the most delightful boy really, but he wasn't any fun to play with at all. There was Robin Douglas-Home, who had a very sexy sister, and who very nearly succeeded in suffocating me by locking me in an antique chest. But I can't remember any other children.

We always lived in beautiful houses, but my parents liked to keep on the move, so we never quite knew which one was 'home', and often ended up feeling more like guests than members of a family. By the early 1950s my father had decided that living in London, with its six million inhabitants, was just too much of a strain. Given time, my mother would become emotionally involved with them all. So in 1955 he sold our house in Hampstead and bought Saltwood Castle in Kent. Saltwood occupies a commanding position over-looking the English Channel, and there are records of a castle there even before the Norman Conquest. The sea used to flow right into the woods at high tide, and this had given the place its name. The huge stone towers and a great hall were added in about 1080, and the knights of King Henry II met there in 1170 to plot the murder of Thomas à Becket. After that it was an army base until it was partially destroyed by an earthquake in 1580, and it remained a ruin until the nineteenth century. It was restored by a family called Deedes, whose punning motto – *Facta non verba* – can still be found on many of the ceilings.

The castle is very large. Its moated walls enclose over an acre of garden, and you can go out of a door in the first-floor drawing room and walk right round on a parapet and back into the tower again on the opposite side of the house. We never counted all the rooms, but there are over sixteen bedrooms in the main house alone. It needed a great deal of work on my mother's part to make it all comfortable and pretty. She didn't mind the work, but as usual it was the people who gave the trouble. Live-in domestic servants were like children, as anyone who saw the television series *Upstairs, Downstairs* will remember. They squabbled among themselves and were always threatening to walk out because their feelings had been hurt. No wonder they have now vanished for ever. At Saltwood there was a secretary, a chef, a butler, a housekeeper and three gardeners, as well as two daily maids from the village and a man called Mr Payne whose only job was to clean the windows. They all seemed essential to the running of the establishment, but they drove my mother crazy.

All her life, my mother was impressed by great men, and she would open her eyes very wide and gaze at them with genuine admiration (like me). There is no doubt that my parents made a glamorous couple, and they were very popular with the rich and famous people who made up London Society. Saltwood was too far from London for them to give dinner parties, but on most Friday evenings the chauffeur would be sent to pick up weekend guests from Folkestone station. Igor Stravinsky, Cecil Beaton, Margot Fonteyn and Paul Robeson made a typically interesting mix. The Queen Mother once came to stay for a night, and she planted a tree in the garden, which subsequently died. (It was replaced many times and is now quite big.) At lunchtime, I would be sent round with a tray of drinks – dry martinis in long fluted glasses, or iced champagne. 'Oh, they look so delicious I think I'll have both,' said Her Majesty, and she did.

My father, who had usually spent part of the week with one of his mistresses, would be in a jolly mood, pottering about and uncorking bottles of wine so they could 'breathe'. He could always escape to his library in the great hall on the other side of the lawn and write his books. But my mother, reduced to a state of nervous exhaustion by the strain of overseeing the servants, would be suffering terribly – the mistresses certainly didn't help either – and by Friday night the alcohol would be starting to take its toll.

My parents had kept a flat in London, and spent three days of each week there. They would be driven to Folkestone station, and from then on they would be treated like royalty. This was because my mother knew all the railway staff by name, and would tip them lavishly on every trip, whether they helped with the luggage or not. Most of us only tip waiters and doormen, who take the tip for granted and who make no effort to remember us. Railway employees are more permanent than they look. When my mother arrived at the station the guards, the inspectors, the porters, the men who clipped tickets at the gate, would each find a ten-shilling note pressed into their hand with a heartfelt and sometimes even tearful expression of thanks from Lady Clark.

On the rare occasions when I travelled with my parents this used to embarrass me dreadfully, but I have now learnt that like anything else, tipping is an art. My wife, who does not have much in common with my mother, being not Irish but Chinese, gives nothing more to doormen than, 'Oh, thank you so much,' and a radiant smile, but she tips every member of the staff who serves her in Harrods, and you can be sure that she never has to wait in a queue on her weekly visit to the food hall there.

It was just as well that my parents took the train to London, as they were both rather old-fashioned drivers. My father would swish along merrily enough, sticking for the most part to his own side of the white line. But he never seemed to notice that there was anyone else on the road until the last moment, which made life rather hair-raising for his passengers.

My mother, on the other hand, preferred to drive very slowly. She was particularly fond of gardening, and on one occasion she was going from Saltwood to Sissinghurst Castle to visit Vita Sackville-West, and show her guests the most famous garden in Kent. She was driving her Morris Minor, with William Walton as her passenger, while his wife Susannah followed with my father in the Bentley. After a few miles of stately progress, Lady Walton could stand it no longer. Ordering my father to stop, she jumped out and ran after the Morris, caught up with it and banged on the roof. My mother was extremely startled to see Susannah's contorted face suddenly appear outside her window. For a frantic moment she thought that she had somehow managed to crash into the car behind. But although she readily agreed to hand the wheel to William this once, she always told the story as an example of Sue Walton's lack of patience rather than of her own lack of speed.

When he was young, my brother Alan was often compared to his grandfather. Kenneth Clark Sr had been a self-indulgent eccentric. He had inherited a vast amount of money from his family's cotton-reeling company in Paisley, and proceeded to squander it on huge estates and yachts. He loved to gamble, and was said to have once actually broken the bank at Monte Carlo. He also drank far too much whisky, and died of cirrhosis of the liver two weeks before

I was born. Like many Edwardian millionaires, his wealth allowed him to be larger than life, and very noisy, but he obviously had more taste than my father liked to give him credit for, and he bought many works of art of great beauty. Whether Alan resembled him or not is hard to say, but he certainly admired him enormously. And so did my father. In fact, his attitude to his father and to his eldest son was exactly the same. He would spend hours telling my mother how much he disapproved of them, while secretly adoring them both.

This quality of being able to excite disapproval and adoration in equal measure has been a constant feature of Alan's life. It is as if he had to have the one, in order to get the other. He started practising his powers of persuasion on my twin sister and myself when we were still in the nursery, and when he was with us we never knew whether to feel excited or scared.

There is a newspaper cartoon strip about small children called *Peanuts*. Anyone who is familiar with it will know the oft-repeated scene in which Lucy, a slightly older girl with black hair, tries to persuade Charlie Brown to kick an (American) football.

'I'll hold it,' she says, lying on her tummy on the grass, 'and you kick it.'

'Oh, no!' says Charlie Brown, remembering the last time she said this, and the painful results. 'Just as I go to kick it, you'll snatch the ball away and I'll fall flat on my back. Do you think I'm a fool, to trust you again?'

'No, no,' says Lucy. 'I won't do that again, I promise.' So Lucy holds the ball, and Charlie Brown runs up to kick it, and, as always, at the last minute Lucy snatches the ball away and he falls flat on his back.

'Rats,' he says, angry not with Lucy but with himself for being so gullible again.

Our relationship with Alan was like that. And yet he was always such wonderful company that we missed him dreadfully when he wasn't there, and we still do.

He had a fantastic imagination, and would think up great escapades for us to do together – wild, improbable places to go and things to see and say. And then he would suddenly get bored, like his grandfather. He would simply vanish, without telling us why, and we would be left to explain to an angry nanny what on earth was going on. He certainly kept the whole household on its toes.

Perhaps because Alan also inherited much of his character from our mother, he would fight with her all the time. His independent attitude drove her to distraction. When he avoided National Service, quite legitimately, because he had been offered a place at university, she regarded it as an act of virtual treason. This was unfair; I knew how passionately patriotic Alan was from an episode when we went to the cinema together in 1946, not long after the war had finished. As was customary at the time, the National Anthem was played at the end of the film, and the audience stood to attention. On this occasion, one man just walked out in the middle of the little ceremony, and Alan, although he had never hidden his admiration for Adolf Hitler, tried to stop him. He got knocked down flat for his pains, but he had shown just how brave he could be.

Such was my mother's goading that when Alan left Oxford in 1959, he went to the RAF and offered to do his National Service there and then. The Air Ministry said that according to their records he had already done two years in the Guards (he had done a six-week training course), and refused to take him, so he joined the RAF Volunteer Reserve. For five years the poor man used to drive off to spend his weekends in an RAF camp somewhere or other. Of course he still didn't get his mother's approval, but I was thrilled because it meant that his service just overlapped with mine. I had become a Pilot Officer, and as Alan was an enlisted man, there was just a chance that we would meet on a parade ground somewhere and he would have to salute me. But it never happened, and now I suppose it never will.

Despite appearances, my brother Alan is not a rebel, any more than my grandfather had been. Both of them were born natural conservatives. Underneath it all, my grandfather wanted, and my brother still wants, to be seen as a prosperous country gentleman. But both of them had a dread of being ignored, and both sometimes felt that rage was the quickest path to love.

In Alan's case this has meant frequent brushes with the law, as well as with the public in general, and these encounters are often a joy to watch. The first that I witnessed was in 1955, when we were driving together through the English countryside in Alan's Porsche. Naturally we were going as fast as we possibly could, and suddenly we were surrounded by police cars. 'Crackle, crackle . . . little silver sports car . . . crackle . . . 100 miles an hour . . . crackle,' went their radios, as four large men in blue marched towards the car, still trembling from the speed they had had to go to catch us.

'Idiots! Fools! Get out of my way!' shouted my brother. I was dumbfounded. I thought we were going to be killed, but now, contrary to appearances, Alan had them where he wanted them. Almost incoherent with rage, the policemen began to yell their own insults, thus revealing their deepest prejudices.

When Alan yelled back, although he seemed to be attacking them, he was actually expressing what they wanted to hear. 'Why are you harassing respectable citizens when you could be catching real criminals? Why don't you go and break the arms of all the local villains?' Soon everyone was slapping each other on the back, as if we were all the best of friends. I had plenty of time, while the policemen escorted us back in triumph to Alan's large Wiltshire country house, to consider that Alan might make a successful politician after all.

A few years ago we went out for a spin in one of Alan's vintage cars (cars did form a very important part of our lives). I forget this one's name, but I think it had four cylinders and twenty-three litres. It also had no number plates, and definitely no MOT. We came to a junction where we had to stop, and found ourselves next to a police car, with two large officers inside. Both men turned to stare as Alan crunched the ancient gears to get going again. 'Bugger off!' he yelled at them, as if to say, 'How dare you look at me?' Two bearded, flat-capped faces snapped smartly round to face the front again and we roared off, unhindered.

My father was not always entirely happy with Alan's method of making friends. On one occasion two police constables actually called on him in his London flat.

'I'm afraid, Sir Kenneth,' said one of them nervously, 'that a very serious charge has been made against you.'

'Oh, really?' said my father amiably, peering over his half-glasses at the two young men in uniform.

'We have a witness who saw you driving your car along the pavement last night, making an obscene gesture with your fingers and shouting "Filthy jewboys" at a group of young men.'

My father looked startled. 'That is bad,' he said.

My mother came to the rescue. She may have disapproved of Alan's behaviour, but she would always defend him like a tigress. 'Well, actually Sir Kenneth was at home with me last night' – she gazed at the policemen with her huge Irish eyes – 'but I think I can guess how this misunderstanding arose. It must have been one of our sons' friends who borrowed our car. Won't you have a glass of sherry?' And the two policemen were persuaded to accept, shifting their feet nervously on the Aubusson rug in front of the eighteenth-century marble fireplace, swallowing everything they were told.

My parents' London flat was in a block called Albany, a large and beautiful building just off Piccadilly. At that point Piccadilly is a one-way street, running east towards Piccadilly Circus, and five lanes of traffic make for serious congestion when one drives out of the Albany courtyard and turns left. When Alan comes out he turns right. He waits for a tiny gap, then surges across the serried ranks of hooting cars and taxis in the wrong direction, swerves into the bus lane, roars past Fortnum & Mason, scattering the tourists, and finally darts down Duke Street to safety.

'It's one-way!' I screamed when he did this for the first (and last) time with me beside him.

'We're not in Saudi Arabia,' he growled. 'They don't cut your hand off in England for traffic offences.'

Alan learned how to do a deal in Warren Street, in the days when it was the centre of London's second-hand car trade, and he was, and still is, a past-master of the art. He will decide what he is prepared to pay, and swiftly knock the price down even lower. Then, when he has negotiated a far more rewarding deal than he had hoped for, his performance will begin.

'You've ruined me,' he will say to his defeated opponent. 'You've taken me to the cleaners. You're the first person who has ever done that to me. I can't stand it – how will I ever explain it to Jane?' (His wife, and his perennial excuse.)

'Why do you bother?' I once asked. 'You got far better terms than you expected.'

'It makes them feel good,' he said. 'And I might have to deal with them again.'

That is why Alan would have made a wonderful Prime Minister. He can make you feel happy even if he's won. Many people have told me that he is the only honest politician they know. Of course, if he wants to, he can lie as well as any of them, and that means very well indeed. I have seen him push away the remains of a roast joint of beef after a hearty meal. 'I never eat meat,' he says menacingly, daring me to refer to what I have just witnessed with my own eyes. But at the same time, he is completely honest about his emotions. Good and bad, they are there for anyone to see.

Under the surface, Alan is as much a believer as I am, even if, like most politicians, he would never dare to admit it. ('Aha!' he shouted when a dinner guest mentioned that I was her church warden at St Peter's in Hammersmith, 'So Colin is a religious maniac!') He used to go to church every Sunday, but as he grew older he could not find a clergyman capable of holding his interest for more than a few minutes. In common with many brilliantly clever people, his attention span is woefully short. I remember an occasion when he asked all the most amusing people he knew to a dinner party at Saltwood. Halfway through, he suddenly announced: 'I'm bored. If this is the best you can do, I'm going to bed,' and he took a large glass of milk and vanished upstairs, not to be seen for the rest of the evening.

Alan is impossible to shock, and that makes him wonderful company. Also, and whether he learned this as a barrister or as a second-hand car dealer I could not say, he can give a succinct and considered reply to any question, without having to begin by uttering all those disclaimers on which more conventional public figures rely. Once, when we were walking over the Kentish hills, I told him that I was worried about the crucifixion. Why did Jesus break down at the last minute and cry out, 'Lord, why hast thou forsaken me?'

'Well, although Jesus was the son of God,' replied Alan, 'He was also a human being. When the pain of the crucifixion grew too much to bear, He cried out for a miracle, just like any other human being. But God said: "Sorry. You've got to go through this on your own. You are going to rise again, and join me here in Heaven, but first you have got to die, and be seen to die, as a man."'

I found that very moving. Imagine having to say that to your son. I don't know if my grandfather ever had a thought like that. My father certainly did not.

My father had started making films on art long before the *Civilisation* series in 1967. He loved talking to camera. He would first carefully write down every word he was going to say, just as if he was writing a book, and then read his words from a teleprompter over the lens. To him, the camera was the perfect audience. However emotional he got, the camera, like a work of art, could not give him any emotion back.

Actually, *Civilisation* very nearly did not happen. I was making television films myself in the 1960s, so my father told me all about the series in advance, and I thought it was a wonderful idea. The filming would mean a year of almost constant travelling, which would suit my mother, and I could see that my father would do it incredibly well. He had already sketched out the thirteen episodes in his mind, and was enjoying putting all his knowledge and wisdom into each one. Then one day when we were walking by the sea at Hythe, near Saltwood, he suddenly told me that he had decided not to do it.

'I don't like the BBC people involved,' he said. 'The director is too bossy.'

'What's his name?' I asked.

'I can't tell you,' my father said. 'It wouldn't be professional. You'll tell someone, and soon it will get to the person involved and he will be hurt.'

'Papa,' I said sternly, 'you have to tell me. I can't bear it if you cancel the whole *Civvy* series just in case one person's feelings get hurt.'

'All right,' said my father. 'It's Michael Gill.'

It so happened that I knew Michael. I had included one of his early films, *Peaches*, in a series I produced for Associated Television on short-film-makers, and I admired him very much.

'You are wrong, Papa,' I said. 'I know Michael, and he is the most wonderful, imaginative man. You are just wrong. Try again.'

It was usually my mother who spoke to my father like this, not me. He was so surprised that he promised to do what I said. Michael was a tough boss, and quite right to be so, but by the end of the series he had become one of the few people whose company my father always enjoyed.

My mother particularly loved to go filming. A film crew is a pretty resilient bunch of people, over whom it is not easy to fuss. They prefer to remain professional, and this means that although they are usually sleeping with each other, they do not let their feelings get involved with outsiders. My mother was simply forced to have an emotional rest. She would go with my father to all the locations and make many suggestions – which Michael Gill received with unfailing politeness – then go off exploring on her own. Since my father had written all the scripts in advance, and only had to read them off the autocue in front of the camera, filming was like a holiday for them both.

Later on, when I was directing my father, this professionalism continued. After six weeks of working together on a series called *The Romantic Rebellion* in locations all over Europe, one of the crew had an inspiration.

'It's a pretty funny coincidence, Colin, you and Sir Kenneth having the same surname. Are you related in any way?'

'Yes, I'm his younger son,' I replied. 'Any other questions?'

I always called him 'Sir Kenneth' when we were filming (just as I had always called Laurence Olivier 'Sir Laurence' and not 'Larry' when we were in the theatre), and my father always referred to me as 'my director'. In fact, in my whole life I never heard him refer to me as 'my son'.

After the success of *Civilisation*, especially in America, my father became more of a 'star', but he was not a bit affected by fame. He had been famous before, as the youngest-ever director of the National Gallery, and he took it for granted. But it meant that he had to travel a lot more, and sometimes he could not take my mother with him. He could see that Saltwood, with its many flights of granite steps, had now become a positive danger, so in 1970 he decided to have a little bungalow built in the grounds for his and my mother's declining years, and gave the castle to Alan – leaving Colette and me rootless once more.

In contrast to the castle, my father wanted the new bungalow to have a completely flat floor, but like everyone else architects have to express themselves, and the man who built it slipped in just one step, between my mother's bedroom and the rest of the house. How many times we could all have throttled him after my mother had had a stroke and was confined to a wheelchair. Apart from that, their new house suited them very well. They crammed in as many of their art works as they possibly could – leaving only the fakes behind – and my father settled down to write, while Alan and Jane moved into the castle and restored it very cleverly in their conservative way, to look exactly as it had done when my parents had been in residence.

I had always been very close to my mother, but as he grew older my father became more remote. As a child I had not sought, or even expected, his love, but I had hoped for his approval. By the time my mother died in 1978, at the age of seventy-five, it was obvious that I was never going to get it, so like any sensible younger son, I emigrated to the United States. Despite all the rage she had shown to Alan in his youth, my mother had left the whole of her estate to him in her will, and I had my living to earn.

My father got married again, rather too quickly we felt, to a lady none of us knew. Perhaps he wanted to start a new chapter of his life before it was too late. Despite all his mistresses, he had never lost his devotion to my mother, and in her final years he had nursed her like a baby. But he showed no emotion whatsoever when she died. He also shed all his lady friends, not because he had found someone to love, as I was to do, but because he was too tired. Mistresses had been an escape from the intense pressures of his marriage, and now that that pressure was gone, he didn't need them. I suppose to some extent, and with the exception of my brother, who lived next door, he wanted to shed his family as well.

On one visit from America I turned up at the Garden House unannounced, and he completely failed to recognise me.

'Now, who are you?' he asked as I advanced towards him across the lawn.

'I am your younger son Colin, Papa,' I replied.

'Oh, yes. So you are. I didn't recognise you. You've grown so stout.'

I think that was the saddest moment of my life.

III

FLYING THE NEST

MY FATHER FELT VERY STRONGLY that his parents had neglected him. He thought of his father as a greedy, reckless drunk, and always described his mother as selfish and lazy. (Quite where his own peerless qualities had come from was never explained.) He certainly did not feel love for his parents, and this may have been why he did not expect to receive love from his own younger son. He had been a lonely child, and his early isolation had caused him to turn inwards, and even to become smug. But I had a noisy, bumptious brother and a sensitive, loving sister, so too much introspection was out of the question.

This meant that I was not really too upset when we children were all sent off to boarding schools in 1939. Even at the age of seven, I felt that it was just a question of adapting to my new circumstances. I missed the company of my twin very much, but I was at Cheltenham Junior School, and I knew that she was quite close by at Cheltenham Ladies' College. I wrote her long and extremely boring letters every week. Most of the other new boys in the school were more homesick than I was, and we all learned, very quickly, how to make friends.

I also found, to my intense delight, that my grandmother, my father's 'selfish' mother, was living in a hotel just down the road. My parents had definitely not chosen the school for this reason. They only mentioned it with gloomy embarrassment, and they made no formal arrangements for me to visit her. But as so often happens, a bad mother can make a wonderful grandma, and on Saturday afternoons, when all the masters had vanished, I would go to see her.

The gates of the school were locked, more or less like a prison, but I could climb over the wall unseen and run up the road to the luxury hotel nearby, which was really a retirement home for elderly ladies. There I would receive a huge welcome, and, just as important to a schoolboy, an enormous tea. My grandmother would nod and cluck sympathetically while I told her of my exploits, between mouthfuls of cake and lemonade. By the end of the afternoon I would be surrounded by an admiring crowd of rich old ladies, all wishing that their grandsons would pop in for tea. My performances became almost theatrical, and I must admit that I have loved rich old ladies ever since.

Parents who send their children to boarding school at an early age simply have to face up to the fact that they are losing them. School life soon becomes more important than home life. School is where you learn to survive, one way or another, for the rest of your life. Home becomes 'the somewhere else', the place where you are spoiled, nagged, neglected, and bored because everything is done for you. I used to dread going back to school at the beginning of each term because of the effort it required – just as one puts off jumping into the sea on a hot August day – but once I was there, I was happier than I was at home.

This was especially true when I got to Eton in 1945, at the age of twelve. Like all the other boys there, I now had a private room. At last I could make my own nest. Eton was completely run by the boys in those days. 'Beaks', as masters were called, were there to teach, and that was all. We could even get rid of a beak if we wanted to. My division, or form, was blessed with a boy called Watt, and another with a very minor tic in his eye. If we had a young and inexperienced beak whom we did not like, the boy with the tic would start by giving him the most enormous theatrical wink.

'Why are you winking at me like that, boy? Are you being cheeky?'

'He's got a twitch, sir,' the whole class would yell. 'He can't help it, sir. He's got a note from the doctor, sir.'

Another huge theatrical wink, accompanied by a leer.

'That's not a twitch. What the hell do you think you're playing at?'

'Perhaps I can explain, sir.' Watt would rise to his feet, looking very serious.

'What's your name?' the master would ask.

'Watt is my name, sir.' Watt would look puzzled.

'That's what I said – What's your name?'

'Yes, sir,' Watt would reply gravely.

'Don't "Yes, sir" me, boy. What is your name?'

'Watt is his name, sir,' we would all yell.

Wink, wink from boy number one.

'What on earth are you playing at, you horrible boys?'

'Yes, sir, yes, sir. What, Watt, What.' Wink, wink etc.

In the end he would put the whole class on report. To do this was a serious sign of weakness, and much disapproved of by the other masters. To have one or two boys 'on report' was fine – they would be beaten. Three or four at a pinch. But the whole class, no.

'Poor Jenkins hasn't quite got the hang of it,' the other masters would say to each other. Imagine Jenkins' feelings when he had to confront the class again next day, and it was he and not they who had been punished.

Going to Eton was like visiting a foreign country. You had to learn the language very quickly in order to survive. On our first day there we were given a booklet packed with information which meant absolutely nothing to us – the names of all the houses, which team had which colours on its cap, etc., and we were told to learn it all immediately. It was as baffling as the Highway Code would be to a non-motorist. Then, after four days, we were given a test on it, which, naturally, most boys failed. This was used as an excuse for a beating, but even for those who passed, another excuse for a beating was quickly found. Caning with a thin, flexible bamboo rod was the accepted way of maintaining discipline in those days, and it was felt necessary to beat every boy in his first week so that he would know how painful the punishment would be if he ever misbehaved.

Each house at Eton was ruled by about five prefects – 'Library', they were known as – who had their own study. For their first two years at the school, junior boys acted as servants to the boys in

Library, running errands, making toast, cleaning their shoes etc. They were known as 'fags', although I should point out that the word is not derived from 'faggot' – the American slang for homosexual – and there were no sexual overtones to the job. Any member of Library who wanted a task performed that he was too lazy to do himself simply stuck his head out of his study door and yelled, or rather sang, 'Boy!' at the top of his lungs. Wherever they were, whatever they were doing, in no matter what state of undress, all the fags had to run like mad rabbits to where the member of Library was standing. The last to arrive got the job. The rest were dismissed; any boy who had not run, and got caught, was punished severely.

If you heard the shout of 'Boy!' after supper it could mean only one thing. Someone was going to be beaten. The wretched victim would be called, quaking, into the Library. His misdemeanour would be read out – no excuses, no appeal for mercy allowed – and the senior boy, or captain of the house, usually chosen for his athletic prowess, would point to a wooden chair in the centre of the room. The culprit would bend over the back of it and grasp the wooden rail below the seat, so that his trousers were stretched over his behind as tight as a drum, while the captain selected a long cane from the rack and gave a few practice swishes in the air. Sometimes he would even run a piece of chalk along the cane, so that he could aim for the same spot with each stroke. The ensuing pain was excruciating, much the most severe that I have ever encountered. It is sometimes said that beating a boy makes him a sado-masochist. Not me.

I managed to get beaten even before the famous test. On my first Saturday afternoon I found myself at a loose end, so I went downstairs to see what other boys were doing. There was nothing on the noticeboard but 'Games', and I had not been told which game to play. I had not yet realised that at Eton you are meant to figure it out for yourself.

'You'd better go for a run,' someone said.

'A run? Where to?'

'Boulter's Lock, of course, you fool.'

I went upstairs and put on my running shorts and gym shoes.

Where on earth was Boulter's Lock? I hadn't a clue, but I thought that perhaps if I went outside I might see someone else running, and I could follow them. Sure enough, I saw a stream of boys heading off across the fields. They all looked fitter than me and ran faster, but I struggled along for about a mile until I got bored. By this time there was also a scattering of boys running back to the school, so I dodged behind some bushes, then ran back in the opposite direction.

The secret of discipline at Eton was that it was run by the boys. Anybody could play a trick like that on a schoolmaster, but other boys are not so easy to fool. That night the call of 'Boy!' after supper signalled that I had not succeeded.

But my beatings did have one good effect. My brother Alan was at the same house as me, and being four years older, was by this time a member of Library. Despite all our fights and quarrels, he found that he simply couldn't bear to watch me being thrashed. The first time he left the room, but on the second occasion he actually managed to put a stop to it, and from then on he became as protective towards me as he had once been hostile. On the whole, with many ups and downs, he has maintained this attitude ever since.

After a year Alan left, and Eton performed the magic trick which it has worked on countless thousands of boys over the last five hundred years (producing eighteen prime ministers in the process) – it gave me the confidence to think for myself. To a teenage boy who had taken it for granted that his father was a god, his mother a goddess, and the word of 'grown-ups' to be followed without question, this revelation was incredible. In many cultures it stems from desperation and leads to rebellion. At Eton it comes from confidence and leads to growth.

I enjoyed my five years at Eton, but I didn't really fit in. In those days Eton was meant for the aristocracy – boys who would inherit titles and the great estates that went with them. My schoolfriends came from this class, but I most definitely did not. When I said my father was an art historian, no one knew what on earth I was talking about, so I had to say he was a professor. Added to this, I was not brilliantly clever and, even more important, I was not that good at games. It was clearly up to me to go my own way, and I looked for a way to do it without incurring ridicule.

Until 1960, all young men had to do two years of National Service in the military when they left school. At Eton it was assumed that we would go into the Guards regiments and become junior officers, and to prepare for this we had to join the Army Cadet Corps. Each week we struggled into ill-fitting khaki uniforms and marched about a parade ground in huge shiny black boots. We also went out on manoeuvres on Aldershot plain with rifles and blank ammunition, to see what a real battle would be like. (Very boring, was the answer.) I soon realised that I could do better than this. When some brave soul from the Air Ministry decided that Eton should have an Air Cadet Corps as well as an Army Cadet Corps, I joined it at once. From then on I was seen as an eccentric. It was not that my friends deserted me, but they sensed that I could no longer be trusted to conform. And the difference between us was plain to see: each week, when they all put on their khaki uniforms, there was I wearing Air Force blue.

At first there were only eight of us air cadets – eight, in a school of thirteen hundred boys – but our number gradually grew to twelve. When the Army Corps went on manoeuvres, we were crammed into some rickety old plane and flown over the 'battle' to provide air support. As soon as it reached Aldershot the plane would start flying in tight little circles on one wing, while we were exhorted to try to spot troop movements on the ground. If there is one way to guarantee that a novice will be airsick, this is it. To the unpleasant rotating motion was added the terror of knowing that the plane was about to flop onto its back and crash at any minute. We had been issued with sickbags, and almost everyone needed them, but luckily not me. I had already flown to Lisbon twice with my family, which had involved crossing the Bay of Biscay in a plane called a Dakota. Designed in 1937, the Dakota was the safest plane in the world, but also the bounciest, and the Bay of Biscay is a very turbulent stretch of sea, so I had got used to ghastly flights. After the first airborne manoeuvres at Eton, only two of the twelve cadets were still thinking of becoming pilots. Then my lone colleague switched to the Fleet Air Arm, which was grander than the Air Force by virtue of its connection with the Navy, and I alone was left to represent Eton in the RAF.

My next venture was to learn to drive. Driving while one was at Eton was almost unthinkable – as well as illegal – but to me driving a car seemed to be the purest expression of independence one could find. When I was seventeen, after many lessons during the holidays, I managed to pass my driving test, and my brother volunteered to buy me a cheap car. Alan could never do anything by halves. One day, as I was walking along the street with my schoolfriends, I saw an incredible two-seater sports car sitting outside our classroom. It was shiny black with bright red seats, and it had a bonnet which seemed to go on for ever. It turned out to be a K2 Allard, designed and built in England with an American V8 engine, and one of the least predictable supercars of its age. As I gazed at it in awe, Alan appeared.

'How do you like your transport?'

I don't think I have ever been so excited, before or since. For the first time, but by no means for the last, one of my dreams had come true. It was certainly not possible to keep the car on school premises, so I enlisted the help of a lady friend of my father who lived nearby in Datchet. She was one of those heavenly people who loves getting up to mischief (I suppose that was why she was a lady friend of my father), and she offered to store the car in her garage so that I could drive it occasionally, wearing heavy disguise.

One day three of us, including Watt, decided to go to Sandown races. We dressed for the occasion as we thought all horsey people dressed, in cavalry twill jodhpurs and yellow rollneck sweaters. Imagine our dismay when we found that everyone else on the racecourse was wearing a grey raincoat. We must have stood out like sore thumbs. If we had been caught we would certainly have been expelled.

Meanwhile, my Air Force career was progressing well. In the next school holidays I was told to report to RAF Hornchurch in Essex for an aptitude test to see if I was 'pilot material', and I drove down there in the Allard. I must have been terribly conceited, as I assumed that the RAF would be thrilled to have an Old Etonian, and that the test was just a formality. I have made this sort of assumption several times in my life, and each time I have, quite naturally, come a cropper. The RAF were happy to get an Etonian, but a pilot requires certain skills in order to survive, and these are not necessarily influenced by which school he has been to. At the end of the test the examiner was undecided. He stood at the window, deep in thought.

'Look at that bloody sports car!' he suddenly yelled. I had parked the Allard in front of the building.

'It's mine,' I said.

'Crikey! Well, if you can drive that, you can certainly fly a plane,' he said, and he passed me right away.

Alas, it wasn't that simple. It rained on the drive back to London. As I drove up Ilford High Street I touched the throttle just a little too hard, and the next moment the car had spun round on the shiny wet tarmac and broadsided a bus. No one was hurt, but it was a bad omen, of which my examiner remained blissfully unaware.

A few months later the Eton College Air Cadet Corps, proud of their new pilot-to-be, sent me down to an RAF base in Sussex to take a ride in a new jet-fighter. I was strapped into the front seat of a big, sleek silver plane called a Gloster Meteor – the main pilot always sits in the rear seat of a two-seater, I don't know why – and we went hurtling off into the clouds. It was a fantastic thrill, even greater than driving the Allard, and I was hooked on flying from then on. But when we came in to land we had a problem.

'Mayday, Mayday, I've got no brakes!' I heard the pilot yell as we shot down the runway. 'My brake lever's broken off, Colin! Try yours!' he shouted at me. 'It's a lever you squeeze by the joystick!'

'I can't find it' – the cockpit was completely crammed with incomprehensible instruments and knobs. 'Can't we go round again while I look?'

'No . . . Feel – grab anything!' he cried.

It is surprising how much you can think and say in five seconds if you think they are going to be your last. By this time we had reached the end of the runway and were still doing about 120 mph.

I reached down and squeezed the first thing I could find. The plane gave a great screech and nearly stood on its nose, then set off again in a new direction across the grass.

'Not so bloody hard!' I heard the pilot exclaim as we skewed around once again. Then he changed his mind.

'Squeeze harder, for Christ's sake!' as we slammed through a rustic stone wall, hurtled across a main road, through another wall, and into a field of corn.

Finally we grunched to a halt. The pilot climbed out without a word, and ran like a lunatic. He knew where the footholds were in the side of the fuselage (the cockpit on a Gloster Meteor was about eight feet off the ground), and he knew how to get out of his parachute in a hurry. He also knew that we were sitting on a few hundred gallons of highly inflammable aircraft fuel. I knew none of these things, so I watched him go with some surprise, and followed in a much more leisurely fashion. A fire engine and an ambulance came charging across the field as I strolled over to where he had taken cover. Perhaps because of his unseemly haste, he was strangely silent on the trip back to the airfield, while I was rather too chatty. It had all seemed to me to be wildly exciting, and I was looking forward to doing it again.

Another test in which I did badly was the entrance exam to Christ Church, Oxford. I was due to go to Oxford after my National Service was over, but I had to take the examination first, and once again I was too confident. It wasn't that I was cocky; I was actually quite nervous. But as usual, because I had assumed that the outcome was a foregone conclusion, I got a very nasty shock. I can still remember the main question in the exam paper: 'Discuss the novel of your choice. You have three hours in which to write your answer.'

Aaaagh!

I should have walked out there and then and said, 'I am not an academic. I am not suited to university life and never will be.'

The most recent book that I had read at that time was a translation of *Les Chemins de la liberté* by Jean-Paul Sartre. It sounds pretty highbrow, but I had actually chosen it because it looked modern and vaguely sexy. I had a horror of all those worthy English novelists like Trollope and Dickens, and I still have – although I've read most of them by now. Sartre's book was about 'existentialism', which fascinated me, even if I did not quite understand it, so I set out to write about that.

Needless to say, the examiners thought I had gone stark, raving mad. By the time I went for my 'viva', or interview, they were extremely hostile.

'Have you ever been abroad?' one of them asked (I had written about a foreign book). Naively, I missed the obvious fact that to these old gentlemen, in 1950, going abroad was tantamount to treason.

'Yes, I have,' I chirruped gaily. (I even thought they liked me.)

'Oh, really. And where, may I ask, have you been . . . abroad?'

'France,' I said.

'Anywhere else?' Icy sarcasm.

'Italy, Switzerland . . .'

'Anywhere else?' Heavy irony now, which, of course, I missed completely.

'Portugal, Spain, Holland . . .' My voice tailed away. Suddenly I realised I was going in the wrong direction.

'Anywhere else?'

'Er, no.'

'Well, thank goodness for that. We don't want to be here all day.' I cursed my father for taking us on all those wonderful, exciting trips, but it was too late – the damage was done. Only a solemn letter from my tutor at Eton to the head of the college prevented me from being barred from Oxford for ever, and they reluctantly granted me a place.

But first I had to do two years in the Air Force, and in 1951, when the time came for me to join, another crisis arose. On the day I was to present myself at the RAF base at Patrington, near Manchester, my father was due back from a visit to Australia, and my mother was absolutely determined that the children should be at home when he arrived. I now know that he had got seriously involved with an Australian lady (no surprises there), and that my mother was quite desperately frightened that she would lose him. If she welcomed him home with all his children, she reasoned, he would remember his responsibilities and stay. As it turned out, she was right, but at the time we all thought she was just making a fuss.

My mother sent a telegram to 'The Commanding Officer, RAF, Patrington,' asking for permission to delay my joining the RAF by two days. No doubt she signed it 'Lady Kenneth Clark'. Soon we got a telegram in reply: 'Granted. J. Finch. Air Commodore,' and that was it. But huge, unwieldy organisations like His Majesty's Armed Forces simply do not work like that. By the time I did arrive, no one was expecting me, or had even heard of me. This was hardly surprising. At a base like Patrington the Commanding Officer was as remote to 'other ranks' as the man in the moon. The RAF was taking in about six hundred recruits a week, and most of them were coming in through this one reception centre. Since I had come on a Thursday instead of a Tuesday, I was a forgotten man; but I had to be put somewhere, so I was sent to a hut with the others who had arrived that day, all of whom were very much older than myself. It was normal practice to delay doing National Service for as long as possible, in the hope that it might be stopped before one was called up (it eventually came to an end in 1960). These men had managed to put off the evil day for five years by pretending to be, and in some rare cases actually being, apprentices.

Soon after lights out I discovered that although they were older than me, they were far more frightened. They came from that stratum of the working class where you lived with your Mum until you were married, and I was the only person in the whole hut who had ever spent a night away from home.

After ten years at a boarding school, Patrington was a piece of cake. I settled in happily, writing the men's letters home and helping them to fill in all their paperwork. I was still 'different', but not too different, and I had certainly never been more anonymous in my life. I even quite enjoyed being marched about and shouted at – it made us seem like a team – and compared to Eton, the food wasn't bad at all. After three weeks of this we were marched into a hall and given a lecture on the joys of being a pilot. It takes about twenty-five men on the ground – 'erks', as they were called – to keep one man in the air, and most recruits did not expect to fly. Some of my new friends, though, thought that it sounded like a good idea – the pay was better than for working in the cookhouse, at least – and I stayed behind with them, making sure I was last in the queue so that I would get more attention.

An officer moved slowly down the row of men, asking questions.

'Have you ever heard of a Spitfire?'

'It's a plane, sir.'

'Bomber or fighter?'

'Don't know, sir.'

'Can you do decimals?'

'Don't know, sir,' etc.

By the time he got to me, he thought he'd have a laugh.

'Tell me Pythagoras' Theorem.'

'The square of the hypotenuse in a right-angle triangle is equal to the sum of the squares of the other two sides, sir.'

The other officers in the room stopped and stared.

'And you want to be a pilot, do you?'

'I've already passed to be a pilot, sir.'

'What! When?'

'At Hornchurch, last October, sir.'

'What the bloody hell are you doing here? Come to think of it, you don't look old enough to be an apprentice. What's going on?'

'I don't know, sir.'

Now a senior officer came across.

'Get this man into the trainee aircrew course immediately.'

There was a corporal in attendance, and he walked over with me to my hut. Then he actually carried my kit bag over to my new quarters. Success doesn't come much sweeter than that.

The group of men I now joined were completely different. They were all eighteen, like me, and as keen as I was to start training. Soon we were sent off to our first real RAF camp, where we were subjected to three months of intensive 'square bashing'. This involved a lot of marching backwards and forwards on a parade ground while being bellowed at by sadistic sergeants, and was the accepted method of instilling discipline into all military personnel. It might have been a bit more suitable for the infantry, where men must think as a unit in order to survive, than for prospective pilots of single-seater fighter planes, but it did us no harm.

Being in an RAF dormitory was like being back at my junior school. Pillowfights, ribald comments shouted after lights out, some-one farting like a thunderclap first thing in the morning. Most of the time we were suffering from a mixture of hunger, thirst, exhaus-tion and boredom. A typical part of our discipline involved the wooden floor of the barracks. If this ever got dirty, it was a ghastly job to hand-scrub it clean again and put on fresh wax. We would get it up to a high glaze, then leave a pile of little bits of old carpet by the door. When anyone arrived in the entrance he would be greeted with howls of 'Use the pads!' He would then enter like an ice skater, a 'pad' under each boot. Sometimes the sergeants took a malicious delight in marching us into the barracks with our muddy boots still on, so we would have to spend the whole weekend getting the floor back to the necessary mirror-finish again.

'If it moves, salute it; if it doesn't move, move it; if you can't move it, paint it white,' was the RAF motto at that level. Sex, emotion and intellectual thought were banned. Religion was per-mitted only at Church Parade on Sunday. With my cut-glass Etonian accent I was expected to be a little eccentric, just enough to give the squad some amusement at the sergeant's expense.

'What religion are you, Clark?' he shouted.

'Blue domer, Sarge.'

'What the 'ell's that?'

'I prefer to worship God under the blue dome of Heaven than in church, Sarge.'

'C of E,' bellowed the Sarge and moved on.

The camp had its own scruffy cinema, and on Saturdays and Sundays I would sneak away and spend hours watching the old movies that had finally found their way there. (I was particularly interested in trying to work out how they were made.) Very occasionally we would be given a pass to go off the base. Then, using money from my grandfather's trust, I could invite all my friends to a slap-up meal. We would all pile into the local taxi and head for the nearest grand hotel. We did not have any civilian clothes, and the management very much disliked having four scruffy aircraftmen sitting among the old ladies and the potted palms. But I had spent many hours in such establishments with my parents. The Avis Hotel in Lisbon, the Crillon in Paris, the Danieli Palace in Venice, had all been subjected to my childish whims, so the hotels of Scarborough and Harrogate did not stand a chance. I once invited all my sergeants to such a meal. They sat like little children at a birthday party, and were heartily relieved when they were back in their local pub, but the occasion greatly improved my chances for passes on future weekends.

I assumed that my parents had forgotten about me altogether, but one day they arranged for me to go to lunch with Osbert Sitwell, whose family's country home was quite near the camp. My Allard had long been consigned to the scrap heap, but I borrowed an elderly Vauxhall and drove over in my blue serge uniform, feeling very nervous and out of place.

The house, when I found it, had the most forbidding exterior I had ever seen – just a high brick wall with blackened windows. Inside, it was incredibly grand, with a wonderful view over the garden and the surrounding countryside. The walls were covered with pictures, their frames touching each other so that one could hardly see the red damask behind them. Sir Osbert was a charming host, but it was his sister Edith who was unforgettable. I had been taken to her poetry recitals as a child, and had felt in awe of her ever since. She wore long dresses of medieval design, and had a profusion of gigantic jewels on ears and fingers and wrists. I got the fright of my life when she first appeared, but she turned out to be wonderful, funny, witty company. Like all really clever people she made her guests feel as if they were as intelligent as she was. I expect that I was not too tolerant of my RAF colleagues when I returned to my barrack hut that night.

Finally the Air Ministry decided that it was time for us to learn to fly, and our lives changed dramatically. The classroom replaced the barrack square, and we spent hours studying aerodynamics, navigation, meteorology and the theory of flight. The first aircraft we encountered was an elderly biplane called the de Havilland Tiger Moth, which was of an extremely old-fashioned design. It had two seats which were open to the wind, so you had a most wonderful view, but when you looped the loop you found yourself hanging upside down, held in by two thin straps of webbing which stretched alarmingly. Luckily the 'Tiger' was not very fast. It took off at about 25 mph, which meant that if it was loosely tied down in a 30 mph wind, it could take off all on its own. Its fuselage and wings were made of fabric, wood and wire, all of which protested furiously when it was put into a dive, but it was actually one of the safest planes ever built. If you had a co-pilot, you could climb out on to the wing and mend something in mid-air. The Tiger Moth was designed for the First World War, not the Second, and certainly not the Third, which was the war that we were presumably being trained for. It bore absolutely no relation to modern jets, but we learned a lot about being in the air.

After twelve hours of flying time, which is much more than it sounds at those speeds, we progressed to the Chipmunk, a sleek little silver plane with low wings and an enclosed cockpit, which was much more up to date. The Tiger Moth had to be started by the extremely risky method of swinging the propeller by hand, rather like cranking an old car. The Chipmunk was much safer. A large cartridge was loaded into a sort of gun in the engine. You pulled a wire loop in the cockpit, the cartridge fired and the engine burst into life. The only trouble was that the cockpit was very small. As one clambered in with a parachute strapped to one's backside, it was all too easy to catch the firing loop by mistake. Then it was to be hoped that no one was standing near the propeller, or they would be neatly sliced up and distributed all over the airfield.

The Chipmunk was probably the easiest plane to fly ever designed. The Airspeed Oxford, our next mount, was definitely one of the nastiest. To make matters worse we were sent to the most dangerous place in the British Isles to learn to fly it. Dalcross Airport – now Inverness Airport – is on the Moray Firth in the very north of Scotland. The weather there is atrocious for eight months of the year, and it is surrounded by mountains which plunge straight into the sea. Avoiding these mountains in thick cloud and rain was extremely difficult, but was absolutely essential if one wanted to survive. Nobody flies into the side of a Scottish mountain more than once. The only landing aid we had – i.e. the only way of getting back safely over the airfield and finding the runway – was a radio device called 'the Beam'. As your plane got near to base, you started to hear different noises over the headphones. 'Beep bip, bip beep' meant you were too far south, and must turn north. 'Bip beep, bip beep' meant you were too far north, and must turn south. A steady note meant you were 'on the beam', directly lined up to land. Or then again, you might be going away from the airfield in completely the opposite direction. The difference, as an astute reader will have already spotted, between 'beep bip, bip beep' and 'bip beep, bip beep' is a pretty fine one, and it was very easy to get confused. But the designers of the beam were not finished yet. If you were in the perfect spot, over the beacon, there was a zone of total silence. And of course that was also what you heard if you were in an imperfect spot, out of range of the whole contraption. It must have been the most confusing system ever designed, and looking back it is a mystery that any of us survived, but when you are all alone and running out of fuel in ten-tenths cloud, it is amazing how hard you concentrate on those beeps.

Despite all this, we were happier at Dalcross than at any other camp. My Uncle Russell and his family lived nearby in Inverness, and my Aunt Margaret would cook huge meals for me and my friends every weekend. I had now acquired a new MG sports car, and four of us would cram into its little two-seater interior and set off to explore the Highlands (and, in particular, the pubs). Those mountains were as beautiful in the sunshine as they were dangerous in the clouds.

The countryside was almost deserted, and while we were meant to be learning to navigate in our planes we would often return to our favourite spots and do a bit of low flying, to get a different perspective. There was a little railway line running from village to village, and when we got lost, which was pretty often, we would fly down the line until we got to a station. If we flew slowly right between the platforms we could read the name from the board on the railings, then look it up on our maps. This did involve a certain danger, because station masters do not really approve of a couple of tons of noisy metal zooming down their line at 100 mph unless it is attached to the rails. It is true that they were not used to reacting very quickly, as their stations probably had only two trains a day, but if they were fast enough to read the number on your fuselage, you could be in very bad trouble indeed.

Our flying course had started with sixty young men. In 1952, after a year of training, those of us who remained were due to be presented with their 'Wings'. This was a tremendous achievement. During that period three of us had died in crashes, ten of us had just lost their nerve and quit, and another eight had been turned down for one reason or another.

I had nearly been thrown out quite early on. In the course of parachute training we were taken to Inverness public baths and made to jump off the highest diving board in full flying kit and with a parachute and a dinghy strapped to our rear. When I got to the end of the board I simply froze. I had never told anyone, but actually I was terrified of heights.

'What's the matter?' shouted the instructor, far below. 'Are you frightened?'

I thought about it for a moment. What the heck, I was an Old Etonian. 'On balance, I have decided that I am more frightened of jumping off this board than I am of you,' I replied, and carefully retraced my steps. For some reason this was taken as a display of initiative. At least I had made a decision for myself, and the truth was that if a pilot did go down in the North Sea, the water was so cold that he would be dead in five minutes anyway.

We survivors were given a big ceremonial parade, with an Air Marshal to do the honours. My mother and sister came up for the event, and caused quite a sensation, what with Colette flirting with all my pilot friends and my mother flirting with the instructors. Everyone got very over-excited, and I nearly failed again on the very last day. I had decided that my uncle and aunt might be feeling a little left out, so I flew over to Inverness and did a series of very tight turns a few feet above their house. That certainly made my poor aunt feel involved, but it also drew a lot of attention from her neighbours. When I got back to the airfield, I felt I might have gone too far. Sure enough, half an hour later I got the dreaded message: 'Pilot Officer Clark. Report to the Commanding Officer immediately.'

'Sir?'

'Pilot Officer Clark, I'm afraid there is bad news.' And he handed me a yellow envelope. It was a telegram, which in those days was very expensive, and only used by those of modest income to inform each other of a death.

Trembling with relief that I had not been caught low flying and summarily kicked off the course, I tore the envelope open and looked inside. 'Congratulations to our intrepid bird man,' it read. 'From Laurence Olivier and Vivien Leigh.'

'All right, Clark?'

'Yes, sir. Thank you, sir.' I stuffed the paper in my pocket and stumbled out.

I was sorry to leave Scotland. My uncle and aunt had looked after me with more kindness and concern than I had ever received at home, and I loved them dearly. The only area where we disagreed was drink. My friends and I were very fond of strong Scottish beer, and my uncle and aunt were strict teetotallers.

When my mother came up from London to stay with her brother and sister-in-law for the Wings parade, she definitely felt in need of alcoholic refreshment.

'Don't you have anything at all to drink in the whole house?' she asked.

'Well, as a matter of fact we do,' my uncle and aunt replied with pride. 'You gave us a bottle of sherry when we got married [sixteen years earlier], and we haven't opened it yet. You can have that.'

'Good,' said my mother, and to their horror, and with my help, the bottle was finished next day.

Our new base was at Driffield, on the Yorkshire coast. The fact that the aeroplane we had trained on, the Oxford, had two engines, made the Air Ministry think that the transition to a twin-engined jet-fighter, the Gloster Meteor, would be a simple one. The fact is that aeroplanes with jet engines behave completely differently to aeroplanes with propellers. If you cut the throttle on a propeller-driven plane, it almost stops in mid-air. When you do this on a jet plane, nothing happens at all and you just go sailing on. The 'lag' is dramatic. In tight situations, like formation flying for example, you have to learn to react a few seconds ahead. To add to our problems, there were not enough training aircraft – dual-control Mark VII Meteors like the one I had crashed in while I was at Eton – to go round. We were taught all sorts of tactics in the classrooms, but did not get much instruction in the actual art of flying a jet plane. After a couple of hours of 'circuits and bumps' – take-offs and landings – we were simply sent off in a single-seater (Mark IV) and told to get used to it.

Early jets used an enormous amount of fuel. An Oxford could fly for five hours at a stretch. A Meteor was limited to forty minutes in the air at a high altitude, and twenty-five minutes at sea level. This meant two things: firstly, we had to taxi round the perimeter track of the base absolutely flat out, actually lifting off every now and then, so as to become airborne as soon as possible; and secondly, when we did get back to the airfield after a mission, we only had one chance to land. There simply was not enough fuel to go round and try again.

As we were to be fighter pilots, who might well be used in a ground-attack role at some time in the future, we were now actually encouraged to 'low fly' – over the sea and the Yorkshire moors. This made flying much more fun. We were nineteen, and we loved to pretend that we were going into battle. There was a Butlin's holiday camp on the cliffs not far from the base with a huge open-air swimming pool. The trick was to come in towards the pool at a hundred feet above the water, doing about 350 mph. Half a mile before we reached land, we would cut the throttle and pull back hard on the joystick. Jet planes 'mush' – that is to say, they keep on going in the same direction for quite some time after they are given a sharp command. With a bit of luck, two tons of silver twin-engined jet fighter, standing on its tail, would arrive about fifty feet over the pool, in total silence.

Simultaneously we would push the throttle fully open and the 25,000-horsepower jet engines would open, pointing downwards. The blast was just about enough to empty the pool of water, not to speak of people. As the plane was now going vertically upwards, no one could read the numbers on the wings, and so, in theory, one was safe from detection. Levelling out at five thousand feet one could see absolute carnage below, and I now realise how dreadfully irresponsible we were. People could easily have been killed in the panic, although I don't believe that anybody was.

'Who the hell was low flying over the sea today, chaps?' the Commandant would say on our return. 'Butlin's are in an uproar.'

'I was, sir. Perhaps I misjudged it a little coming home. But you know how those trippers exaggerate. They've never seen a plane before in their lives.' And we all laughed. On the whole we were a devil-may-care lot. A few more of us crashed and died, but that was taken as a matter of course.

After three months at Driffield we progressed to squadron training at RAF Stradishall in Suffolk. It was a horrible place, and was later converted into a holding camp for illegal immigrants. A few years ago I read that the inmates had gone on strike over the conditions, and particularly the quality of the food. It's nice to know that some things don't change.

It was at Stradishall that the instructors decided I had had enough. The truth is that I was never quite as brave as a fighter pilot has to be. I couldn't chuck that plane around the sky as if it was part of me, as a good pilot must.

I certainly wasn't sad to leave Fighter Command. Apart from my lack of courage, I had never fancied shooting at anyone, and if I had passed the course in 1952, that was beginning to look like a necessity. Britain had lots of little native uprisings to put down in those days – Malaya, Aden, Kenya and so on. Many people in the Air Force considered the chance of taking potshots at defenceless wogs too good to miss, so when I had 'Not suitable material Fighter Pilot' written in my logbook, I was rather proud.

But that was not the end of my flying career. Very flatteringly, if naively, the Air Ministry took the view that when you had got your 'Wings' you could fly any aeroplane built. I was transferred to Transport Command, and found myself back in Yorkshire at RAF Dishforth, flying a lovely old four-engined propeller plane called a Hastings. There was an 'emergency' in Malaya at the time, and my first job was to fly to Singapore, carrying troops out and married families back. It took us five days to get there, flying for eleven hours at a stretch, and we landed in Malta, Iraq, Karachi and Sri Lanka en route. When great stormclouds blew up over the

Bay of Sharks in the Indian Ocean, the turbulence was so severe that we had to fly at only fifty feet above the sea for many hundreds of miles, often through waterfalls of rain. Considering what was just beneath us, we were very glad that the Hastings did not let us down.

On one trip two of our engines seized up, but luckily we were over the desert. We staggered into Sharjah in the Trucial Oman, and I have never seen such a godforsaken place in my life. Just a few huts, around a runway carved out of the sand, and some Arabs hiding in the dunes. Unlike Stradishall, I believe Sharjah has now changed a great deal.

Our passengers must have had a ghastly journey, as the planes were very slow, with no pressurisation, no air-conditioning and no soundproofing. On one occasion when we came back from Egypt with a senior officer's car on the plane, we took it in turns to sleep on the back seat. With all the car's windows shut it was relatively peaceful.

On another flight I took a terrific fancy to someone's sixteen-year-old daughter. Of course her mother greatly disapproved of a nineteen-year-old Pilot Officer chatting up her little baby and told me to leave her alone. But I discovered that the mother was very prone to airsickness, so just before my break started – we had two pilots and flew one hour on, one hour off – I would rock the plane around like a cork in a rough sea. Then when I went back to flirt, Mum would be groaning under a blanket. I actually arranged to meet my young lady later, in London, but although her Mum had become less hostile, the magic had gone.

I V

PAÇO DA GLORIA

IN 1953, WHEN I HAD COMPLETED my National Service, I knew that I had to get a job. I was not due to go up to Oxford for another eight months, and I certainly could not spend that time hanging around with my parents. They had a new and larger house in Hampstead, with a beautiful garden, but I found it claustrophobic. They both led busy social lives, and they hardly recognised this young man who had spent the last two years flying round the world. My parents' servants, too, resented the extra work my presence entailed. There was a housekeeper, a butler and a cook who had no intention of providing hot meals for me if my parents were out. (Years later when I was filming with Prince Charles at Windsor Castle, I found he had exactly the same problem.)

I looked round for something to do, and decided on birds. Ever since I had been a little boy, I had been interested in birds. I suppose that for me they represented a form of escape – the ability to fly away (perhaps this was why I had joined the Air Force). I also thought of them as vaguely sexy – I can't imagine why. At any rate, I decided to get a job working with birds, and applied to the London Zoo for a job as a keeper. Surprisingly enough they did need an extra keeper – working with the monkeys. I signed on, and trotted straight round to the Tropical Bird House.

'We didn't ask for an extra helper,' said the head keeper there.

'The office thinks you did,' I said.

No one turns down extra staff in that sort of situation. The more staff you have, the more important your department becomes compared to other departments. So they took me in, and I was duly trained in the art of looking after tropical birds. Somehow the Monkey House survived without me. I detest monkeys.

In the next six months I learned a lot – about humans as well as animals. When we prepared the food, for instance, we had to be unbelievably clean and careful. A waiter in a posh restaurant can put almost anything in the food, with the possible exception of ground glass. The worst that can happen is that the customer will get indigestion. If one speck of dirt gets into a tropical bird's dish, or one implement is used that hasn't been boiled, the next morning 'the customer' will be lying on its back on the floor of the cage, with its little claws sticking up in the air. And the zoo hates a dead tropical bird. One thing all my wives have agreed on is how tidy I am in the kitchen. Some of my American friends have accused me of being 'anally retentive', but it isn't that, it is just training.

Another important thing which you learn when you work in a zoo is how to observe. Animals spend a lot of time watching you. If you are prepared to watch them back, it is much easier to build a relationship. I have enjoyed watching people ever since, and that has definitely been a help when I have been making programmes for television.

When October came, I had to make another dramatic switch. I went up to university to read Modern Greats – Politics, Philosophy and Economics – but I could not settle down. Oxford was enormous fun, but it was an almost total waste of time. Many of my friends from Eton were there, and I shared beautiful rooms in Peckwater Quad at Christ Church, with my great friend Tim Rathbone (later Conservative MP for Lewes, in Sussex), who had just spent two years in the Army. All we wanted to do was go to parties, get drunk and chase girls – we had yet to learn that if you do one, you can't do the other.

What a waste. What a mistake. My parents never said anything. They must have seen what was going on, but they didn't seem to feel involved. For most people, their three years at university is the most formative period of their whole life. To me it meant nothing. I felt very disappointed at the time, but I now realise that for some people Oxford can be just another stage in growing up, and not a very important one. I had two wonderful tutors, a philosopher called Gilbert Ryle and an economist called Sir Roy Harrod. I also had Robert Blake, now Lord Blake, for Political History, but he was not remotely interested in his students' progress, and we weren't interested in him.

Despite all these advantages, university life was like going backwards. I had been an officer in the Air Force, and had flown jet planes; I had my brand-new sports car (an Austin Healey), and I did not want to revert to being a schoolboy again.

During the long vacation of my second year at Oxford in 1954, I found myself staying in a little palace in the mountains of northern Portugal, and the course of my life changed once more. I had planned to go on a driving tour of Europe with my room-mate, but at the last minute he had backed out. Tim was, and still is, a more serious and diligent character than I am. He saw that this trip could easily deteriorate into another drunken waste of time, and he did not want to be led too far astray. I was left with nothing planned for the whole summer, and this must have been an even greater threat to my parents than it was to me.

One evening they invited an American architect called Norman Bliss to dinner in Hampstead. Norman was pale and earnest, and about twenty years older than me. He had been a lieutenant in the US Army and was stationed in England during the war. He was actually something of a figure of fun in London society, because he was a persistent social climber. (Most social climbers were known as 'Je suis partout', but Norman had been elevated to 'Presentez-moi donc'.) That night he said that he had also planned to go on a European driving tour and had just been let down, in his case by his mother, who had fallen ill. Why didn't Norman and I team up, my parents suggested. I had the car, and Norman had the hotel reservations for two.

The fact that an unmarried man of forty had planned to go off for a month sharing a room with his mother should have rung warning bells, but I was almost totally naive. It wasn't until we set off for Paris that I realised that Norman's physical urges lay in the opposite direction to mine. At the very moment that I wanted to go in search of girls, Norman was keeping an eye open for sailors. Soon the differences between us started to multiply. My car was a convertible Bristol 402, which I had bought from the actress Jean Simmons. Norman thought, correctly as it turned out, that the sun would make his nose go bright red, but I couldn't stand to have the top up in that glorious summer weather. By the time we got to Santiago de Compostela in Spain, we were hardly on speaking terms. This was extremely awkward, since we were driving together all day and sharing a room, sometimes even a double bed, at night, and were scheduled to do so for the next three weeks.

We had driven to Santiago to witness the fantastic ceremony that is held there every year on St James's day. A burning brazier is hung on a chain from the tower inside the cathedral, and during the service the priests start to swing it up and down the aisle. They manage to get it going right up to the top of the roof, and soon it is roaring between the pews at sixty miles an hour, only a few feet off the ground, belching flames and incense. It is incredibly impressive, but it is just as well that they only do it once a year. Talk about 'smells and bells'! It must be one of the most dangerous religious experiences you can find anywhere.

After Spain, our next stop was in the mountains of the Minho region of north Portugal, at the house of an old Englishman to whom Norman had a letter of introduction but whom he had never met. The Portuguese roads were appalling. They were like dry riverbeds, which is what they become when it rains, and there were no signposts. I was suffering from 'Spanish tummy', and by the time we found the house – by bellowing '*Inglese*' at the startled peasants, although '*Inglese*' is Italian – I was in a state of total collapse.

I got a quick impression of a huge stone house, a grey-haired host and a clean bathroom before I passed out – alone, thank God – in bed.

The owner of the house was called Peter Pitt-Milward. His appearance was that of a military man – a colonel recently retired from the Indian Army, perhaps – and his manner was of gruff courtesy, but he had a wicked sense of humour. In his youth he had been part of the Capri literary set, with Somerset Maugham and Noël Coward. He had also been very, very handsome, and had become the boyfriend of a French millionaire called Alphons Khan. In 1938 Khan had been clever enough to see that there was going to be a world war, and that Portugal might be the only safe place in Europe for a rich Jewish banker to hide. He had told Peter to search for a suitable house, and Peter had found Paço da Gloria and bought it in his own name. Khan sent out his collection of Impressionist paintings, but never went to Portugal to see them installed, deciding to stay in London after all. When he and Peter had their inevitable falling out, Khan had not been able to get the house or paintings back. He died in 1946, and Peter stayed in Portugal.

The morning after we arrived, Peter came to see me in my room. We chatted for a while, and I could see that he was a very cultured man. I was still feeling ill, and he said I must stay in bed until I had been seen by the local doctor.

Norman Bliss was furious. We were meant to be driving down to Lisbon that very day, and Norman had worked out a strict timetable for the next two weeks. Any delay would throw it into chaos. In the end, Peter pacified him by sending him off with the chauffeur to look for sailors at the local port. (I don't think there were any sailors there, so Norman seduced the chauffeur instead, which kept him quiet for the night.)

The next morning Peter reappeared with a doctor, who examined me carefully, then he and Peter gabbled away in Portuguese for a few minutes.

'He says you have a serious case of amoebic dysentery, and you must not get out of bed for a week,' Peter told me after the doctor had gone.

I greeted this news with relief. I didn't know what amoebic dysentery was, but I didn't feel that ill, and I certainly didn't want to drive down to Lisbon with Norman.

Norman, on the other hand, was in despair. 'We can't miss another day. Our reservations and our arrangements all round Europe will be put out. I'll take the car and go on ahead, and you can join me when you're better. Give me the keys to the car, and I'll leave at once.'

Luckily, even in my weakened condition I had had the foresight to hide the keys. My reply came into the modern category of 'expletive deleted'.

Norman nearly had a fit, but the chauffeur was called, again, and told to drive him to the railway station at Oporto, about forty miles away. He could hire a car, Peter told him, when he reached Lisbon. As it turned out, Norman could not hire a car. There was no such thing as car rental in Portugal in those days, and I have no idea how he completed the trip.

As soon as Norman had left, Peter came back into my room.

'All right. He's gone. You can get up now.'

'Get up? What about my amoebic dysentery?'

'Oh, that's all nonsense. I made it up,' said Peter. 'The doctor said there's nothing the matter with you at all. You did want to get rid of that awful man, didn't you? Now, what do you want for lunch?'

Paço da Gloria was, and still is, one of the most beautiful houses in the world. It is built high up on the side of a lush green valley in the region where Portugal's best white wine, Vinho Verde, is produced. Peter was the only Englishman – the only foreigner – for miles around, and he was very much the local *grand seigneur*. He had four loyal servants: a cook, a butler, a chauffeur and a gardener, all of whom had been his boyfriends when they were young but had now married and settled down in houses which Peter had given them. Peter had spent the nine years since the war getting Paço da Gloria exactly as he wanted it, with as many as fifty local stonemasons on his payroll at any given time. The hall on the first floor was a hundred feet long, lined with tapestries and with four enormous chandeliers. There was an excellent library, and a music room with a grand piano and a harpsichord.

In front of the house, across a wide lawn, Peter had built a huge granite water-tank, eighty feet long and five feet deep, which he used as a swimming pool. It was fed by a local stream, pouring in through a fountain, so the water was always cool. Many years later, when the pool was cleaned out, it was found to contain over ten thousand quite large fish, two thousand frogs, and five hundred snakes. No one had ever been bitten, but it was surprising that there had been room to jump in.

I stayed in that idyllic place for two months. Peter was a wonderful companion. He spent a lot of time in his bedroom, into which I was not allowed, reading and writing and seducing the local boys.

Luckily, at twenty-one I was just too old for his taste. He and I would meet each evening under the arched stone *loggia* (another Italian word – '*loggia*' means shop in Portuguese) for a drink before dinner, and watch the sun go down over the unspoilt green valley below.

For all his sexy little companions, Peter was really very lonely. He had been a classical scholar at Oxford and could speak, and write, fluently in six languages – Portuguese, Spanish, French, German, Italian and English. Of course, he had nothing else to do.

The only problem with Paço da Gloria was the dogs. Peter bred Doberman Pinschers, and he always had at least three. On my first visit, the house was absolutely ruled by one called Edo, which had just won some championship in France. Edo was a massive black brute, very fierce and mindlessly aggressive. Peter was completely unafraid of him, even though Edo bit him as often as he bit anyone else, but I was scared stiff, and realised that I had to work out a method of survival. I noticed that the garden boys always carried sticks, not to hit Edo with – he was a hundred pounds of solid muscle – but to throw for him whenever he charged. This seemed to work fine: Edo was easily distracted, and would chase the stick instead of the boy, happily crunching it into matchwood before trotting off. I decided to follow the same plan as the boys, but I worked it out a little more carefully. By the pool, the lawn was held up by a granite wall, and at the edge there was a sheer drop of about six feet. The ground then continued to fall away very steeply, so that the oleanders whose flowers surrounded the far side of the pool were actually about twenty feet high. One morning I came out of the french windows of my bedroom carrying a particularly tempting stick, and, instead of scuttling straight round the corner and into my car, I walked across the lawn and stood at the edge of the drop. Edo must have thought his luck had changed. He came racing out of the house, and headed straight for me at full gallop. At the very last moment I threw the stick and jumped aside. Edo took off like a swan, and landed with the most terrible crash about twenty-five feet down the hill. A yelp of pain and surprise told me that at least I hadn't killed him. Then a lot of frantic crashing about made it clear that he was very much alive, and that he was on his way back. Sure enough, after a few minutes he came limping up the hill. He had that blessed stick in his mouth, too – he wasn't a Doberman for nothing. Finally he dragged himself across the lawn to where I stood, and leaned against me, breathing hard. What could I do? In the end I bent down and gave him a pat.

'You stupid dog,' I said.

Edo gave me a look of enormous gratitude, and he never went for me again. I think Peter was quite disappointed.

Just in case animal-lovers think that I shouldn't have been cruel to a dog, they ought to know that many years later I remembered my success with Edo, and did much the same thing to a cat. My girlfriend in New York had the prettiest little marmalade cat, which purred and made a fuss of visitors – until they stroked it. Then it would flick itself over onto its back and sink its claws and teeth into their hand, causing a nasty wound before it let go.

'Don't stroke the cat!' we would cry as soon as anyone came in. 'The cat bites! Look out!'

'Purr, purr,' the cat would go, looking forward to its moment of revenge for the boredom of its life in a New York apartment.

The visitor would bend down. 'What a pretty pussy!'

'Don't stroke it!'

Stroke, stroke. 'OW!' And we would all have to join in to prise the cat's claws out of the visitor's skin.

One day the cat did it to me. I wasn't even stroking it, I simply had my hand dangling over the arm of the sofa. I leapt up and shook it off, and kicked with all my strength, just catching it in its furry rear. The cat soared across the room, hit a picture over the mantelpiece, and dropped onto a pile of books. For a while I nursed my sore hand and the cat nursed its injured pride. Then it walked over, climbed onto the sofa, and went to sleep on my head. From then on it always liked to sleep there if it could, and I was the only person who was allowed to stroke it as much I liked. I have always prided myself that I get on well with animals.

Peter was by far the best employer in that region of Portugal. The peasant farmers and their families were often close to starvation in those days, and Peter would look after them and help them.

When their children were ill he would send his car to take them to the local hospital – such as it was – and in fact I never knew him refuse any request, however far-fetched. The local people forgave him his love of boys – although if it had been their daughters that he was after, he would have been dead within a week. Any sort of heterosexual promiscuity was unthinkable in that devoutly Catholic country, which meant that I too simply had to go without. This was a terrible strain, but I did manage to resist sleeping with the boys. I had a strong feeling that if I gave in and started an affair with one of them, I would never have gone home again.

At the end of the summer I simply had to leave, to get back for my last year at Oxford. I drove to Vigo, the port in northern Spain, and there, by pure chance, I found myself in a huge crowd waiting to greet General Franco, the Spanish dictator. The populace in Vigo all hated Franco, and were looking forward to throwing rotten fruit – some said even bombs – at him as he went by. They were completely taken off guard when the very first car in the motorcade contained the General himself. There he was in his white uniform and his little red phalangist beret, a small man with beetle brows, a hooked nose and a moustache. Next came a couple of police cars, and then another limousine, and it too had General Franco in the back, uniform and all. By the time the fifth identical General Franco had gone by, the crowd realised they might all be 'doubles', and that they had no chance at all against such a cunning opponent.

Nevertheless, the people around me were extremely jolly, and they admired my car, the convertible Bristol, like mad. We had a few glasses of wine together and I took them all for a ride. We finally ended up in their apartment, which was in a very poor area of the town. I could speak no Spanish, and they, of course, no English – but I managed to convey to them that I had been staying in Portugal. The only problem, I told my new friends, was that there had been no girls.

'Don't worry,' they said. 'You can have our sisters.' Two very bouncy young ladies were produced, and after a lot more wine, I spent a very agreeable night in a small bed, squeezed between them. The next morning they all presented me with a beautifully carved wooden model of the first experimental jet plane which the

Germans had built at the end of the war. You never know what you will find.

After a holiday like that, Oxford seemed dull and almost irrelevant. I struggled on, but my heart was not in it. Peter wrote me a ten-page letter every week, telling me what was happening at Paço da Gloria, and I often wished that I had had that affair, and stayed there for ever. I wrote back faithfully whenever I could. I had started to keep a diary while I was in Portugal, and after I left university for my first real job I kept a journal specifically to amuse Peter (it was later published as *The Prince, the Showgirl and Me*), although in the end I never sent it to him.

The memories of Peter and Paço da Gloria gradually faded into the background, but they never vanished completely. In 1975 I heard that Peter had fallen ill, and I flew out to see him. He was very depressed. He was being blackmailed by his new servants, who had taken some Polaroid photographs which even the Portuguese police could not have ignored. I had managed to make a little money by this time, so I bought the pictures from the servants.

I also agreed to pay Peter the sum of ten thousand American dollars every year until his death. Then, and only then, Paço da Gloria and the whole estate would be mine, lock, stock and barrel. Lawyers were called in and a lengthy document was drawn up – painfully slowly, as the legal team was terrified of the dogs. Peter was thrilled by the arrangement, and so was I. He was seventy-seven, and his future was secure. I owned the house of my dreams, even though I could not yet take possession.

When Peter died two and a half years later it came as a terrible shock to me, a preparation I suppose for the death of my own father. I was in Hollywood, working on a film, but I sensed that if I didn't go back to Portugal immediately I never would. I had a twelve-hour flight to Lisbon via New York, another flight up to Oporto, and then a two-hour drive up into the hills. By the time I arrived, I felt exactly like Mole in *The Wind in the Willows*. There stood that great stone palace, completely empty, dripping in the rain. There was no heating and no electric light. Everything inside was damp and dark. Even the dogs had gone, all dead but one, which had been adopted by the cook. Somehow the servants had heard that I was coming – the bush telegraph in the Portuguese countryside is much faster than any telephone – and they were gathered in a mutinous little circle on the steps.

'Go home,' I said. 'I'll see you in the morning.' And I went in to what was now my house to spend a very spooky and uncomfortable night alone. The next morning the servants were back. They had ransacked the house on Peter's death, and found his will. He had no property, of course – that all now belonged to me – but he had kept a little money in a Swiss bank, and this he had left to be split among the four of them. They assumed that I was going to steal it from them, and so they had decided to kill me.

This was a situation with which I was completely familiar. Little groups of rebellious servants had been a constant feature of my home life ever since I had been a baby.

'Don't be so silly,' I told them. 'I'm the only person who can get that money out of the Swiss bank. If you kill me, you'll never see it. I'll go to Switzerland tomorrow. In the meantime, I want you to clean up the house completely. I've photographed all the rooms' – a lie, there were twenty-seven rooms altogether – 'and if anything is missing, I'll put you all in jail.'

The next day I flew to Geneva. By coincidence I had an account at the same bank as Peter. Like all good Swiss banks, they understood the situation completely, and they handed over Peter's last remaining £8,000, in cash, without any paperwork whatsoever. I returned to Portugal the following day, changed the money into escudos and solemnly handed over the equivalent of £2,000 to each of the astounded staff. 'You are all fired,' I said pleasantly, and that was that.

Pedro, the son of the old chauffeur, appeared, on the run from the secret police, and he became my great friend and helper. It took almost two years to clear the house out. One medicine cupboard turned out to be a room ten foot square. When Pedro and I emptied a little stable behind the garage we discovered that it was sixty feet deep, with room for five horses and a wine press. Electricity finally arrived from the valley below, and even a very wobbly telephone wire came looping over the trees on tall, hand-carved poles.

I love the people of northern Portugal. They work incredibly hard, and are as friendly as children. Soon the whole village became involved with my restoration. They were still very poor, so that anything I threw out, they would welcome. Their church, which was the centre of village life, had become as scruffy as my house, so when my chapel was repainted, I arranged for the church to be repainted too. Although it was always full at every service, the church only had two pews. A few very old ladies sat on them (and so did I – the priest often gave sermons of half an hour). Everyone else simply stood, like tree trunks planted on two feet, with the men in front and the women behind so there could be no fraternisation between them. When the time came to sing a hymn, they all lifted up their voices to heaven with such a total lack of inhibition that it nearly raised the roof. I adored that racket, and when television finally arrived in the local café I paid for a complete set of wooden pews to be installed in the church, in an effort to make it more tempting. At the time they were all touchingly grateful, but in the end I fear television will win.

The other great joy for the people of that region was fireworks. The Portuguese are the greatest firework-makers in the world. It is their skill which makes Macao, near Hong Kong, the biggest exporter of fireworks in the world. In the Minho valley, each tiny village had its own saint's day, its 'festa', and this had become the excuse, after an interminable communion service, to dazzle the neighbouring villages with the most dramatic fireworks it could afford. The bigger the bang, the higher your fireworks went into the air and the more the surrounding villages would be impressed. Their ambition was to get a rocket to the moon – not to carry scientific instruments, but to burst in a shower of red and gold stars so that the whole world would go 'Aaah!'

The way to make a firework go higher is to put in more gunpowder – it is as simple as that. But in order to stop every little village blowing itself to smithereens, the Portuguese government had passed a law limiting the amount of gunpowder that could be used. Naturally this did not stop villagers from adding just that little bit extra at the last moment. As soon as the rockets started to go higher than normal, the neighbouring villages would call in the police. In fact, since there were no telephones, they would probably have had the police standing by in anticipation. A few stalwart '*guardias*', already copiously bribed with wine, would advance into the offending village carrying clumsy brass scales with which to weigh the gunpowder – itself a tricky process. The organisers of the *festa*, also drunk by now but not wishing to be led off to prison, would panic, and rush around letting off every overweight rocket they could find, not necessarily in a vertical direction. Now was a good time for a spectator to keep his head down. The ensuing display was very impressive, but I often retired under a table to watch.

In rural Portugal the village priest is still the law, as he has been for centuries. When an army marched across the country – it really didn't matter whose army, they were all the same – who was it who stopped the soldiers from looting all the property and raping all the wives? The priest would go out, armed only with his faith, and threaten eternal damnation on anyone who sinned; and very often it would work. No wonder that in my village, even in 1980, the priest was held in such high esteem. In thirty years I never saw a policeman (except on fireworks night), or heard of the need for one.

The church was the centre of village life. Mass was held there every morning at six o'clock, and the church was always completely full. I would go on Sundays, when Mass was held at eight so that everyone could have a lie-in, and I could see why it was so popular. Outside, the rain would be driving down, with a cold wind coming straight off the Atlantic. There was no electricity in the village, and no running water, so the villagers would not want to linger too long in their homes. But inside the little church, all was light and warmth and joy. Hundreds of candles would illuminate golden angels, paintings, carvings and lace. The crush would quickly warm everyone up, even more so when they all began to sing at the tops of their lungs. And the priest would tell them about their immortal souls, tell them about another world outside their wet fields and gloomy toil. He would remind them of how important they were to God, and he was right.

I once even had my own small miracle. It was 1982, and I had just arrived in Portugal for the summer from the USA, bringing with me a group of students for a tour of Europe. As well as making films, I was teaching art and film at the University of California, Los Angeles, and anyone who has taught at an American college will know that the students there vary greatly in age and social class. They also get very bored in the long summer vacation, and like to travel abroad. Some of them are prepared to pay to take their lecturer with them as a guide. I would take groups of ten at a time, and we started by staying at Paço da Gloria, although it was badly in need of restoration.

On the first Sunday morning of our stay, I walked down to the village church for Mass, and squeezed into my usual pew in front of the statue of St Anthony of Padua. St Anthony was Portuguese. He left Lisbon in 1220 to follow St Francis of Assisi, and became that saint's right-hand man. Although he is buried in Padua, St Anthony has never been forgotten by his country of birth. He is the patron saint of Portugal, and a great many Portuguese boys are still christened Antonio. The church that morning was filled to capacity with the local peasant farmers and their wives, all of whom were very poor but extremely devout. When the time came for the collection plate to be passed round, I realised that I had absolutely no money. This was extremely embarrassing. The congregation took enormous pleasure in observing everything that their strange foreigner did, and while they could only afford to give a few escudos each, they did look forward to me dropping in the equivalent of about a pound.

In panic, I looked up at the statue in front of me for help. A voice inside my head said: 'You have a hundred-dollar bill in your hip pocket.'

I couldn't put a hundred-dollar bill in that plate. Nobody in the church that morning had ever seen such a large amount of money in their lives. It would cause a sensation, and besides, it was my emergency cash, intended to last the whole trip. I explained this to St Anthony as politely as I could.

'If you can't put it in the plate, give it to the priest after the service.'

Well, you can't argue with a saint in a Catholic country. After

I emerged from the church, covered in embarrassment at being thought so mean, I went round and offered the banknote to Padre Evelino.

'Quite so,' he said, putting it in his pocket without listening to a word of my explanations. He no doubt thought I was trying to buy forgiveness for something that I was ashamed of, and I walked back to my house feeling pretty hard done by, as well as rather poor.

As soon as I arrived I was met by one of my American guests. She was a rich, elderly lady who wore a wig, and I had already wondered if she was going to be strong enough for the trip.

'Oh, Colin,' she said. 'I've just had a very strange dream. If I tell you, will you promise not to laugh?'

'I promise not to laugh,' I said. The truth was that I already knew what she was going to say.

'I dreamt that I met St Anthony of Padua, walking in the garden, and he told me to give you $10,000 for your house. Would you allow me to do that?'

'You must always obey a saint in a Catholic country,' I said gravely. And she did.

I couldn't stay in Portugal all year round – I had a house in Hollywood, and I had to earn a living too – so I used to rent out Paço da Gloria to people who appreciated peace and quiet (except for firework night) and beauty. I once returned to find that the pianist Alfred Brendel had moved in with his family, and had brought with him a wonderful Bechstein piano from Oporto. I wasn't allowed into the house during the day – no one was – but I knew how to sneak up onto the roof unobserved, and I would lie in the sun for hours, listening to him playing Beethoven and Mozart beneath me.

I have been fortunate to have owned many beautiful houses in my lifetime – the villa which I built on the cliffs on the Italian island of Ischia, the 1920s beach house in California, and an eighteenth-century manor house in Kent among them – but Paço da Gloria was far and away the most beautiful of them all. It was the most terrible wrench when I finally had to leave it for ever. By 1987 my young son was beginning to grow. He needed a stable, normal home, next to a school, where it was safe to drink the water and the nearest doctor wasn't over an hour away. What Paço da Gloria needed was a large Portuguese family living in it all year round. Every winter, when I left the house for six months or more, Mother Nature would creep in and start to take over again. Snakes and bats, to say nothing of mice and creepers, would greet me on my return; the pool would take a week to drain and two weeks to refill. There was a strange and never-identified family of cat-like animals in the roof which fed on fruit, and when the warm, wet winds of spring blew in from the Atlantic, the cold stone walls ran with water for ten days, even in the bedrooms, and the lights all fused. But when the sun shone hot in the summer, the great house stayed cool and dark, the perfect place from which to enjoy the orange trees and the pool and that incredible view.

Nevertheless, Paço da Gloria had to be sold, and for me it is now just a dream. But at least it is still there. It will never go away.

V

SEX AND MARRIAGE

GROWING UP IN THE 1930s, my brother and sister and I were meant to be of an enlightened age, but our upbringing was still Victorian. We were given no sex education whatsoever, from our parents or our schools. All we managed to learn about was guilt. At my first school, Cheltenham Junior, where I started as a boarder at the age of seven, there was absolutely no privacy, and I found this the least agreeable part of my life. There were twenty boys to a dormitory, which was natural enough, and there were communal showers. But there were also large communal lavatories, with no doors on them, which a 'nicely brought-up' boy like me found insulting. Of course the idea was to stop any hanky-panky, which, as far as I was concerned, it did. What it also caused was a lot of constipation, as one tried to wait for a quiet moment. There is nothing more humiliating for a tender soul than being mocked while one is actually, and inescapably, on the 'loo'. So I was still completely innocent when I arrived at Eton, and I pretty much remained so for the five years I was there.

There are about thirteen hundred boys at Eton, and unlike other big public schools, every boy has his own private room. My house-master took a delight in barging into mine last thing at night and bellowing some inane but highly provocative accusation, which was guaranteed to make me jump out of my skin.

'I hear that you have been having intercourse with the Italian maids!'

Of course, Mr Jaques meant *social* intercourse. Chatting to the maids in the corridors was strictly forbidden. But since I had spent the last two hours thinking about sexual intercourse with the Italian maids when I should have been studying Latin verbs, the effect was electric.

'I – er – gulp – what, sir?'

'Talking to the maids is strictly forbidden, boy, don't you realise that?'

And impossible. 'I – er – I don't speak Italian, sir.'

Big 'Aha, gotcha' leer from Mr Jaques.

'I thought you'd been there on holiday. Don't you learn anything, Clark minor? Disgusting boy.'

And he would slam out of the room, leaving me in confusion.

The Italian maids were about the only women under fifty whom we Etonians ever saw. They had fat brown faces, curly black hair, and huge greasy breasts which hung down in the most tantalising manner when they were on their knees scrubbing the floor. But they were strictly for the imagination only – as remote as hippopotami from a little, top-hat-clutching schoolboy, half their age and size.

The need for a love object starts in the early teens for boys, as it does for girls. Just as schoolgirls have fevered crushes on their older classmates in girls' schools, the real sexual tension in our all-male world was between the boys.

For the last three years of my time at Eton, most of the boys, including me, were in love with the same boy. They may have forgotten it now, after busy, successful heterosexual lives, but that is the way it was. The boy's name was Jeremy Huggins, and he sang in the choir. He had the most beautiful treble voice you could imagine, and he was remarkably handsome. In his white vestal robe, with his brown hair brushed until it glowed, his eyes gazing heavenward and his mouth open in pure song, he could make his audience swoon away during the psalms. Quite a few boys did actually faint, but no one took any notice. Church attendance was compulsory at Eton in 1948 – every weekday morning except Saturday, and twice on Sundays – and we all flocked in gleefully, hardly daring to hope that Huggins would be singing a solo that day. Eventually his voice broke into a mellow tenor, and his looks, if anything, improved. But all that attention must have been a terrific strain on him, just as it was to be on Marilyn Monroe, and he seemed to have great difficulty settling down. He became an actor and changed his name to Jeremy Brett. He played various good-looking but rather uninteresting young men, like Freddie in the London stage version of *My Fair Lady*. At one stage he married the actress Anna Massey, whose brother, the actor Dan Massey, had also been at Eton. Finally he took on the role of Sherlock Holmes – a character as eccentric as himself – giving some wonderful performances on television. To millions of people his tortured, lined face became what Holmes actually looked like. He even suffered the same depressions that the great detective was supposed to have been prey to.

Since he and I were both in show business, we used to meet every now and then, and although I never referred to it, he seemed to be aware of the role he had played in my early affections. He was sweet and sad and sincere, and still very good looking. When he died, tragically young, in 1995, I suddenly felt guilty. I've no idea whether anyone actually seduced him when we were at school, but there is no doubt that he had been the idol of hundreds of his contemporaries. In a sense I felt that he had been abused, and I had been part of it. I suppose that his beauty had been a curse, as well as a blessing.

Finally, when I reached the age of seventeen, girls came on the scene at last. My twin sister Colette was persuaded, very much against her will, to 'come out' as a debutante in the 1950 London season. This involved buying lots of long white dresses and going to endless parties and balls. The idea was for poor upper-class and rich middle-class girls to find suitable husbands. This meant upper-class girls looking for rich husbands and rich girls looking for upper-class husbands, and it worked quite well. Colette had been head girl at Cheltenham Ladies' College, and had already secured a place at Oxford, so she was not at all enthusiastic about meeting the typical debs' delights.

As her brother, I was invited to a lot of the dances, and I should have had a wonderful time. There were the girls at last, gift-wrapped and waiting to be swept off their feet. But it wasn't that simple. We were rigidly chaperoned – even a furtive grope in a taxi was considered grounds for scandal – and anyway, if one of the girls had accepted my clumsy anatomical advances I would have dropped dead with embarrassment and fright. What a shame! What a lot I missed! What a lot of time I spent propping up the bar and guffawing with my school friends, lonely and frustrated and pretending I didn't care. Who knows how the course of my life would have changed if one of those giggling feminine creatures at whom I occasionally lunged so clumsily had decided to embark on an affair. Boys and girls are all beautiful at eighteen, and it does seem sad that we were not allowed to behave like the healthy young animals we were. All too soon the tyrannies of the conscience and the intellect take over, and the innocence goes.

So when, in 1951, I went into the RAF to do my National Service, I was still a virgin, and my ignorance was intact. The armed forces do not encourage sex, or even acknowledge its existence except in married quarters. Booze is an accepted substitute, and drunken squaddies made a nuisance of themselves then as now. There were very few public-school boys in the Air Force in those days (I was certainly the only Old Etonian), and I acquired a reputation as a 'smoothie' with the gift of the gab. Soon my virginity became like a lead weight around my neck. Others boasted of their steady girlfriends at home, or the large number of village lasses they had seduced, while I could only hint at the number of my conquests – 'But of course gentlemen don't tell tales.'

In 1952 we were awarded our 'Wings' and officially confirmed as pilot officers. To celebrate this important event, I invited my three great friends to go on a pub crawl round the West End of London. As we had been stationed in the north of Scotland for the past six months, we had become pretty good bumpkins. We started by exploring the pubs around Piccadilly Circus, and by midnight we were drunk and randy. To our surprise and delight two women, older than us it is true, and only beautiful through a haze of alcohol, but women nonetheless, agreed to take us to their flat for 'a good time'. All six of us piled merrily into my car and weaved off in the direction of Notting Hill Gate. It was only when we arrived that the ladies mentioned money. Evidently they were expecting us to pay for their favours. Some noisy shouting on the pavement ensued before my friends and I piled back into the car and sped off, leaving the women very angry indeed. This rather sobered us up, which was just as well because twenty minutes later we found ourselves driven off the road by the Metropolitan Police. Before we could protest, we were yanked out of our seats and dumped unceremoniously in the back of a Black Maria. When we arrived at Notting Hill Gate police station, we were told that we would be charged with assault and battery, and were then left in separate cells to cool off.

At 8.30 the next morning, after an uneasy night, we were marched into an interview room and confronted by two plain-clothes detectives. They told us that the police had been given our car's licence number by the women, hence the arrest. Now, it so happened that the detectives already knew these two women. While they may have been prostitutes, and had probably only made the accusation out of spite, they could still press charges, which might ruin our Air Force careers. What the detectives suggested, therefore, was that we pay the women off. If we could arrange to get £100 in cash – equivalent to about £500 today – within an hour, then they would see that the whole thing went no further.

We had a quick conference. I had been the host, and I was also the only one from a wealthy family, so I agreed to ring home. My mother was relieved to hear from me after an unexplained night away, and she was immediately sympathetic to our problem. She promised to scrape together the money somehow and to send my brother Alan to the police station with it as soon as she could. Not having that sort of cash in the house, she promptly rang the richest man she knew. This happened to be the author Somerset Maugham, who was staying at the Savoy Hotel. My mother explained the situation to him. 'Willy' Maugham was no fool. Yes, he did have that amount of cash and would be happy to lend it, but he also had a friend called Ronnie Howe, who was the Commissioner of Police, and he rang him up. An hour later, as I was looking out of the window of the police station, I saw Alan drive up in his white Jaguar XK 120 sports car. At the same moment, a new lot of very stern men in raincoats marched in through the door. I noticed a look of consternation cross the faces of our original tormentors, but by this time I was fed up.

'The money has arrived and I want to go home,' I said. 'I'm not answering any more questions.'

'Oh yes you are,' said Sir Ronald Howe. 'You're going to tell me every single detail.' And we did. It was a victory of a kind, I suppose, but it was not at all what I had planned.

My parents took it well, and invited Sir Ronald to their box at the opera several times in order to repay him. My brother was the only one to tease me about it – something he still likes to do, very occasionally, after forty-five years.

My next sexual encounter was equally unsatisfactory. I had failed to make the grade as a fighter pilot for reasons already described, and been assigned to fly transport planes instead. After my first long-haul trip to Singapore I felt I deserved a treat, so I decided to sample Lavender Street, the famous red-light district of that exciting city. Lavender Street itself was out of bounds to all forces personnel, but hostess bars had sprung up all round it, so off I set. I got into a taxi outside the camp, and explained my problem. The driver didn't seem to listen. After a long drive he stopped in a quiet, leafy street and took me into a large house. I had already paid him, but I saw the lady in the foyer pay him some more. I was ushered unceremoniously into a small bedroom, told to undress and then left alone. This wasn't quite how I had pictured it. Where were the bright lights, the cool glasses of beer, the sexy hostesses queuing up to seduce me? I sat on the bed in my underpants with my apprehensions growing as fast as my sexual urges diminished. This was a war zone, after all. Perhaps I was going to have my throat cut by terrorists? After ten minutes, a pretty little Malaysian girl came in and explained the price structure. I got out my passport, in which my money was concealed, but she just grabbed the whole thing and went out again. After another wait she came back, gave me some change and started to take off her clothes. She had a lovely little body and my hopes rose. Was I going to be initiated at last? But before I could sample her delights, there was an almighty bang on the door.

'Open up! Military Police!'

The girl squealed and pulled her clothes on again – my pants hadn't even come off – as the flimsy door burst open and two gigantic sailors in white uniforms came barging in.

'Get your clothes on. Show us your papers. You're under arrest.'

'I'm an officer,' I said with as much dignity as I could muster, given that they were stamping around in shiny black boots and I had bare feet.

'Oh yes? Then get your bloody clothes on, SIR. Show us your bloody papers, SIR. You're under arrest, SIR.' Once again I found myself in a Black Maria, feeling very miserable indeed. Then another problem arose. 'I've left my passport behind!' I yelled at the sailors through the wire hatch separating us. 'Can we go back and get it?' Somehow this struck a chord. We turned round, charged back and burst in again. There was my passport lying on the front desk. This seemed a great triumph to my captors, and they now became quite friendly. I had been too close to Lavender Street, they explained, definitely out of bounds. I told them that I was an Air Force pilot who had only arrived from England that morning, and had no idea of the rules. So they took me to the taxi station instead of the police station – pausing only to beat some drunken soldier unconscious with their truncheons and throw him on top of me in the back. I then had the long and terrifying journey back to Changi Air Force Base at 3 o'clock in the morning. As we drove through the impenetrable pitch-black jungle, the driver praying just as hard as I was that there were no terrorists around, I had time to reflect that my sex life was in very bad shape indeed. I had expected to get rebuffed every now and then, but not arrested.

When my two years' National Service was over, I knew that something had to be done, however drastic, to break that bloody ice. I had arrived at Oxford University at the age of twenty-one, and I was still a virgin. The thought of going that extra yard with one of the society girls I knew filled me with terror. I was 'smooching' with the assurance of a practised lover. How they would laugh when they found it was 'my first time'! Indeed, what a muddle we would make if it was their first time too. The very thought was out of the question.

My brother Alan has often got me into trouble, but he has often got me out of it, too. I went to stay the weekend with him, and I explained the situation in despair.

'All right. I'll help,' he said. 'But you've got to do exactly what

I tell you. There is this girl called Priscilla. Lovely girl, good family. The trouble is that she is desperate to get married. So any boy who approaches her is dragged into bed and then told that he has got her pregnant. The trick is that after you have slept with her a few times, you must pass her on to someone else. She has just told me she's pregnant by me, so I'm going to pass her over to you. All you have to do is turn up and tell her that I've sent you. Make any excuse. You can leave the rest to her. But don't forget the rules. I'm not having you marry Priscilla.'

So off I went, and it worked just as Alan had said. Actually I got quite fond of Priscilla. I was much too young to get married, but she did get me over the hump, as it were, and I was grateful. I don't think she thought of me with much affection. She hardly seemed to notice who I was. She did just seem to think 'I need a husband, and he'll do.' One day, sure enough, in the Randolph Hotel in Oxford, she broke the news. Even though I was expecting it, I got a bit of a shock. Up to then, it had never occurred to me that I could ever be a father. I had to remember what Alan had told me, that it was probably nonsense, and that I must do something about it as quickly as I could. It so happened that a great friend of mine, who was at Christ Church with me, was still in the virginal state that I had left only a few months ago. I explained the situation carefully to him just as Alan had explained it to me, and he announced that he would be delighted to take over. Needless to say, he was a much more honourable, and gullible, person than Alan or me. When Priscilla told him the news – the same news – three months later, he got in the most terrible flap. I suppose she was gradually getting better at telling the story, and he believed her. But I wasn't having him throw himself away, so I put my foot down hard, and we quickly found someone else for Priscilla. And why not? All I can tell you, gentle reader, is that Priscilla has been happily married to some jolly upper-class gent for over forty years and is now a much-respected grandmother. There are many ways to heaven, after all.

'There are three great mysteries,' my father once wrote: 'Sex, fear and death.' Although he never explained this oracular pro-nouncement, I think I know what he meant. But surely sex should not be so complicated. According to the theory of evolution, sex is a natural act, more or less pleasurable, like all natural acts, which we share with the whole of the animal world. Of course, you have to remember that it isn't all that simple in the animal world either. Think of those mad ritual dances by birds of paradise, weighed down by so many feathers that they can hardly fly. Think of the mole rats. There are huge colonies of mole rats where only a few males are ever allowed to mate, and even they are restricted to the queen. That is certainly not an evolutionary system which would go down too well in London at the moment. Think of the great matriarchies – the elephants, the dolphins and the bees. Think of those snakes in North America which roll themselves into a ball a hundred strong in their effort to mate with a single female. I once spent half an hour observing a magnificent pair of tigers in a small cage. They were already mates, the parents of many sets of cubs. Clearly the female was 'in season' again, and the male was doing everything he could to seduce her. At first she would have none of it, snarling and spitting and lashing out at him whenever he approached. In the end, he got bored of this treatment and slumped down in the sunlight to sleep. Immediately she changed. She licked his face, she purred, she ran round him in skittish little circles. She was absolutely irresistible. Up he got to his feet and tried again. 'Oh no you don't, buster.' Slash, snarl, slash. Down he sat. Lick, purr, wriggle. Up he got. Slash, snarl, spit. Down he sat, and so on for over fifteen minutes. Finally he lost his patience. He gave a mighty roar, grabbed her by the neck, and in a few seconds the deed was done. I suppose nature has a good reason for all this, but it must have been very frustrating. If he had been a man he would have got fifteen years.

My next problem at Oxford was that I fell in love. This was a new experience for me and I had no idea how to deal with it. Her name was April, and she was pretty and vivacious and funny and delightful. I won't say that she was in love with me, but she was flattered by my attention and she needed the love of a boy as much as I needed to fall in love with a girl. For a whole year we danced and partied and kissed and cuddled – but that was all. The sexual revolution of the sixties was still some years away. Birth control seemed to be a complicated gynaecological process, designed for married couples. The trouble was that in those happy far-off days, nice girls simply didn't. It wasn't as if they were saving themselves for their husbands on their wedding night. That would have seemed like a quaint old Victorian idea and been greeted with hoots of laughter. It was just that the idea of living with a boyfriend in a full sexual relationship was simply unthinkable.

Finally, after months of heavier and heavier petting and parting, the moment came. I went round to collect April from her (absent) mother's flat, and she was still in bed – warm and cuddly and straight out of one's dreams. And what did I do? I fled. To my eternal shame, I simply did not have the confidence to advance, to caress her, to slip off my clothes and climb in. Perhaps it was because I was in love this time, and despite Priscilla's generosity I was still frightened of being laughed at or getting it wrong. What a tragedy. But who knows? If we had made love, we would certainly have had to start thinking of getting married, and the course of our lives would have changed completely. As it was, what could have begun a new phase signalled the end. April found a more dashing partner, while I found satisfaction in a series of girls of easier virtue, whom I didn't love at all.

This was a paradox which faced young men – and women – all over the civilised world before the arrival of 'the pill'. Nice girls didn't. You only wanted to marry a nice girl, of course, and you spent most of your time trying to seduce one. But if you succeeded, it meant that she was a naughty girl, and then you no longer wanted to marry her. It was the original catch-22, and I could no more solve it than anyone else. I would fall in love, get totally frustrated by my own lack of courage as much as by the young lady's modesty, then charge off to a nightclub, get drunk and pick up a 'hostess' for the night. How disreputable. After a while my sins would be discovered by the loved one, and there would be tearful recrimi-nations, which would only lead to more frustration. How could I explain that I wanted a loving relationship, which included sex, without making an irrevocable commitment to marriage? That is a problem for many a teenager, but by twenty-five, I felt it was one I should have solved. When I did finally propose marriage to

LEFT: My father, a great lover of music, in the library at Portland Place in 1934. This gramophone used wooden needles which had to be sharpened for every record.

ABOVE: My mother, drawn by my father during their honeymoon in 1925, although he later denied it.

RIGHT: Overawed by art. My twin sister Colette and me in 1934. Our brother Alan was to sell the picture to the Tate Gallery.

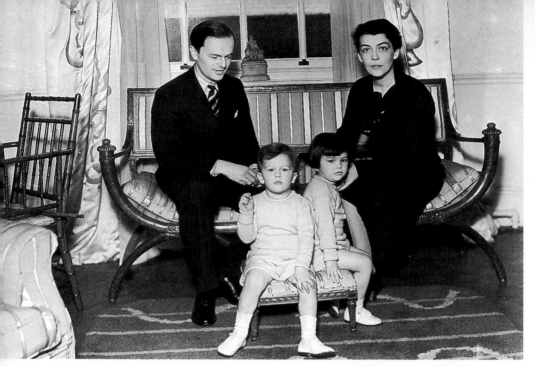

Colette and me with our parents at Portland Place in 1934.

BELOW RIGHT: Studio portrait of myself in 1943, aged eleven.

Henry Moore drew this pencil sketch of me when I was ill in bed at the age of nine. 'It's bloody good,' he said when I showed it to him years later. 'Who did it?'

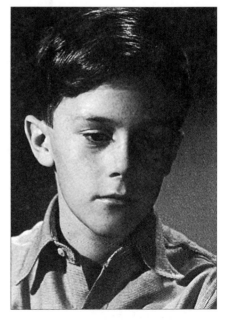

ABOVE: A picnic at Eton.
Left to right: my brother Alan;
the Countess of Crawford and
Balcarres; my mother; myself;
my father; the Earl of Crawford
and Balcarres (*front*); the Hon.
Patrick Lindsay.

LEFT: With Vivien Leigh at the
Oliviers' Buckinghamshire home
Notley Abbey in 1947. Already
in love.

LEFT: Gabriel Pascal on the lido with Jean Simmons during the 1947 Venice Film Festival (*photograph by the author*).

BELOW: Vivien Leigh at Notley Abbey in 1950 with the actress Linda Christian, wife of Tyrone Power (*photograph by the author*).

my first wife I added, by implication if not in words, 'And if you will let me have sex with you now and again I would be jolly grateful,' which wasn't the best basis for a marriage either.

By that time I was working for Granada Television in London, and my sister had begun her life in the ballet world, so I was able to meet all the dancers.

Violette Verdy was a talented and quite famous ballerina who joined the Sadlers Wells Company as a guest artist from Paris. When I saw her on stage, I was besotted. This was by no means the first time I had been dazzled by a ballerina. My parents had often taken me to Covent Garden where, from the Royal Box, I would imagine – wrongly – that I could see down into the dancers' bodices. I worshipped Margot Fonteyn, and had a crush on almost all of the principal dancers and at least six members of the *corps de ballet*. I now know that most ballerinas are absolutely adorable and worth all the trouble, but at that time it was just a beautiful dream, and I had not worked it out.

Violette was equally confused. She thought that marriage into a rich English family would give her class and stability, which means that she did not look very hard at me. We had a splendid wedding at Saltwood, presided over by the Dean of Canterbury, Dr Hewlett Johnson, who was a committed communist. I had arranged for a Rolls-Royce to drive us up to the Dorchester Hotel, where we would spend our first night, and I had found a beautiful little house on the island of Ischia for our two-week honeymoon. Once again, things did not go well. The Rolls-Royce turned out to be ancient and smelly, and poor Violette felt sick. We were forced to stop many times for fresh air. When we arrived in London, the Dorchester tried to put us in a little back room. I produced a letter confirming that I had booked the Oliver Messel Suite, and won the ensuing discussion, but it made me feel edgy, and Violette got very tense. Once we were in the suite, Violette ordered an enormous meal – something all dancers do if they are nervous – at which I only dared to nibble. When she finally got into bed, she was looking forward, I suspect, to getting a good night's sleep before the journey to Italy. Of course I had other ideas. I leapt on top of her like an idiot, but before I could get far I was interrupted by the unmistakable sounds of washing up. Donning a dressing gown, I discovered two members of the Dorchester staff crashing around in a kitchen which was part of the suite and only separated from the bedroom by a swing door. I angrily dismissed the bolshie waiters, and returned to bed with my ardour considerably dampened.

The journey to Ischia involved a taxi, a plane, another taxi, a boat and then a car, so we were both exhausted when we arrived. Violette came from country stock, and she was not as impressed as I was by the rustic beauty of the house. After two restless days (and nights), she announced that we must return to Paris immediately.

'But what about our honeymoon?'

'Surely,' she said severely, 'you don't think our marriage is going to come before my career?'

Well, yes, actually I had. It was certainly going to come before my career. But Violette would have none of it, so off we set to Paris, where Violette could keep in close touch with her mother, and even more important, her ballet teacher.

Eventually we had to return to London, where I had a house and my modest television job, and then almost immediately Violette was invited to join the New York City Ballet in America. This was a terrific compliment for a foreign dancer. David Balanchine, whose company it was, preferred tall, thin, impossibly elastic young girls as his leading ladies, and he had a tendency to fall in love with each of them in turn. Violette was anything but tall and thin, but she was brilliant at the flashy, quicksilver roles which are in all the great Petipa ballets. *Casse Noisette* formed an essential part of Balanchine's repertoire every Christmas, and Violette was excellent in it. (She was one of the few dancers I have ever known who actually listened to the orchestra while they were on stage.) Violette also wanted to escape from me, and quite rightly. I must have been nothing but a nuisance. She immediately accepted Balanchine's offer and left, with her mother, for New York. I was to join them there as soon as I could wind up my job with Granada, sell my house in London, get an immigrant's visa for the USA and find a job in New York. That was a pretty tall order. In practice it meant a minimum of six months.

By this time even I could see that the marriage was not going to work out, but I decided to go to America anyway. It seemed a good opportunity to enhance my career, so I pressed on with the plans as if nothing was wrong.

In the meantime, I had a stroke of luck. I was driving through Chelsea early one morning when I saw a tall, skinny girl battling along the pavement in what was clearly a state of distress. She was a striking mixture of beauty and ugliness – what the French call 'belle-laide' – with very big eyes, a wide mouth and a mass of unkempt blonde hair. I obviously couldn't do anything to help her, but her face, and her distress, stayed in my mind all day. That evening I went to Muriel Belcher's famous Colony Club in Soho, where Francis Bacon held court, and there was the same girl, perched on a bar stool, laughing and smiling but apparently unattached. I walked across and looked into her eyes. 'This is fate,' I said. 'You can't fight fate,' and I held out my hand. For a moment she gazed at me with blank unrecognition, but then she grinned like a kitten.

'No. I suppose not,' she said, and accompanied me down to my car and straight to my house without saying another word.

Shelagh was a bit crazy, but a wonderful mistress. She was hopeless and helpless, which was a nice contrast to Violette. She liked to party all night and make love all day, and although this was dreadfully tempting, my bank manager was getting restless and it was not something I could afford to do for very long. In the end, my US visa came through. I had to leave Shelagh to fend for herself which, I'm glad to say, after a few false starts she did.

My life in New York was much as I had expected. Immediately after my arrival, Violette went off with the ballet company on a five-month tour of Europe and Russia. I stayed in a tiny apartment with Violette's *Maman* and her little dog. But I did manage to get a job with the newly formed educational TV station Channel 13, and I made some new friends who helped to compensate for the misery of a non-marriage. When Violette returned, we agreed that there was no future in it, and went our separate ways.

Two years later, when I was a bachelor again, I went back to Ischia to stay with my godfather William Walton, and one evening I drove across to the idyllic little house which Lady Walton had arranged for me to borrow for that disastrous honeymoon. By pure chance, the owner, whom I had never met, was there. She was a beautiful Italian Contessa, about ten years older than me, tall and tanned. Her husband and children were in their palace in Rome and she was alone. We sat for hours on the terrace, sipping wine and talking about life and love. I told her all about my failures, and especially the disaster of my last visit to her house. Finally she stood up and took my hand, and led me to the bedroom.

'Try again,' she said, and as only an Italian Contessa can, she made me feel like a real man at last. The next evening, the Waltons were giving a party and the Contessa was there. We were solemnly introduced and she gave me a look almost, but not quite, devoid of emotion. I remembered the coolness of her body as she had slipped between the sheets, and the fire that had blazed there later, but I barely returned her gaze. 'Buona sera, Contessa,' I managed to murmur before she moved on.

Meanwhile, back in New York, I had met a lovely, sympathetic Irish girl and we had become 'a couple'. Serena was the most undemanding girlfriend I have ever had. She quietly accompanied me to dinners, theatres, parties, country weekends and filming locations, seeming to ask nothing more than that I took her home with me at the end of the day. We lived in separate apartments, but we used to have dinner together every evening after work. On weekends and holidays we slept together in her apartment, or went away to stay with friends, just as if we were married. I was enormously fond of Serena, but I can't say that I was in love with her, and I was frightened of becoming committed again too quickly and too soon.

My apartment in Manhattan was in a brownstone house on 94th Street, between 5th Avenue and Madison Avenue, near Central Park. I had often noticed a strikingly beautiful young lady who lived on the top floor and whom I took to be a fashion model. Although we were such close neighbours, she had never addressed a remark to me, nor indeed given me the slightest glance. One evening we found ourselves climbing the stairs together, and on this occasion she suddenly spoke.

'You're British, aren't you? I've just been to see the funniest British picture, called The Knack.'

'Yes, excellent.'

'Directed by Tony Richardson.'

'Well – er – yes. Richard Lester, actually. But it's a wonderful film.'

American ladies do not like being contradicted.

'No. It was Tony Richardson. I've been a great admirer of his ever since *Tom Jones*.'

We had reached my apartment.

'Well, actually I worked with Tony Richardson in London,' I said, 'and I admire him like crazy, but it really was Richard Lester who directed *The Knack*.'

She glared at me, wrinkling her perfect porcelain nose. 'Have you got an arts section in there?' (That's the bit of the Sunday *New York Times* with all the theatre and cinema listings.)

'No.'

'Come upstairs.'

We trudged up. No arts section.

'I tell you what,' she said. 'What do you bet?'

I felt a bit of a cheat. I knew Dick Lester directed *The Knack*. No doubt possible. I knew it. I beckoned her to the window.

'Do you see my car down there?'

My new dark-blue Fiat 600, which I had had specially imported from London, was parked outside the house.

'I'll give you that car if I'm wrong. Here are the keys.' And I threw them on the table.

She really was tempted. She must have seen that little Fiat outside many times, much cuter than her battered Volkswagen Beetle.

And she knew that it was Tony Richardson, right? She'd just seen the film.

'What can I possibly bet you in return?' she asked.

'If I'm right I spend the night up here, with you.'

'Hmm.'

She looked at me afresh. I'd never seen her bring a man up here, so obviously she did not have a steady boyfriend.

'Hmm.' But she knew she was right, right?

'OK,' she said. 'It's a bet.'

She was a lovely girl, not a model as it turned out, but a medical

85

illustrator. She took defeat very graciously, and we passed the most delightful night together.

'Perhaps I won the bet after all,' she said as I prepared to leave, but as with the Italian Contessa, we never made love again. Ships that pass in the night. Just a case of being in the right place at the right time, I suppose.

Poor Serena took all this with total calm. She could see that I was an absolute sucker for a pretty face, especially after a couple of drinks, and she knew it was never serious. The truth was that by the spring of 1965 I was beginning to drink too much, and my behaviour could be erratic. Although I admit that I am an obsessive, addictive character, I am convinced that my dependence on alcohol started with fear of women. For two years I had had no idea of what a woman was. I was scared witless by the very object of my desire. It had been easy to let alcohol become a substitute for sex, and finally a habit. At that time, drinking large amounts of alcohol was socially acceptable in New York. Triple dry martinis with lunch and half a bottle of whisky before dinner almost seemed the norm.

That summer I decided to go back to England for a holiday, alone. At eleven o'clock on the morning after I arrived at Saltwood, my first thought as I got out of bed was to get a drink. Then I stopped. Perhaps this was a very bad idea. I suddenly felt really scared. What had I become? I went back to bed, took two sleeping pills and passed out. I was woken in the early evening by someone playing a radio in the garden outside. Tourists did occasionally walk round outside the castle walls, uninvited, but I'd never met one with a radio. I squinted out of the window, but there didn't seem to be anyone there. Then the music stopped, and I heard the radio station call sign – WABC. That was odd. WABC was my favourite radio station in New York. That tourist must have a very powerful multi-frequency receiver to pick up WABC in England. I went back to bed, but soon my sleep was disturbed by the voices of my parents' servants gossiping in the corridor outside. I even caught my own name. How dare they? I climbed out of bed and stormed across the room, but they had obviously heard me coming, because by the time I had opened the door they had gone.

Finally my parents came up to see me. Was I all right? Didn't I want anything to eat or drink? I had jet lag, I explained, and would prefer to sleep it off. I would be fine by tomorrow.

In the middle of the night I woke again. It seemed that I had left the light on, and by now the room was full of wire animals, I simply could not imagine why. But it all seemed perfectly logical at the time. The next morning, I simply asked the staff to move me into a bigger room so the wire animals would have more space.

Of course all this will be familiar to anyone who has read Evelyn Waugh's autobiographical novel *The Ordeal of Gilbert Pinfold*. I, like Waugh, was in the early stages of delirium tremens, or the DTs.

My beloved twin sister Colette came up to see me. When she sat on the end of my bed and asked what was the matter, I suddenly stopped talking.

'Now what is it?' she asked.

'You know, I'm not really sure whether you are actually here or not,' I said. 'Perhaps you are just an illusion.'

'Oh, Col, you are absolutely impossible,' she cried, and walked out. She was actually in London at the time.

The next night things got very bad. Some of my friends came to visit me, and they ended up by having a party in my room. Finally they decided to go out for dinner, and they persuaded me to join them. I jumped out of bed and ran across the room and — crash! Since the room in my head bore no relation to the room I was actually in, I hit a real piece of furniture very hard indeed. When I came to my senses I was in pitch dark, and I had absolutely no idea which country I was in, let alone which room. I could not even guess where the walls were, or where a light switch might be. I was completely and utterly terrified. For over an hour I groped around that strange room, growing more and more desperate. When I finally found the door, I vowed I would never drink alcohol again — and I never have.

The reason I describe these events here is that they had a dramatic effect on my love life. For some unknown reason — it almost seems chemical — no one who successfully gives up the booze can bear to go back to the partner they had before. You need three clear months after DTs before you can bear to touch anyone. Every nerve in your body is shrieking 'leave me alone' so loudly that it is painful even to shake hands. This is especially cruel for those patient partners of alcoholics who have nursed their loved one back to health, and then find themselves rejected for no reason. It was very hard on Serena. I still feel guilty about it, but there was nothing I could do. The need to start a completely new life is overwhelming. I knew that I could not go back to New York. Serena came over to London to see what on earth was the matter. Finally her patience ran out, and I was alone again. Serious and sober, I joined Associated Television and lived like a hermit in a tiny house in Pimlico which I had borrowed from my sister.

If it be virtuous to live without a sexual partner (except when married of course), I managed to live a virtuous life for about a year. I directed a lot of very inferior soap operas for ATV, and ate large quantities of Rowntrees fruit gums until my two harmful addictions (to alcohol and nicotine) had passed. I took long walks in the country with my brother Alan – whose sex life had always seemed so much more interesting than my own – and generally tried to settle down.

But Mother Nature abhors a vacuum, and in the end I was deflected from my best intentions by another of those ships in the night. I still missed my life in America, and in the winter of 1966 I decided to visit my friends there. It was time to lay the ghosts of a disastrous marriage and a failed love affair. On the flight out I was lucky enough to be seated next to a pretty English girl, and we began to chat. She was travelling alone, she said, because she was going to spend a week of passion with her boss – who was married, of course – in Bermuda. They had to take separate planes, or the office would be suspicious, and she was going via New York. Was she in love with him? No, but he was very handsome. She had had a crush on him for many months, so why not? It so happened that Kennedy International Airport was closed by a snowstorm, and after much anxious circling around, the flight eventually landed in Toronto. All the passengers had to go through immigration control ('What is the purpose of your visit to Canada?' seemed absolutely impossible to answer), and we were then taken by bus to a large modern hotel. I stuck closely to my new friend, just for company, and she did not seem to mind. On arrival, we were the last two people in the hotel reception line.

'I've only got one room left,' said the clerk.

To my amazement, I heard my own voice: 'We'll share it.'

The girl seemed too startled to say anything.

'Are you married?' asked the clerk.

'Not yet,' I said.

'Well, we can't book unmarried couples into a double room,' he said snippily. 'I have a small single room in the annexe. You can take that,' he pointed to a building at the other end of a snowbound footpath, 'and the lady can have the double.'

By this time, the girl was giggly.

'Well, let's have dinner together anyway,' I said.

'OK,' she said. 'But I have to go to my room first to get out of these smelly clothes. You can leave your suitcase there for now, and go to your annexe after dinner.'

Needless to say, I never made it to the annexe. We had a lovely dinner, and then, since it was very late, we never bothered to go to sleep at all. I only hope 'the boss' enjoyed her company as much as I did.

When I got back to London, I found myself invited to take part in an orgy. A friend of mine called Jim Lipton was staying in my house in Chelsea. Jim is an American impresario who knows everybody, and he had been asked to drinks by someone who was involved with setting up the Playboy Club in Park Lane. We went round to a beautiful house in Mayfair, where the chief topic of conversation was who had applied for Playboy membership. Huge guffaws greeted each name as it was read out – Lord this, Lord that, even the Reverend so and so. I had seen the application form for membership, and it had stressed the absolute confidentiality with which it would be treated, so I was very glad that I had resisted the urge to apply. After a bit, our host got bored.

'How about an orgy?' he asked. 'Let's have an orgy.'

There didn't seem to be enough ladies present to me, and I said so.

'No problem, boy. I'll ring the bunnies.'

After half an hour a few seedy, plumpish blondes began to appear.

Our host may have been American, but he shared the very English view, as reflected in the popular press, that any healthy woman with a large bust and a round bottom is a sex object. And the young woman offered to me was not even healthy. The poor girl had the most dreadful cold.

'You should be in bed at home,' I told her. 'What on earth made you come here?'

'Oh, when the boss calls we have to come, or we won't get a job at the club.'

'I thought bunnies weren't allowed to have sex with customers.'

'Oh, get away!'

She had used a variety of strong-smelling rubs and lozenges to try to cure her bronchial problems, and the thought of making love to her anywhere, let alone in this very mixed company, was impossible.

'I'm just going to the little boys' room,' I said in language she would understand, and fled.

Jim caught me at the door. 'Chicken?' he said.

'Definitely not my scene,' I replied and drove home.

I took a wrong turn at Knightsbridge and thus spent a little longer than usual on the trip. When I got to my house, I could see that there was a light on in Jim's room, which clicked off just as I got to the front door. So Jim had been chicken too, eh? His bedroom door was shut, and I was too discreet to knock.

'You don't know what you missed, Colin,' he said later.

Then there was Tina. Tina worked in the accounts department of Associated Television, which was on the same floor as my office in the production department, and we used to meet at the water fountain in the centre of the building. Tina was very tall, and thin to the point of being skinny. She had high cheekbones and huge brown eyes (the result of being thin, I suppose) under a mop of black curls, which made her look exotic. The office where Tina worked was open plan, and all the girls there spent most of their working hours trying to figure out who might be having a romance with whom. Any flirtation had to be carefully concealed, but the human eye can pick up infinitesimal signals if it is looking for them, and Tina soon picked up mine. In a short time, she and I were both drinking much more cool water than we needed to, and the tension between us was rising. By pure coincidence we would arrive at the machine together. I would wait for her to take a cup, she would wait for me. Then we would both stretch out our hands at the same time. Our fingers would meet, and touch for a split-second longer than was necessary. We would look each other in the eye, and smile, and give a nervous laugh. It was all standard romantic stuff, only dangerous if it is taken too far.

It is not often that I have tried to seduce a girl purely on the basis of her physical appearance. The world is full of beautiful young ladies. There has to be a feature which catches the imagination, a facet of the personality which appeals in a particular way. In Tina's case I was absolutely desperate to kiss her, although all I knew of her was her face and her figure. In the end I bucked up my courage and spoke — or rather whispered, because the whole accounts department were flapping their ears like water buffalo.

'Will you come out with me this Saturday?'

'Yes.'

'Give me your home phone number on a piece of paper at lunchtime.'

'All right. When I drop an envelope, you pick it up.'

'I'll collect you in the morning and we'll drive down to the country. OK?'

'OK.'

Tina was as friendly and naive as a puppy, but she wasn't quite 'me'. She thought mainly in clichés. She believed things were nice if they matched. She preferred things if they were shiny. When I collected her on that Saturday morning I made sure that my car was spotless, which was more than could be said of my intentions.

'My parents have a castle in Kent,' I said. 'Shall we go down and see it?'

'A castle? A real castle? Like the history books? How could they live in a castle?'

'Well, let's go and explore it, shall we? Hop in.' And Tina hopped in.

It was a glorious sunny day. We had lunch on the way down

and Tina had two sherries. By the time we arrived at Saltwood, she was feeling amorous.

'Are you sure your Mum and Dad aren't here?' she said. 'I tell you what,' she giggled. 'As soon as we get in, let's go to bed.' This seemed a really excellent idea. We dashed up the stone steps at the entrance, but the great wooden door was locked, and banging on it brought no response.

'There are two gardeners,' I said. 'We'll go and ask one of them to let us in.'

'Ooh,' said Tina.

There weren't two gardeners working that day. There was no one.

'I can break in,' I said. 'It's my house too, after all.'

But Saltwood was built in the eleventh century expressly to keep people out. I got ladders and hammers and long bits of wood, but nothing made any difference. Soon I was getting desperate.

'Let's go back to London,' said Tina. The sherry was wearing off.

Oh no. And miss spending the afternoon in Tina's long thin arms. We climbed into the car and drove to the gardener's cottage. No one. We tried the under-gardener's cottage.

'I don't have a key to the castle, Master Colin,' said Woollett. 'You'd have to ask Miss Marsh for that.'

'What is her address?'

'She lives in Dover, Master Colin.'

'Tell me the name of the street.'

Miss Marsh was my mother's secretary – a prim, pinch-faced spinster who had disapproved of every move I had made for the last ten years, but by now I was a man possessed. Off we set to Dover, a twenty-mile round trip, with Tina resigned to the fact that she was stuck with a maniac, and getting very bored.

To my great relief Miss Marsh was at home, and after many snoopy protests, she let me have the key. Finally I got Tina into the castle and into my parents' huge double bed. But a success it was not, romantically or even physically. By the following day we had both learned a lesson about office romance.

By 1967 I knew that I had to find a steady girlfriend again. I had to admit that, morality notwithstanding, living alone was just not my natural state. One of my great friends had a beautiful fiancée. She was tall and slim (again), with straight dark brown hair and long white arms. I absolutely adored her, and set out to find someone as like her as possible to be my permanent companion.

Susannah fitted the bill perfectly. She was modest, quiet, self-contained and extremely beautiful, with a figure which any man would die for. We spent a happy time together and we even talked of marriage, but after a year she was offered an excellent job in Switzerland. I visited her as often as I could, and we continued to spend holidays together, but there had always been one problem which we had not been able to solve. She was an adorable person, and I worshipped her, but she could never, at least with me, completely enjoy the sexual side of a relationship. When she moved to Geneva she shared a flat with another woman, who seemed to be very jealous of me. Whether or not I was right, I will never know. Susannah was not someone who found it easy, or indeed possible, to discuss that sort of thing. But it meant, inevitably, that our affair had to end.

Back in England, I simply wanted to settle down, and in 1970 I married Faith, the half-sister of my old Oxford friend Tim Rathbone. She already had two children, so I acquired the most wonderful ready-made family anyone could ask for. I had parents-in-law whom I had known and loved since my days at Eton, and a ravishing, clever, witty wife who was more lovely than a summer day. For the first time I felt completely relaxed. Seven happy years went by, but clouds were gathering on the horizon, as they so often do, and tensions were beginning to creep in. My wife had always been restless, and in 1978, when my work seemed to be stalled (I had my own film company now, making documentary films) we decided to move to Hollywood and try our luck there.

This was a mistake. If your marriage is failing, go to Hull, not to Hollywood. Escaping to somewhere glamorous is rarely a satisfactory solution to any problem. But at the time it seemed to be a huge release, a breath of fresh air after the stuffy corridors of England.

I flew out ahead of my family to set up a production office and find us somewhere to live. The first effect of Los Angeles on a pale, thin Englishman is incredible. You simply can't believe that such a place exists – miles and miles of blue sky and ocean, waving palms, wide roads, beautiful houses, and friendly people with seemingly endless prosperity. It was like a dream come true. An important Hollywood agent had frequently invited me to stay in his home in the Hollywood Hills, and this also had a dreamlike quality. Richard Kahlenberg had first telephoned me in London about a year before. He was coming to London, he said, and would dearly love to see me again. This was fine, and I invited him to dinner at our home in Chelsea. Richard was a serious man who looked and spoke like Charlton Heston. The only problem was that I had never met him before in my life, nor even heard his name, and I have no idea to this day where he got my telephone number. Despite this, his visit had gone quite well, in a very British sort of way.

So when I needed a bed for my first visit to Hollywood, it was Richard whom I called. 'You are welcome, but you cannot stay more than three weeks,' he said. 'I like house-guests. I hate lodgers.' Fair enough, I said, guessing, correctly, that I would be extremely grateful for even Richard's unfamiliar face. Then, on the first morning after my arrival, he announced that he was taking me to lunch with one of his clients, and we set off for some fashionable bistro in Richard's old classic Studebaker.

When we arrived, no guest was there for Mr Kahlenberg, so we settled down to wait. Soon, into the restaurant came the most attractive girl I have ever seen in my whole life. I had often watched Goldie Hawn in *Rowan and Martin's Laugh-In* when I was living in New York, and I had fallen in love with her then. Now here she was, breathtaking, and apparently not a day older. Goldie was not the first film star I had met, by any means, but she was the most unspoilt. She could see that I was completely infatuated, and was perfectly prepared to flirt over the lunch table. Richard sat back like an amiable nanny, watching the kids with a tolerant smile and proud of his role as matchmaker. Mind you, I did not flatter myself too much. Goldie was and still is such an incredible charmer that I suspect everyone leaves her company feeling as if they are on a cloud. She told me all about her love life – or lack of it at that precise moment (she was to meet Kurt Russell a few months later) – and offered to drive me back to Richard's house. She had a silver Mercedes sports car outside, of which she was extremely proud. 'I was sheltering from the rain in a doorway in San Francisco,' she said, 'when I looked through the window and saw this beautiful car. I looked at the price tag and suddenly I thought, "Hey, I can afford that," so I went in and bought it.'

One thing that I do not think Goldie had done was to drive the car from San Francisco to Hollywood. She was an atrocious driver. She didn't go fast – she simply pointed the car in the same general direction as the other traffic and let it choose its exact path for itself. But I was so excited to be in a sports car with Goldie Hawn that I quite forgot to be frightened. The roads of Los Angeles are wide and relatively empty, and somehow we got back to the house unscathed. And then – did I invite Goldie in for coffee? Or to admire the view? Or to go to bed? I did not. All my old awe of film stars came flooding back. I had once worked for Marilyn Monroe and Vivien Leigh simultaneously – two of the most influential beauties of the century – and I had been in love with both of them. But the very thought of laying a finger on either of them was unthinkable. I had danced with Jayne Mansfield in a New York nightclub. She had the most voluptuous figure you could imagine – like Jessica Rabbit – but I might as well have been dancing with a statue. Film stars were psychologically out of bounds. So I froze to the door handle of Goldie Hawn's Mercedes, mumbled 'Goodbye,' and fled. I have kicked myself ever since. It wasn't that I even dreamed that I could keep up with someone like Goldie, or had any illusions that I could have partnered her in her superstar career, but at least I could have tried.

Hollywood is not conducive to an uneventful married life. I was making films in conjunction with a public relations company, and they knew all the beautiful stars. One of their clients was Cheryl Ladd, who was starring in a television series called *Charlie's Angels*. I tend to use too many superlatives when describing the fair sex, but I must say that, with the possible exception of Vivien Leigh, Cheryl Ladd had the most exquisite face I have ever seen. When I was first introduced to her and she held out her hand for me to shake it, I was so stunned that I nearly fell over backwards. I can only suppose that she had encountered this reaction before, because she held my hand hard, and even gave a little pull to keep me upright. Cheryl was not sexy like Marilyn or gorgeous like Goldie. She was like a Cartier watch.

Dana Wynter was different. She had starred in the original version of *The Invasion of the Body Snatchers*, and when she played a Wren in *Sink the Bismarck* she had caught the eye of Earl Mountbatten of Burma. Her beauty was smooth, dark and regal, and she was reputed to have gypsy blood. She became a terrific chum of mine, and I would visit her nearly every day on my way home, for a chat.

All this beauty and excitement probably made me a less attentive husband than I should have been. Hollywood was very much a 'company' town. If you weren't in the movies, you felt out of it. Showbiz can exact a pull as strong as any mistress. My wife felt excluded, and we drifted apart in more ways than one. Finally, in 1981, we decided to divorce – neither of us knew quite why. Faith returned with her children to London, and I stayed in California alone.

VI

THE OLIVIERS

AFTER LEAVING OXFORD IN 1956, my first job was as 3rd Assistant Director on the film *The Prince and the Showgirl*, produced and directed by Laurence Olivier, and starring him and Marilyn Monroe.* The filming had been extremely traumatic for Olivier. Marilyn had upset him much more than he was ready to admit – she was a phenomenon that he simply could not understand. What she did in front of a camera had challenged his whole notion of what an actor should be.

Olivier was a total professional. He thought of acting as a trade, or at least a tradition. It was something you learned, practised, polished and refined. He thought that the best training for actors was British repertory theatre, where you had to learn three plays a week and perform to hostile audiences in cold, half-empty theatres in provincial towns. He could see that this experience often turned his less successful colleagues into old 'hams' who kept on repeating the same mannered performance no matter what play they were in, and he took enormous pains to vary his approach to each role he took on. But even he, the greatest actor of his generation, had acquired mannerisms which were impossible to shake off – the elongating of the vowels, the sing-song intonations, the sudden little bursts of rage, controlled or uncontrolled, serious or mock. These tricks worked very well on the stage, and theatre audiences had grown to love and expect them, but they were less suited to film.

* The diary which I kept during the production of the film was published in 1995 as *The Prince, the Showgirl and Me*.

97

The very first movies were made to record theatrical productions. Famous actors had continued to give, in front of the camera, the performances which had made them successful on stage. The earliest existing full–length feature movie is of *Richard III*, and the performers simply revelled in exaggeration, as did almost all the actors in the silent films that followed it. Olivier's early films were 'talkies', but they had been in the same genre. *Wuthering Heights* was hardly a story to underplay, and when he made *Hamlet* and *Henry V*, the public wanted to see a great Shakespearean actor. It never occurred to anyone to wonder what a Danish prince or an English king would really have been like in those far-off times before everyone used a hairbrush and a razor every day.

Marilyn Monroe came from a completely different tradition. She had never been on a stage in her life, but had wandered into films in Hollywood on the strength of her beauty, her figure and her sexy smile. She had discovered that the camera – any camera, still or movie – simply loved her just as she was. In each of her films (by the time of *The Prince and the Showgirl* she had made twenty-four) she simply had to walk on and be herself to have a great success. But no one could be contented with that, so of course she dreamed of becoming a 'real' actress, just as Olivier would have liked to become a natural movie star. So Marilyn decided to take acting lessons – which Olivier would have considered a contradiction in terms – at the Actors' Studio in New York, where Lee Strasberg was teaching 'the method'.

Olivier thought this was nonsense. He could not see that although 'the method' wasn't much help on a stage, it suited the new type of Hollywood films perfectly. The giant close-ups, often held on screen while other actors are talking, showed up the tiniest mannerism, and made glaringly obvious anything that looked like 'an act'. The set of the jaw, the furled brow, the artificially curled lip would give the game away at once. In the modern movies, an actor simply had to immerse himself in the part 100 per cent. The story of Olivier telling Dustin Hoffman on the set of *Marathon Man*: 'It's much easier to act, dear boy,' as Hoffman tried to work himself up to feel like a torture victim, shows that Olivier had never learned this lesson. Of course it's easier to act; but that is why Olivier never became a truly great film star.

For all these reasons, when Marilyn arrived on the set of *The Prince and the Showgirl*, Olivier felt very threatened indeed. She couldn't act, dammit. She was just a silly little girl with a big bosom – rude, lazy and unprofessional as hell. Oh, all right, she was a big star. Perhaps he could seduce her to help get her into shape. And yet, and yet, there was something more going on than that. What was she really thinking, behind that beautiful mask? Was she listening when he gave her direction, or was she just 'doing her own thing'? Whatever it was, the results were amazing. In real life, on the set, she had been ghastly. She was hesitant and forgetful, with nothing but fear in her eyes. But on the screen, as Olivier could see, she was delightful. Sometimes, although no one would dare say so, she came across much better than Olivier himself. Was it a trick of nature? Surely it couldn't be art. Olivier was not stupid, but Marilyn was talking a language that he could not understand. (Some years later I experienced a similar situation when I took my father to the studio of the Pop artist Andy Warhol in New York. My father was an art historian of the old school, used to the canvases of Rembrandt and Titian. He simply could not conceive that Andy's silk-screened Brillo boxes were serious art.)

It was with enormous relief that, with *The Prince and the Showgirl* behind him, Olivier sank back again into the arms of the theatre. At first sight, the play he had chosen for his return to the stage – *The Entertainer* by John Osborne – was the most controversial decision Olivier had ever made. Osborne had been branded a dangerous revolutionary by the British theatrical establishment. After many years of polite drawing-room comedies, when even Noël Coward and Terence Rattigan sometimes seemed rather risqué, the violent 'kitchen sink' dialogue of Osborne's *Look Back in Anger* had given everyone a nasty shock. But when Olivier read the first act of *The Entertainer* in January 1957, he was delighted. Here was a chance to prove that he was not a theatrical dinosaur, and to ally himself with the new *avant-garde* that was transforming the British stage. At the same time he could see that the role of Archie Rice would suit him perfectly. It was exactly like the sort of role that he loved so much in Shakespeare – the tragic hero forced to play the fool.

Olivier realised that, despite the tag of 'angry young man' which had been pinned on him by the press, John Osborne was actually a traditional playwright – just as Olivier was a traditional actor. Both of them wanted to extend the boundaries of British theatre, but neither wanted to go outside them. And so *The Entertainer* was conceived traditionally – a three-act play, set behind a proscenium arch, with a cast of five.

I had officially been 3rd Assistant Director on *The Prince and the Showgirl*, but I had become Olivier's unofficial personal assistant as well, and he asked me to carry on in that role as he prepared for the new play. After the tortures of Pinewood studios, it was wonderful to see him back in his element again. He started by learning the entire play by heart – not just his own part, but every single word of the script, including the stage directions. He would go over and over the lines no matter where we were, throwing the script to me in a car or in a restaurant and rattling out the words in a low voice, like a tape recording. He loved Osborne's sudden changes of thought, but was very quick to pounce on anything which appeared to him to be out of character. Whenever he found anything that grated, he would ring up Osborne and they would discuss it at length.

In those days Osborne was very polite – meek, even – and anxious to please. He had been, and continued to be, a very capable actor himself, and he always understood exactly what Olivier was thinking. 'I'm not an angry young man,' he would say, 'I just write about angry young men.' In many areas he was already extremely conservative – more like the angry old man he was to become than an angry young one.

Eventually Osborne and Olivier were joined by the director of *Look Back in Anger*, Tony Richardson. Tony was delightful company. He had the reputation of being brilliantly talented, although I could not see much imagination in the direction of *Look Back in Anger*. The three main characters seemed to be rooted to the spot while they took it in turns to give soliloquies, and with a few obvious exceptions, *The Entertainer* was the same. Perhaps it was Tony who inspired the performances of the actors in *Look Back* – Kenneth Haig as Jimmy Porter, Alan Bates as his friend Cliff, and

Mary Ure, later to become Mrs John Osborne, as Jimmy's wife Alison. But in the case of *The Entertainer*, Olivier was already inspired by the time Tony Richardson came along, and he had decided exactly how he would play his part. It was also Olivier who chose those two wonderfully professional British actors Brenda de Banzie and George Relph to join him as the main characters, and I never saw either of them vary their performances by a hair's breadth once Olivier had 'suggested' to them what to do. Nothing Tony Richardson could say made the slightest difference.

Olivier's role in *The Entertainer* was that of a deadbeat old music-hall artiste, and Tony suggested that he go to see Max Miller, a stand-up comedian of the old school who was playing in a variety show in Southend. I went down with Olivier in the car, and I could see that in a way he felt insulted. He didn't need to see the real thing, even once. He already had the characterisation in his head, bulging eyes, gap teeth, baggy check suit and all.

In those days stand-up comedians used to include a 'soft-shoe shuffle' in their act, and Olivier decided he must do this too, even though he had never tap danced before and was beginning to suffer from gout. We went off together to a tiny dance studio, rehearsing the script in the car as usual, and were met by a most attractive* lady choreographer who was a tap-dance expert. Olivier made her go right through each routine several times, while he watched her feet intently. Then he simply stood up and started to do it himself. Of course the lady had to correct exactly where he put his feet, but the rhythm, the balance, the inflexion were all completely accurate. He was such an incredible mimic that you couldn't tell he wasn't doing it perfectly the first time he tried.

When we moved into the Royal Court Theatre, where *The Entertainer* was to be performed, I encountered a problem. The people who were in charge of the Royal Court in 1957 thought of it as the crucible of revolutionary British theatre, which indeed it was, and like all little bands of revolutionaries, they did not welcome outsiders. When Olivier asked the head of the theatre company, George Devine, if he could bring me with him, Devine simply said

---

* I mention this because I think it helped.

'No.' There were already two stage managers, and there was not room for another. But Olivier was the most loyal man I ever knew. Once you were part of his extended family, you were there for life. I also think that Vivien had decided that it might be useful to have me keep an eye on Larry for her, just as Larry would want me to keep an eye on Vivien later on. It wasn't that I could ever do anything or even say anything, but each liked to feel that they had an ally in the other's camp. In the end, Devine agreed to ask Tony Richardson. 'Oh, I don't mind,' drawled Tony, surprised and flattered to be asked, so I was in.

The Royal Court offered me a wage of £3 per week as an assistant stage manager. Even in 1957 this was not enough to live on, but I accepted, and Olivier, who had been paying me £10 a week out of his own pocket, agreed to make up the difference until we moved the play into the West End.

Tony Richardson was a great ally, but it was hard to see him as a great director. He would drape himself languorously over a row of stalls in the darkened auditorium, while on stage Olivier did exactly what he had already decided to do.

'Larry darling, can you just alter this or that a tiny bit?' Tony would call out.

Olivier would click out of character as sharply as a needle being lifted off a gramophone record. 'Do you mean like this?' And he would drop the needle down and become Archie Rice again. If he was in the middle of a scene, even in the tragic last act with the tears rolling down his cheeks, he could switch from the part to real life and back again without any apparent effort. One thing he would not forget, after all the times he had recited the whole script to me, was his lines.

Most people in the theatre like to 'camp it up', women as well as men. I suppose the theatre naturally attracts homosexuals. There is already the tradition of people pretending to be what they are not, and in the claustrophobic atmosphere of backstage, high theatrical camp can often smooth over a difficult moment. Big stars have large and fragile egos. The stage crew, the stage managers, the understudies have to be there all the time, and while the actors are performing they have to stay out of the way. A sense of humour is essential. No one wants to laugh all the time – that would be too disruptive – but irritability has to be defused somehow. The easy banter of the gay community is often the least offensive way of dealing with conflict. The result was that we all minced around like fairy queens – as camp, as they used to say, as a row of tents.

One day Tony Richardson came into the office and caught sight of himself in a mirror. 'Oh dear,' he said. 'I must get my hair cut. People will start thinking I'm queer.' That really caught us out. We had already assumed that he was queer anyway, and despite his having several children, it did turn out that Tony's sexuality was confused. But most of us were aggressively normal outside the theatre, and this was also true of Olivier. He and I once found ourselves sharing a bed for the night, but I never saw him exhibit the slightest signs of homosexuality. If anything, he had a tendency to fall into bed with rather too many ladies. It was not that he was lecherous – I never saw him actively pursue a lady – but he was himself very frequently pursued. Then he would be tempted to sink into the arms of his female admirer, as if to say: 'And who will give this weary warrior a bed?'

By this time Olivier's relationship with Vivien Leigh had become very stormy indeed. When, in the middle of our rehearsals, Vivien announced that she was going on holiday to Yugoslavia with her ex-husband Leigh Holman and their daughter Suzanne, the newspapers began to speculate that Vivien was going to leave Olivier for her former love. This was total nonsense. Leigh was a friendly, dried-up old stick whom Vivien treated as if he was a favourite uncle. Their daughter was about to get married, and they simply wanted to spend some time with her first. Nevertheless, the whole press corps decided that if Olivier did not meet Vivien on her return, it meant that their marriage was over. Vivien had guessed this – as indeed she always guessed everything – and she charged me with getting Olivier to the airport in time. ('You must!' she had said, in her best Scarlett O'Hara voice, so I had no alternative.)

Ten days later, when the moment to leave for the airport arrived, Olivier was caught up in discussions with Osborne, and I had a hard time persuading him to go. In the end I drove him down to Lydd airport in Kent in my own car (at that time a Lancia Aurelia

Grand Turismo coupé). It was such a fast car that we even managed to arrive a little early, and in order to avoid the waiting reporters we stopped at a pub near the airport to get a drink. As we walked in, I saw to my horror that every single member of the press had had the same idea. They all recognised me immediately as Olivier's assistant, and clustered round.

'Colin, are you meeting Vivien? Is Olivier coming down? Is he going to be there too? Does he still love her? etc.'

'Where the hell is Olivier?' I thought. 'He walked in here with me. Has he vanished into thin air?' Yes, was the answer, he had. There was a crumple-faced, middle-aged man standing by my elbow whom I scarcely recognised.

'Who is this with you?' the reporters asked suspiciously.

'Oh, he's my parents' gardener,' I said. 'He's come to help with the luggage. What will you have to drink, Fred?'

'Half a pint of bitter, please sir,' said 'Fred' in a Kent accent.

When the press rushed off to meet the plane, now happily convinced that Olivier wasn't coming – one paper even filed that story without bothering to go to the airport – the gardener turned back into Laurence Olivier. 'Not bad bitter,' he said, completely unmoved after having given one of the great performances of his life in front of my very eyes.

As always, Vivien was overjoyed to see that 'her darling Larry' had not let her down, but by then the situation between them had gone too far. As it was late in the evening, we drove over to my parents' home at Saltwood Castle to stay the night. I was showing Olivier up to his and Vivien's room when he suddenly stopped. 'Where's your room, Colin?' he asked. 'If I have to spend a whole night with her, I might strangle her.'

I showed him my door. 'I'll make a space for you, in case,' I said. 'And I'll leave the lights on.' Sure enough, in the early hours Olivier came down. He slumped into the empty half of my bed with a groan, and when I awoke next morning he had gone.

The Entertainer was an enormous success. It was only scheduled for a run of six weeks, and by the time it opened, on 10 April 1957, it was already sold out. Kenneth Tynan gave it one of his best reviews, and every celebrity in London decided they had to see it. Princess Margaret, as unchanged over the years as her mother, demanded the best seats in the house, and some unfortunate couple had to be kicked out.

Olivier had taken a terrific risk. His role on stage was that of a really bad comedian, an old has-been who is reduced to performing in the seediest possible seaside vaudeville show. All actors are terrified of becoming parodies of themselves. In *The Entertainer*, Olivier was acting his own 'bogeyman', and if his portrayal of Archie Rice was so subtle that it actually fooled some of the audience, that only went to show what an incredible genius he was. It was as if, just as in the pub in Kent, he wanted to show that he could play absolutely anything — even his nemesis.

There was another shock in store for the audiences at the Royal Court. Every night a small bunch of musicians, led by that talented composer Marcus Dodds, sat in the orchestra pit doing what Olivier was doing on stage — that is to say, pretending to be bad. When they got to the interval of Archie Rice's vaudeville show they would give a huge, tinny drum roll, and the curtain would go up to show a nude woman. In those days, if you showed a naked lady on stage, she was not allowed to move a muscle, otherwise the theatre would be shut down. The Lord Chamberlain was longing to do this to the Royal Court anyway: the establishment hated Osborne's unorthodox style, and considered that Olivier was a traitor to appear in such a scandalous production. Several lines in the text had already been censored. 'The old church bells won't ring tonight 'cos the vicar's got the clappers,' which I thought rather funny, had to be changed to ''cos the vicar's dropped a clanger'. Olivier always delivered the line with a particularly horrible leer, making it sound even more suggestive than it had originally been.

The nude was meant to be vulgar. She was played by a large red-headed actress called Elizabeth, and she sat on stage draped in a Union Jack, with a trident and a helmet, in the pose of Britannia on a penny coin. Elizabeth was also a part-time artist's model. She didn't mind a bit taking her clothes off in front of an audience, but I was never quite sure whether she realised that she was meant to be a figure of fun. I slept with her a few times, more out of mutual loneliness than anything else, and I expect Olivier did too.

Working with Olivier on *The Prince and the Showgirl* had been very hard work for everyone. I had to be at Pinewood studios by 6.45 every morning, and I often stayed there until seven o'clock at night. But once a play is into its run, working in the theatre is almost too easy. Unless there was a matinée, we never turned up at the Royal Court until about five o'clock in the evening. The other stage managers and I would then check that everything was working, and lay out all the props for the performance. In *The Entertainer*, Archie Rice has a very common wife, and he feeds her with gin and Dubonnet throughout the play, so we had fresh bottles of Dubonnet delivered every week – the Dubonnet company didn't realise it was the subject of a joke – and Gordon's kindly kept us supplied with sealed bottles full of fresh water. I can't imagine what this did to their production line, but it certainly livened up a few parties when I opened a new bottle of Gordon's and drank it straight down without any apparent effect.

All the actors in the play had been hand-picked by Olivier, and they were so professional that none of their performances ever varied. As in most of John Osborne's plays, there were only three main characters, one of whom dominated the other two. There were also a couple of very minor parts for young actors, but they had so little to do that we would spend our time gossiping together during the long periods when they were waiting to go on stage. Richard Pascoe and the late Bobby (Sir Robert) Stephens both understudied Olivier, and both became my great friends. Dorothy Tutin played Olivier's daughter. She was as slim and serious as a beautiful boy – as well as being a wonderful actress – and she once asked me to tea on her houseboat on the Thames. I wasn't quite sure if she was expecting me to make advances towards her (she was not), and I sat in a panic of indecision on the edge of a chair, as the whole room gradually settled at an angle of thirty degrees on the mud. Joan Plowright replaced Dorothy when we took the play on tour, and I suppose she began her relationship with Olivier then (they married in 1961). She certainly concealed it well. She must be the least flirtatious actress I have ever met. When I went to Granada Television I worked with her brother David, and he was no more flirtatious than his sister.

The success of the play and the scarcity of the tickets meant that I became quite popular in London society. I was sharing a flat in Mayfair with two other bachelors, and since I did not have to get up and go to work until after lunch, I could and did stay up very late. Nightclubs, champagne and ladies took up all of my spare time. One of my flatmates, Dominic Elwes, suffered dreadfully from lack of money. In the end he decided to marry an heiress, but her family disapproved.

'Should I elope with her, Col?'

'No. I don't think you'll get the money anyway,' I said. But he did, and he didn't.

When my other flatmate went to work in New York I sold the lease, to Christian Dior, and moved into the servants' quarters of my parents' flat in the Albany. Albany's porters do not allow high-jinks with nightclub hostesses after midnight, so from then on my bad behaviour had to be curtailed.

When *The Entertainer* finished its short run, Olivier decided to revive the production of *Titus Andronicus* that he and Vivien had starred in at the Shakespeare Memorial Theatre at Stratford two years earlier. Just as my parents liked location filming, Olivier and Vivien loved touring (but for the opposite reason – Vivien always felt that she could drink more on tour), and they planned to take the play all round Europe before going into the West End.

It had originally been directed by Peter Brook, who was the only theatrical director whom Olivier genuinely admired. Brook had designed every element in the play, including the music, and he had given Olivier a new insight into what an actor could do on stage. The Shakespeare Memorial Theatre was a very grand repertory company. There was a resident group of about forty actors who performed all the plays, and stars were invited to appear with them as guests, for very little money. Occasionally, when a production had been a great success, it would be moved to the West End, and then everyone could be paid a more reasonable wage – including the Oliviers.

Almost all the actors from the original cast of *Titus Andronicus* were still working at Stratford in 1957, and they were rehired for the tour. Rehearsals began in London, and I was employed as an assistant stage manager. Once again I found myself injected into a theatrical 'family'. This time I was doubly unpopular, because I had unrestricted access to the two great stars. But Olivier insisted. He knew by now that I was totally loyal to Vivien, and that he would need someone to look after her if she got into trouble on the tour.

Our first stop was the Théâtre Sarah Bernhardt in Paris, and there we opened on 15 May 1957. Peter Brook's beautiful set was extremely complicated to build, and we had brought with us two carpenters, two electricians and six stage managers. The theatre was vast – it has since been pulled down – and when we first arrived we all went up on to the roof to have a look at the city. The senior stage manager was inspired by the magnificent view. 'Allo, Paree!' he shouted at the top of his voice. Then he thought for a moment. 'Ici Keith Green.' I thought that was very endearing, and we soon became friends.

There is some debate about whether Shakespeare actually wrote *Titus Andronicus* or not, but there is no mistaking the effect which the play has on the audience. Titus is a Roman nobleman whose daughter Lavinia is captured and raped, on stage, by the sons of his enemy Tamora, the Queen of the Goths. The young men cut off Lavinia's hands and tear out her tongue so she cannot tell her father who did it. After much grieving – 'Thou hast no hands to wipe away thy tears' – Titus surrenders his own right hand, also cut off on stage, in order to ransom his captured sons, but it is returned to him with their heads. Lavinia manages to write the names of her abductors in the sand with a staff held in her mouth. Titus invites Tamora to a great feast. At the end of the meal he tells her with relish ('Why, there they are, both baked in that pie') that she has just eaten her sons.

Olivier loved all this gore, and gave the audience its money's worth. His face streaked with grief, he laid his hand, palm up, on a slab, and Anthony Quayle, blacked up like a Moor, struck it off with his axe. After many experiments I had found a box which made a loud and sickening crunch when hit with a hammer, and I would make this noise in the wings just as Quayle brought down his blade. It was a great success. Many people in the audience were sick, and on the opening night in Paris Douglas Fairbanks Jr. swallowed his chewing gum.

While Larry and Vivien were in Paris, all their expenses were met by a millionaire called Paul Louis Weiller. There were rumours that Weiller had a very doubtful war record – something to do with selling fighter planes which he knew would crash – and most of Paris society would have nothing to do with him. Vivien could not have cared less about that sort of gossip, and even insisted that Weiller should find somewhere for me to stay.

I was sent to a huge empty house called l'Hôtel des Ambassadeurs d'Hollande, on the top floor of which Weiller's construction company had built a tiny flat especially for me. Each night when I finished work I would walk up to bed through this dark and deserted mansion.

On the fourth day it suddenly filled with about three hundred workmen who set about transforming the bare walls into an eighteenth-century palace, complete with gold-leaf mouldings, chandeliers, tapestries, carpets and furniture. Two nights later, Weiller gave a sumptuous party in the house for the Oliviers. I heard him telling Vivien of the years it had taken him to do the restoration, and I knew that I had only to take her through the little door to my attic room to reveal that the whole creation was artificial, as artificial as Peter Brook's beautiful set for *Titus* in the theatre round the corner, or, indeed, as Paul Louis Weiller's friendship with Vivien herself.

Although Olivier was giving a towering performance every night, and the whole company absolutely worshipped him, it was Vivien who soon became the focal point of the tour. Her energy was incredible. She had arranged some social occasion for every day, and another one every evening when the play was over. She and Larry were the toast of Paris, and she had a great many invitations to choose from. When all these parties were finished, she would collect the survivors in Paul Louis Weiller's Rolls-Royce and drag them off to nightclubs. She liked to greet the dawn drinking onion soup in the open-air market of Les Halles.

That was really the biggest problem with Vivien: she simply hated to go to bed. She has sometimes been accused of sleeping with too many men. Not in my experience. Although she had a very passionate nature, she never seemed to enjoy sex or place much importance on it. She was much more likely not to go to bed at all. It was as if she was terrified of falling asleep, determined to put off for as long as possible the moment when oblivion took over and she lost control. Vivien suffered from bouts of manic depression, which affected her about twice a year and lasted several weeks. She would gradually get more and more excitable, and she was clearly beginning the cycle during the first week of the tour. To start with, her mind became like a razor that you could not blunt. Alcohol and drugs had very little effect. She would sleep for only two or three hours a night before blazing away again, as beautiful, brilliant and dangerous as before. This was absolutely exhausting for all of us, but especially for Olivier. He simply could not keep up. After all, the reason he and Vivien were being made such a fuss of was his magnificent performance as *Titus*. He could hardly, as he pointed out to me continually, be expected to give that performance every night, unless he had had some 'SLEEP'.

'You've got to stay with her, Colin. Get her back to the hotel before dawn, somehow, if you can.'

Poor Larry. On the third evening in Paris, I came across him sitting all alone backstage, his head in his hands.

'What's the matter, Larry?' I asked. 'It can't be that bad.'

'It is, Colin, it's worse than you can imagine. I'm giving mine back.' He waved a newspaper in my face.

'Giving what back?'

'It's my fiftieth birthday today,' he moaned – there was a big party planned for later, which he was dreading – 'and as if that wasn't bad enough, THEY'VE GIVEN FUCKING DONALD WOLFIT A KNIGHTHOOD!' And he let out a great howl of pain.

Meanwhile, Vivien was in full swing. A famous French actress, Marie Lohr, invited her and Olivier to a dinner party on a *bateau mouche*, one of those floating restaurants which go up and down the Seine by night.

'How lovely!' cried Vivien. 'What time shall I tell the company to be there?' 'The company' comprised sixty-two people, fifty of whom were young male actors who were unreliable, to say the least, off stage. Marie Lohr went pale.

'I just meant you and Larry,' she said.

'Oh, I wouldn't dream of coming without the whole company,' said Vivien sweetly, her eyes like steel. So all the plans had to be changed. The company flocked into the lower decks of the boat and proceeded to get as drunk as Marie Lohr had feared they would, while the grand party ate dinner upstairs.

My duty was to keep up with Vivien no matter what. The Oliviers were staying at the Plaza Athenée hotel, and I would wait there in the lobby every morning. Vivien would come down at about 11 a.m., looking exquisite, for some brisk shopping before her lunch party. With luck I would not be asked to the meal – certainly not by the hostess, and hopefully not by Vivien either – and I could have a quiet chicken sandwich in a bar round the corner. Then we would be off again – a museum, another shop, an art gallery, a tea party, back to the hotel to change, on to a friend's house for drinks, and, finally, to the theatre.

Vivien's speaking part in the play was drastically restricted by the early loss of her tongue, but now my work as assistant stage manager was just about to begin. Peter Brook had designed the production in such a way that the same set could be transformed from a palace to a forest and back again. The external walls were covered with long arrows on springs, wired flat into the surface. When these springs were released from behind by pull wires, the arrows flicked out so quickly that they appeared to have been shot from the back of the theatre. It was a magical effect but, like all illusions, it took long and careful preparation. A highly camp Australian actor called Frank Thring was on stage when these arrows were released. He would lean against the set so that the arrows sprang out just beside his head, and each night his reaction was merely petulant, as if someone at a party had dropped a glass of champagne, rather than been caught in the middle of a deadly hail of arrows. By the end of the tour his feebleness had got on my nerves so much that one night as I pulled out the wires, I also pushed a spare arrow through a crack in the scenery, on a level with his behind. For once he let out the shriek of horror which I felt was appropriate, but I have been ashamed of myself ever since. He was acting a part, in front of a large number of people, all caught up in the same illusion. It is absolutely unforgivable to allow reality to intrude at a moment like that, especially in such a tender spot.

As soon as the performance was over, I would change into a dinner jacket and dash up to the Oliviers' dressing room to greet and pour whisky for a stream of important guests. A dinner party would follow and, of course, no one would take any notice of me at all. I just had to make sure to squeeze into the car afterwards when Vivien set off to sample the night life, and Larry had gone back to his hotel.

One night, at Maxims, Vivien lost an earring. 'Colin, darling, would you be an angel and look on the floor?'

It is more peaceful than you would think under a dinner table, hidden by a long white cloth, among all those silent feet, and I could not resist a nap. When I emerged about half an hour later, the earring had been found and nobody noticed that I had been missing.

After a week in Paris, when we all boarded the Simplon–Orient Express for Venice, there was no disputing that, although Olivier was the star, it was Vivien who was in complete control. We couldn't take our eyes off her. We couldn't stop talking about her. We spent our whole time wondering what she would do next. There were only twelve other ladies in the company, including three actresses and the wardrobe staff. I don't expect they liked Vivien very much, but all the men were simply at her feet. It was as if we had our own private royalty. Vivien Leigh was also much better known to the general public in Europe than Laurence Olivier. A few of Olivier's films might have been translated into Italian or German, but everyone in the whole world had seen *Gone with the Wind*.

When we arrived in Italy, Vivien's night life had to be curtailed. It was spring, and Venice out of season is a very quiet town. I had been coming there with my parents ever since 1948. We had been in a box at La Fenice, where *Titus Andronicus* would be playing, when Toscanini had given his first concert in Italy after the fall of

RIGHT: My first plane, a de Havilland Tiger Moth. It felt alarmingly insecure, but actually it was one of the safest planes ever made.

BELOW: A pilot at last. With my MG TD sports car (0–60 mph in 23.9 seconds) in 1952.

Saltwood, 1954. Sir Colin Anderson poses as a Henry Moore sculpture, observed by Moore himself and his wife Irina, Katriona Anderson, my mother, myself and my father.

A typical house party at Saltwood in 1956 (*photograph by Cecil Beaton*). *From extreme left*:
Loelia, Duchess of Westminster; my sister Colette; myself; Margot Fonteyn; my mother;
Margot Fonteyn's husband Tito Arias; Gerard André, First Secretary at the French
Embassy; my father.

Paço da Gloria, in the Minho region of northern Portugal, is one of the world's most beautiful houses. When I first saw it in the summer of 1955, I little imagined that one day it would be mine.

Peter Pitt-Milward on his Lippizaner at Paço da Gloria, with Edo, the fearsome Doberman Pinscher.

fascism. (He was eighty years old, and he had seemed to me more like a tired old dog than a great conductor.)

La Fenice was one of the most beautiful theatres in the world. It contained three tiers of little gold boxes, hung with white flowers, surrounding a sloping horseshoe of plush red stalls. Like all eighteenth-century theatres the stage was very steeply raked towards the audience, which presented us with a terrific challenge, as our set had been built to swing open on a level floor. We had our own carpenters, but if they recut the bases of the towers on a slant for the Fenice, the set would have sloped backwards at the next theatre on the tour, with equally disastrous results. In the end, we all pushed and pulled and lifted until wedges could be inserted to make it work, and none of us got much rest.

Added to this, the Fenice, full of elegant ladies and the scent of tuberoses, was not the best place to perform Shakespeare's wild tale of blood and vengeance, and our stay in Italy was not a great success.

One week later we set off by train again, this time for Belgrade. Western cigarettes were not available in Yugoslavia in those days of Tito's communism. Nor were chocolates or whisky – and actors have a great need for all three. When we stopped at the border town of Trieste, we all dashed into the station to stock up.

'Oh, Colin, how sweet of you. You've bought me some cigarettes,' said Vivien as I returned to the carriage.

'My pleasure, Vivien,' I replied, handing them over, her slave as usual. I had trotted back to the kiosk to buy some more, when I noticed to my horror that the train was beginning to pull away. Dropping everything, I ran like a lunatic, and as the train gathered speed, I caught hold of the last rail of an open box car, and swung myself on.

It was a glorious sunny day. For twenty miles I had the most incredible views of the Dalmatian coast as the train wound its way up into the hills, with me sitting on its tail. There was no way in which I could rejoin the other carriages, so I just sat on the bare boards and rattled along. The trouble was that Vivien assumed that I had missed the train, and a search failed to find me. As soon as the train stopped at the border, she jumped out and phoned the British Consul in a panic. (No one likes to lose a slave.) When I then came sauntering up the line from my box car, I nearly got a slap. The fact that I had lost my cigarettes did not seem to count in my favour.

Yugoslavia went to Vivien's head. She had reached the manic stage of her depressive cycle, and her behaviour began to get very erratic indeed. It was just as well that her part in the play was of a young girl driven almost mad, because that was really all she could play. She wore a beautiful white costume, with red ribbons pinned on it to show where her tongue had been torn out and her hands cut off. Her black hair – a wig of course – hung down round her face, half shielding it from view, as she drifted around the stage in a daze. Olivier was genuinely much more worried about her health than about her performance, but she did have to turn up at the theatre on time, since at least half the audience had come to see her rather than him.

On the fourth night in Belgrade, it was announced that President Tito himself was going to pay us a visit, and a large number of his secret service men came to a matinée to assess the security risks. Being simple people, they were completely fooled by the arrows which Peter Brook had designed to flick out from the walls of the set, and they refused to believe that we didn't have a group of archers hidden in the back of the stalls. They searched the whole theatre from top to bottom, and when they could not find them, they demanded our solemn promise that we would leave our mystery bowmen at home. When the arrows did appear during the play they flung themselves noisily in front of the President, which greatly annoyed him.

Before Tito arrived, a regiment of armed guards was posted in front of the theatre, and a crowd gathered to watch. There was the usual long delay, and I popped out of the stage door for a quiet smoke in the late evening sunshine. To my intense surprise (and his) I nearly collided with President Tito coming in. Accompanied by only two bodyguards, he had decided to slip in through the rear entrance instead of the front one.

(On the poster advertising *Titus Andronicus* in Belgrade, I was billed as an '*Inspicigenti*'. I have no idea what it means, but it sounds about right.)

After a week we all went by coach to Zagreb, and there poor Vivien went to pieces completely. Luckily – and Vivien was always lucky – the chief of police in Zagreb had fallen in love with her, so he made sure she had a clear field. Nightclubs were emptied when she arrived, curious crowds were kept at bay, and cars were laid on to whisk her to the theatre from wherever she (and I) had ended up. It would be unkind to chronicle all the problems which occurred. Suffice it to say that when the time came to leave Zagreb, Vivien refused to board the train. Flags were waved, whistles blown, and frantic stationmasters ran up and down, but to no avail.

In the end the doting police chief simply picked her up and plonked her into the carriage. Vivien may have looked fragile, but she was actually very strong. Whop! She gave that fat policeman one of the nicest black eyes I have ever seen. And I did see it too, because he then got in his car and followed the train all the way to the border, to say a final farewell to Vivien – albeit with one eye.

Vivien always packed a mean punch. Years later I visited her after a performance of the musical *Tovarich* in New York. When I arrived she was on stage, having a blazing row with her co-star, Jean-Pierre Aumont. As neither of them could sing a note, the strain of being in a musical together must have been terrific.

'Vivien, you must do what you are told,' he said in that famous French accent. Fatal.

'Must I?' said Vivien, hopping onto a lighting box in the wings. '*Must I, little man?*'* and she banged him a beauty.

'Vivien, you can't do that!' he cried, putting his hand over his eye.

'Can't I?' said Vivien, and promptly shut the other eye with a straight left. She then came out to dinner with me without a tremor.

Half an hour after our train had left Zagreb it stopped, for no apparent reason, in a cutting between two tunnels. Vivien promptly opened the carriage door, climbed down and wandered off along the line. Olivier got out. The company manager got out. I got out.

* A quotation from Queen Victoria, and a favourite of Vivien's.

The train started to move again. Olivier got on, the company manager got on, and the train rolled slowly away.

Soon Vivien and I were all alone between two tunnels in the mountains of Yugoslavia, with nothing but the larks for company. Once again, the weather was glorious. Vivien sat down on the grass, and I sat beside her.

Poor, darling Vivien. Suddenly she looked very frail and miserable. 'It will be over soon, Colin,' she said. Then she pulled herself together, stood up, squared her little shoulders and began to march back up the track. To my astonishment, as if on cue, our train reversed out of the tunnel until it reached us. I gave Vivien my hand and we silently rejoined the company. When you were with Vivien things just happened like that.

As soon as we reached Vienna, a famous doctor was called and gave Vivien – I suspect by force – a serious injection. 'That will make her sleep for two days,' he pronounced. She was up and about again after two hours, but her mental cycle was beginning to turn again of its own accord, and she gradually returned to her former self.

The Burgtheater in Vienna had a very impressive modern stage which could hold two full sets at once and revolve them up and down. We could build our great forest/tower complex, light it, and leave it for a few days' break while the Vienna State Opera continued to perform Wagner's *The Flying Dutchman* at night.

By the time we arrived in Warsaw we were spoilt. The nineteenth-century theatre there also looked quite modern, but the gulf between Polish stage hands and Austrian stage hands was immense. Foolishly, I did not take into account the wild optimism of the Polish people. Every time the company had gone to a new city our set and props were packed into enormous crates, which we had loaded onto trains and lorries all over Europe. Warsaw was our sixth stop, and by this time we were thoroughly fed up with putting up the set then taking it down again. 'Don't you worry,' said the Polish theatre crew through an interpreter, 'we are professionals. Leave us the plans and we will put up your set. Come back for the dress rehearsal in two days' time, and all will be ready.' How fantastically kind, we thought, and went off to have a holiday.

As it was very hot, my friends and I decided to go to the country. We commandeered a bus, and made it take us to a lake in the woods nearby. At first the other picnickers stared at us in hostile amazement. I suppose the Poles had had a pretty rough time from foreigners in the past twenty years, and as there were no tourists in those days, they probably thought we were Russians. To break the ice as it were, one of the actors, John Standing, took off all his clothes except his shoes and socks, his pants and his hat. He then walked into the water, and kept on walking until he had completely disappeared, leaving only his hat floating on the surface. It was a very poetic performance, and it brought the house down. Soon we were surrounded by friendly people offering us wine and food.

The next day, the company was offered a trip to Cracow. Only half of us could go, because the plane only had thirty seats, so all our names were put in a hat, and a list of lucky winners was compiled, Vivien's among them, of course. As we were being driven to the airport, our hatchet-faced government interpreter gave us a stern lecture about our (rowdy) behaviour. She really was an unpleasant woman, and I could see Vivien sharpening her claws. When we got on to the plane, there was one person too many. The interpreter counted us. Thirty. What explanation could there be?

'I have here a list of names,' said our guide. 'Whoever's name is not on that list must get off immediately.'

Vivien saw her chance. 'What's your name?' she asked in her most dangerous voice, snatching the paper out of the woman's hands. There was, of course, no Polish name on the list. 'Off!' said Vivien, and literally forced her out of the plane.

An hour later, thirty high-spirited British actors landed in Cracow without an interpreter or a word of Polish between them, or the slightest idea of what to do, or how to get back to the airport when they had done it. Vivien was delighted. We set out to explore the only great Polish town which the Nazis had not destroyed, and to find the best restaurant available.

By 4 p.m. I was seriously worried. Not only had I no idea how to get back to our plane, but Vivien had been recognised and a large crowd now surrounded us as we walked along the street.

Then, once again, I was reminded that Vivien's aura always somehow protected her from total disaster. Through the crowd came nosing a grey Rolls-Royce with a uniformed chauffeur. A Rolls-Royce? In Cracow? In 1957? But there it was, and it wasn't a mirage. I opened the door, and Vivien got in as if she was expecting it. The driver had the glass division up, but it did not matter, as we had no idea what to say. The car just glided off, direct to the airport, and set us down by our waiting plane. Vivien thanked the driver with a gracious smile, and he sped off. We never did find out where he came from, or how he had known where to find us.

'Check, and check again, Colin,' had been the great lesson I had learned from my boss, Mr Perceval, on *The Prince and the Showgirl*. When we arrived safely back in Warsaw, I thought I had better stroll down to the theatre to see how the Polish stage hands had got on. The whole building was in darkness, and I had great difficulty getting in. Then I saw what the stage hands had done. Nothing. Absolutely zero. The seven great crates containing our scenery were lying on the empty stage, exactly where we had left them two and a half days before. A full dress rehearsal was scheduled for the next morning, followed by our first performance that night. The set took a minimum of twelve hours to construct. I went back to the hotel and summoned the company manager, the crew and every sober actor I could find, to come to the theatre and help. We spent the entire night building the set ourselves, and it was more or less ready by the time the stage hands turned up the next morning.

'Where have you been?' we asked in a rage. 'We thought you were going to build our set for us.'

'Oh, we were going to build it this morning.'

'But we've got a dress rehearsal in two hours.'

'We would have built it in less than two hours. You should have trusted us.'

Since they hadn't even taken the instructions out of their packets, words failed us. From then on we did everything ourselves.

The Polish people were very friendly and hospitable, but in 1957 Poland was still very much an Iron Curtain country, under the Soviet thumb. In the centre of Warsaw, in the middle of a huge square, stood the Palace of Culture, built by the Russians with a red star on the top to show who was boss. One night, after the performance, my three great friends in the company – David Conville, John Standing and Johnny MacGregor – and I thought we would teach this building a lesson. It was seven hundred feet high, and was reputed to have a famous Olympic-sized pool in the basement, so we decided that we would go for a swim.

Fortified by a great deal of Polish vodka, we marched across the square and banged on the front doors. The whole enormous building was in total darkness, and to start with we got no reaction. We went on banging. Finally two sleepy and, luckily, Polish guards opened a spy hole and demanded to know what we wanted. Then came the tricky bit. We did not speak any more Polish than they did English. We had somehow to explain, in mime, at 2 a.m., on the pavement, drunk, that we were members of a famous Shakespearean theatre company who had to swim, there and then, in their Olympic pool. It was difficult, yes, but not impossible. One must never underestimate the talent of British actors. David and the two Johnnies were magnificent. They even managed to add that we were flying back to London the next morning (a lie), so we could not come back the next day, during more normal swimming hours.

Of course the guards were adamant. Even Poles would not be so crazy as to let four drunken Englishmen in to swim in their prized Olympic pool in the middle of the night.

Very well. Could we just come in and look at it? Admire it? So we could tell everyone in England about it when we got back? Oh well then, said the guards, just to admire it.

The great doors were swung open at last, and in we went. Down in the basement the lights were switched on, and there lay the pool in all its glory. As one man, we dashed towards it, tearing off our clothes, and dived into the water. Poor guards. They ran round the edge; they implored us to get out; but they couldn't very well shoot us. We had the most enjoyable swim, and when we did eventually climb out, we had to pour on the charm like naughty schoolboys. In the end the guards even fetched towels for us, and we parted the best of friends. We promised faithfully to tell the whole world what a wonderful pool we had seen, but, of course, not swum in.

The Warsawa Hotel was another Polish muddle. It had sixteen floors but only two elevators, so the problem of getting up to our room on the sixth floor was acute. There were always about fifty people in the lobby ready to fight – literally fight – for a chance to get in to a lift.

We soon had a better idea. If we went up to the first floor by the stairs, we could stop an empty elevator on its way down and then wait inside for it to go up again. This was fine, but we were not the first to think of it. On the first floor were about twenty people with the same plan. On the second floor about six people, and on the third floor only a couple. This arrangement ensured that when the lift did get down to the ground floor it was already completely full of people who wanted to go up, hence the fisticuffs in the lobby. In the end we decided that by the time we had walked up three floors it was really easier to climb another three to our rooms than to descend to '*l'enfer*' and risk a bloody nose.

What the Polish people lack in efficiency, they make up in enthusiasm. They were a wonderful if noisy audience – many of those who did not understand English sitting with translations on their knees and clapping energetically at the bits they recognised. There was a permanent crowd of young women outside the stage door waiting for any autograph they could get – even mine. I fell in love with one extremely pretty little blonde. I could speak no Polish and she could speak no English, but we held out our young hands to each other in desperate yearning. Like a wartime romance, we knew nothing could come of it. (And nothing did. The Poles are ardent Catholics.) But we both enjoyed ourselves enormously for a full four days.

By now Vivien had largely recovered her equilibrium.

'It's so nice when it's over, Colin,' she said. 'Thank you so much for looking after me.'

'I would die for you, Vivien,' I wanted to say, but of course I didn't have the courage.

After the final performance, we all went off to a nightclub to celebrate. Olivier came with us for the first half hour. It must have been a great relief to him that the tour was over, although I am forced to admit that in all the years I knew him, it was always a great relief to Larry when anything was over. It was as if each episode in his life was part of an obstacle race, a mountain range which took all his energy and courage to surmount. He did not whinge all the time, the way Prince Charles does, but he did roll his eyes, and groan, and square his shoulders quite a lot.

As dawn neared, on that last night in Warsaw, and the nightclub was about to close, Vivien summoned me to dance with her.

'I've got no money left, Colin,' she giggled. 'How are we going to pay the bill?'

'I'll handle it, Vivien,' I said.

'I knew you would, Colin, darling,' she said – you can see why I was in love with her – and we danced on until the band stopped playing. I had already noticed two grim-faced men in blue suits sitting at the back of the hall. These same two men had been in the lobby of our hotel for the last four days, and I did not think they were fans. I walked into the middle of the dance floor and called for quiet.

'Ladies and gentlemen. On behalf of all the actors and actresses of the Shakespeare Memorial Theatre, I wish to thank these two gentlemen here' – I pointed to their table – 'for being such gracious hosts tonight. Next week their names will be famous all over England.' The whole company started to applaud, Vivien blew them kisses, and soon the nightclub was in an uproar.

'These gentlemen will take care of our bill,' I told the head waiter, who had been hovering nearby. The two 'gentlemen' scowled and squirmed. They were actually quite senior secret policemen who had been detailed to keep an eye on us, but in the end they could only bow and acquiesce. Our bill vanished, never, I am afraid, to be paid at all, and the whole company escaped, whooping delightedly, into the first light of our last morning in Poland.

By the time we got back to our sixth-floor room it was already daylight. It didn't seem important to go to bed now. All we had to do that day was to catch the aeroplane back to London, and then we could collapse for a week. John Standing and I were gazing out of our window, saying goodbye to Warsaw, when we spotted another member of the company coming furtively down the street towards the hotel. Alan Webb had been a very distinguished actor in his youth, but by now, although he had an important role in *Titus*, he was a fussy and often drunken old queen. Goodness knows what mischief he had been up to that night, but he was clearly very apprehensive, so we decided to make his dreams, or rather his nightmares, come true.

Just as he drew level with the hotel, we dropped a very small bottle of fizzy pear juice out of the window. Room service had been giving us these bottles every morning since we arrived, under the impression, I suppose, that if the fresh orange juice on the menu was unavailable, fizzy pear juice was better than nothing at all. Since our trays had never been cleared away for a whole week, we had accumulated a great many bottles. When the first bottle hit the pavement, it went off with the noise of a gun. Alan Webb nearly fainted. He jumped back into the shelter of a doorway and waited with bated breath. He was in a communist country. Perhaps there was a curfew. Perhaps one of his lovers was out for revenge. I don't expect his mind was very clear, but he knew, as he was to tell us on the plane later, that he had almost been shot.

Finally he plucked up the courage to peer round the corner of his doorway. Wait until he puts his foot out. Another bottle. CRACK! Now Alan knew they were out to get him. In desperation he made to run across the road. CRACK! CRACK! CRACK! And he bolted back to the safety of his door.

And so on. Finally we ran out of bottles. The poor man only just caught the flight back to London, but what an exciting story he now had to tell his friends about the dangers lurking behind the Iron Curtain.

The success of the *Titus Andronicus* tour was followed by a ten-week run at the Stoll Theatre in the Aldwych. This enormous old barn of a theatre was due to be pulled down immediately after we left, but we managed to fill it for every performance, so I suppose that made back some of the cost of carting us all around Europe. Both Larry and Vivien soon settled into a routine, arriving just in time to get their make-up on, and leaving for their country home, Notley Abbey, as quickly as they possibly could. Each night their dressing rooms would fill up with a stream of visitors, and I was continually amazed at how patient and polite they were, even with the stupidest guests.

'Larry, darling,' people would say as they squeezed in. 'It's us.'

I would have already checked who had sent flowers and made a list of people to expect.

'Darlings!' Larry would cry, nothing if not a great actor. 'How lovely to see you. Thank you for those wonderful flowers. You really shouldn't have.'

'No. We nearly didn't. You've got so many flowers already. But we wanted you to know we were out front.'

As if.

'How are you?' Larry would say.

'Well, Henry has had the most terrible toothache all day, but we didn't want to waste our seats even though Melissa is on half term and her horse has gone lame ... etc. etc. etc.' Not one word about Larry's performance or whether they liked the play. It was incredible.

'For heaven's sake, Larry,' I implored him when we were alone again, 'don't ask people how they are.'

'They're going to tell me anyway,' he groaned, and he was right.

I suppose this might have been partly because the roles Olivier played – like Titus and Archie Rice – were such towering personalities. Those smart and important people, who knew Larry well enough to be able to come round to see him, had had to sit still in the theatre and to suppress their egos for much longer than they normally would. They desperately needed to assert themselves again as soon as the play was over, and when they got to Larry's dressing room, they did.

Vivien's role in *Titus* was much more modest, and mostly silent, so she did not get the same boorish response. She often came to Larry's dressing room, and she was always absolutely wonderful. Outside the theatre she could not resist teasing and taunting him, but inside she never failed to defer to him as the great actor that he was. 'Wasn't Larry wonderful?' she would say to the noisy guests, and she would bill and coo over him like a loving mate, genuinely happy and proud.

This contradiction in Vivien was very hard to reconcile. Whenever they were apart, she seemed to miss Olivier dreadfully. Right up until her death in 1967, when they had been separated for over five years, she would keep her rooms covered with his photographs, and would sigh over them like a mother who has lost her child. I often heard her pouring her heart out to him on the telephone – when she did not know I was there, so it wasn't done for effect. But when they were together she would torment him as if her very life depended on it, and she could behave very badly indeed.

Vivien was not an alcoholic or a nymphomaniac, as she has sometimes been described. She suffered from bouts of manic depression from which, occasionally, alcohol or sex could give temporary relief, and she would bitterly despise herself for this afterwards. She showed incredible courage in continuing to act when confronted with this affliction. She never flinched from roles – Blanche DuBois in *A Streetcar Named Desire*, or Mrs Stone in *The Roman Spring of Mrs Stone* – which seemed to illustrate the dark side of her temperament. She faced the decline of her incredible beauty with great dignity, and finally accepted her fatal illness without bitterness or complaint. The only thing in her life that she regretted was that she could not make Olivier happy. That was beyond even her formidable powers, and I am not sure that it was entirely her fault.

As we were finishing the West End run of *Titus Andronicus* we were already preparing to restage *The Entertainer*, first on tour and then at the Palace Theatre at Cambridge Circus. The same cast was lined up for the principal roles – Olivier of course, Brenda de Banzie and George Relph. They were all such professionals that they could do the play in their sleep. Only the minor parts were changed. The role of Archie Rice's daughter, originally played by Dorothy Tutin, was given first to Geraldine McEwan, and later to Joan Plowright (it was the most ghastly part, so I suppose no one wanted to keep it for too long). Great though Olivier was, his performance also never varied once it had been set, which I now think indicates rather an old-fashioned approach. Perhaps it is the only way an actor can stay sane for the whole of a long run. Olivier was such an intelligent man that it was hard to admit that he could behave like a super-efficient machine. If it troubled me, it was because each audience thought that he was giving the performance of his life that night, just for them; and of course even Laurence Olivier could not do that. So the magic was – had to be – a sort of conjuring trick.

The Entertainer's tour round the provincial theatres of England and Scotland was nothing like taking *Titus Andronicus* round Europe. By this time Olivier and Vivien were clearly getting on very badly indeed. Vivien came up to Edinburgh to join us for her forty-fourth birthday – always a difficult moment for a lady, especially one who has been famous for her beauty. We celebrated the event at a dinner party which was of a horror not even contemplated by Edgar Allan Poe. The chef had decided to name each dish after one of Vivien's famous roles. This was fine for 'Soup Lady Hamilton' or 'Soufflé Scarlett O'Hara', but became macabre when we got to 'Boeuf Blanche Dubois'. We were all painfully reminded of the passage of time – and not all that smooth a passage either. Vivien was grim and miserable. At least she was not going through the manic part of her cycle, so she was lucid, but Larry was clearly – clearly to Vivien as well as to me – having an affair with somebody else.

I had become accustomed to such situations with my father. I did not realise then that great and successful men often need to spread themselves very thinly among the opposite sex. Olivier was a natural performer, and my father was too. Both of them found it very hard to show their emotions except when they were on stage. My father sometimes described Olivier as a clown, but perhaps that was because he was jealous. Neither man was vain, but they both felt that, in the face of difficult wives and a demanding world, they had shown the patience of Job, and each of them used to sink into the arms of an adoring admirer as if it was their due. Surely, they seemed to say, I deserve the reward of a few hours of peace, of being able to take instead of endlessly giving. This did make life very difficult for their partners, and I must admit that I rather sympathised with Vivien; as I did, indeed, with my mother.

On the night *The Entertainer* finally closed its run at the Shaftesbury Theatre, there was a party on stage. The curtain was raised on the empty auditorium, and everyone did their party piece, encouraged by plenty of champagne and beer. It was the sort of situation in which Olivier usually shone even brighter than usual, but this time he was obviously depressed.

In his dressing room afterwards, he told me the bad news. He and Vivien were separating, probably for ever. It seemed very sudden, even though they had been spending most of the past few months in despair about each other – 'Oh, Colin, I'm afraid I've upset my darling Larry dreadfully this time. Do you think he will be terribly cross?' 'What am I going to do about Vivien, dear boy? Tell me I'm not going crazy. I just don't know how to help.' And so on, virtually every day.

'I'm off to Hollywood next week,' Olivier said (he was going to act in the film of *Spartacus*). 'I loathe Hollywood, but I've got to get away. Vivien will be staying here. I'm not sure what her plans are.'

I was struck dumb. Vivien had left Larry on several occasions, but he had never left her. I had seen them close to splitting up many times, just as I had my parents. Both had begun as golden couples. In both cases the wife was as intelligent as the husband, and as ambitious, if not as wise. Larry and Vivien did not have children, and they were ten years younger than my parents, but I still thought of them as too old to make drastic changes, and the news came as a tremendous shock.

Olivier took an Asprey cigarette case out of a drawer. 'I'm saying goodbye to everyone, dear boy. But we will work together again, I promise.' In the lid of the cigarette case was inscribed: '*The Prince and the Showgirl, The Entertainer, Titus Andronicus*, for a start. SLO.'

Now I had to find another job. Actors in long-running plays can be refreshed by the ever-changing nature of each audience. They get rewarded by a different reaction every night, and by the applause. Backstage you get no such recognition, nor do you deserve it. In the end you even feel guilty for taking wages in return for so little work. It was rather a relief to rejoin the real world.

After Olivier had returned to London I would go to see him give his wonderful performances at the National Theatre, and then pay him a respectful visit afterwards. We would sit in his dressing room, gossiping and sipping whisky. I was determined not to behave like those other visitors who told him their life stories, but soon I discovered that Larry did not want to talk about himself. He would happily list his problems, his frustrations and his fatigue (Larry was always tired), but his 'self' − if indeed he had a 'self' after all the roles he had assumed − seemed to be buried for ever.

It has been said that no one should ever contemplate becoming an actor unless they have a desperate need to be someone else. Olivier was at his happiest when he was on stage, wearing a false nose, leaping about, manipulating the emotions of his audience with his incredible skill. At the end of his long life, when he ran out of roles, he almost seemed to vanish − a little man with a gingery beard and a quavering, high-pitched voice. But Olivier in his prime was an extraordinarily strong character. Vivien Leigh was the most beautiful, brilliantly clever woman I have ever known, but she must surely have been one of the most difficult of partners. The critic Kenneth Tynan, who worked with Olivier at the National Theatre, was a precocious genius, but he was hardly an easy person to get along with. Olivier managed to cope with both him and Vivien and, indeed, to dominate them. Vivien had won her first Oscar, for *Gone With the Wind*, in 1939, long before Olivier had won his Special Academy Award for *Henry V* in 1947 (he was awarded the Oscar for Best Actor for *Hamlet* the following year). She knew full well that she was the cleverer of the two, but she always acknowledged that Olivier was the boss. Even Tynan knew that he could not tell Olivier how to act. In the end, both Vivien and Tynan self-destructed, but Olivier carried on. He saw the stage as a profession. He knew that he had an enormous talent for acting, and for recognising talent in others. He despised amateurs in any field, but he never hesitated to encourage those he felt were willing to work as hard as he did. All the prima donna actors and actresses who criticised Olivier so much were secretly longing to be asked to join the National Theatre under his direction. He was a king not by birth or accident, but by strength and skill and courage. If he demanded loyalty, then he himself was loyal to a fault.

Olivier was always perfectly conscious of his powers − and of his power, but I never once saw him abuse it. He was thoughtful, considerate, gracious, warm-hearted and wise. Perhaps this is why he still casts such a giant shadow. He has become a bogeyman at whom many of his successors cannot resist to tilt. If you want to get a laugh in a room full of actors, make an unkind joke about Larry. Say that he was cruel, egotistical, sexually impotent, and they will all be quick to approve and agree. Say that he was a very great man, which is the truth, and they will look at you with scorn.

This book was not written for actors, so I can tell you that Olivier was one of the greatest men I have ever known, and I have been lucky enough to know quite a few.

VII

FROM POPEYE TO PBS

I FIRST MET SYDNEY BERNSTEIN, the head of Granada Television, at a very grand party in Venice during the *Titus Andronicus* tour. The party was being given for the Oliviers, and my job was to remain as inconspicuous as possible, but Bernstein had a relentless curiosity which one could not escape. His broken nose, combined with his enormous charm, made him look like a gangster, which in a way he was.

'Who are you?' he asked me, probably a little out of his depth among all the chic Venetians.

'Oh, I'm no one, I'm afraid,' I replied. 'I work for Larry and Vivien as their assistant. I'm one of the stage managers on their play.'

'I was there tonight,' said Bernstein. 'Very exciting.'

Then, typically of him, as I was to learn later, he asked a question which I didn't expect, but which hit the nail right on the head. 'Where are you staying in Venice?'

'I've been lent a flat by an artist called Graham Sutherland.'

'Oh, you're *that* Clark, are you? Well, I'm a great admirer of your father's.' He paused, and stared at me. 'If you ever want a job after all this,' he waved his hand round the room, 'come to see me at Granada Television.' And off he went.

After that, whenever someone asked me what I was going to do next (a very common question in the theatre), I would tell them that I was going to work for Granada Television. I thought the Oliviers would go on for ever, but it was nice to have something up my sleeve.

The day after Olivier told me that he and Vivien were splitting

129

up, and that he was leaving for Hollywood, I telephoned Mr Bernstein. Not surprisingly, I did not get through to him personally. Sydney Bernstein was trying to make Granada the most prestigious of the independent television companies, and his power, and the autocratic way in which he wielded it, were already a legend in the television industry.

'If you want a job,' his office told me, 'you should apply to the general manager of our studios in Manchester.'

'Well, I met Mr Bernstein in Venice a little while ago, and he offered me something then.' I must admit that it did sound pretty lame.

'His name is Simon Kershaw,' the secretary continued relentlessly. 'You should write to him with your details.'

After all my previous experience with the London Zoo, the Air Force and *The Prince and the Showgirl*, I knew you didn't just write to someone with your details. I rang Mr Kershaw immediately.

'My name is Colin Clark,' I said, as if he ought to know it well. 'Mr Bernstein has offered me a job, and I thought I should come up to see you first.'

'Very well,' said an amiable Mr Kershaw. 'Come in tomorrow at noon. I look forward to meeting you.'

I went up by train. I'd never been to Manchester before, and Salford, where the TV studios are, looked very grim.

Mr Kershaw was a big, bland man, with a podgy handshake. 'Ah, Colin,' he said. 'I've had a word with Mr Bernstein's office, and we are prepared to offer you a job. You can start immediately as a trainee assistant floor manager at a salary of £8.10s. per week, up here in Manchester, of course.'

This was much less money than I had been earning in the theatre. I did not know a soul in Manchester, or have a clue as to where I could live. 'I'll take it,' I said.

'And you won't last a month,' said the production manager, Jack Martin, who had joined Mr Kershaw in the office. 'There are no nightclubs up here, you know.'

'That's why I've accepted the job,' I said. 'I'll be back on Monday.'

Trainee assistant floor manager was a position I knew well. It meant a 'gofer', the very same job that I had had on *The Prince and the Showgirl*. Cups of tea for the senior floor manager, cables all over the studio floor, scripts left in dressing rooms and stars to be collected from make-up, this was all familiar ground to me. I had been Laurence Olivier's gofer. I was the best gofer in the business. I could do it in my sleep. But it was time to move on.

It took three months before I was 'floor-managing' my own programme. (A floor manager wears headphones and organises the studio for the director, rather like a stage manager in the theatre. He, or she, has no influence over the content or direction of the show.) It wasn't much. It was a daily Popeye cartoon show for children, and each film was introduced by a lovely actor called Gordon Rollins. The producer, who was on the way down, of course, or he would never have been given such a modest show to produce, had long since stopped paying attention to what was going on. Gordon was dressed up as a pirate, and he and I and a cameraman were crammed together in a little studio the size of a phone booth. Every day we watched the endless Popeye films while Gordon waited for me to give him the cue to speak. In the end, we decided to get up to mischief. Without any authority at all I wrote Gordon a couple of lines that were not in the script: 'Now, children, if you've enjoyed *Popeye* this afternoon,' said Gordon to camera, 'why don't you write and tell us? And the best letter will get a prize.'

Even in those early days, television was watched by more people than we had imagined. Two days later, a startled mailroom rang up to say they had over three thousand letters addressed to 'Popeye, c/o Granada TV, Manchester'. The producer nearly fainted with fear. What would SLB* say? He kept an eye on everything that happened. Sure enough, the next morning there he was on the phone from Golden Square.

'Was this your idea?' he asked the producer.

'No, no. It was the floor manager's. He did it on his own, without telling me.'

* I use initials because, as anyone who has worked in a big corporation will know, it is the initials at the top of an inter-office memo which show who the memo is going to. They also show how much power you have: anyone who put 'cc SLB' at the top of their memoranda had to have a great deal of power indeed.

'What's his name?'

'Colin Clark.'

SLB had probably forgotten that I was on his payroll. 'Put him on the line. Colin? What's the idea?'

'I thought it might liven things up, Mr Bernstein. Make the children see it as their programme, not just talking wallpaper. We got a terrific response.'

'OK. Well done. But don't ever do it again without asking first. And you've got yourself into this mess, so let's see you get yourself out of it.'

'What did he say?' asked the wretched producer.

'He's furious, of course,' I said, 'but he doesn't blame you. I've got to write in an extra line for Gordon to say tomorrow.'

'Hello, children, Popeye here. You certainly sent me some great letters. I've enjoyed reading every one. And here is the prize for the best one,' holding up a Popeye book. 'It goes to Michael, aged eleven, in Leeds' – a name chosen completely at random. 'And now for another cartoon.' The film rolled, and it was all over.

Television is a pretty ruthless business. Soon I had progressed from *Popeye* to *What the Papers Say*, a weekly fifteen-minute news review programme. It depended on split-second timing to get the right voice coming up with the right newspaper caption, and the floor manager was responsible for making it work. The show was written and presented by a different journalist each week. They would usually come up from London for the night, and after the programme was over (it went out live, as did *Popeye*), the producer, the director and I would take them to the Midland Hotel for copious drinks, while they gave us the lowdown on current affairs. It was not normal procedure for the floor manager to be included in this sort of occasion, but being an Old Etonian I just went, and soon I was making friends in high places.

In every TV station I've known, there are only three or four people who wield real power – the power to commission programmes and to decide who will make them. At Granada in 1960 there were two such people – Sydney Bernstein, of course, and another executive, Denis Forman. Denis was as tough as they come. I once saw him walk into the road in front of a Granada staff member's car. The driver didn't recognise him, I suppose, and kept on going. Denis did not step back and the car went over his foot.

'My God!' I shouted. 'Your foot. He's broken it.'

Denis stayed icy calm. 'It's made of tin,' he said. I had not noticed it before, but he'd had the original leg shot off in the war. The staff member had stopped and rushed back to apologise, but he needn't have bothered. It was his last day.

Denis took a great interest in *What the Papers Say*, and this made it one of Granada's most important programmes. Everybody was jockeying for position then, as they probably are now, eager to improve their careers at the expense of their colleagues, and the ability to catch Denis Forman's eye was invaluable. Denis was a wonderfully able executive, and I liked him very much. After a month on *What the Papers Say*, I found I could talk to him as a person and not just as a floor manager. In the end I took the enormous risk of telling him that I was leaving Granada to join ABC Television in London. I had written to ABC in answer to an advertisement and, after an interview, been offered the position of assistant to the chief executive, but I really wanted to stay at Granada.

Denis looked at me quizzically for a moment. 'Well, what job do you want?'

I said nothing.

'Do you want to be a producer, or a director, or what?' Then he glared at me, correctly reading my mind. 'No, Colin. You cannot have my job,' he said. 'But you can be my assistant. We are expanding so fast at the moment, that I could use some help.' And so I changed jobs again, and this time I had some power.

I had also found a new home. My digs in Manchester were pretty claustrophobic. I was working such long hours at the studios that all I needed was somewhere to sleep at night (alone), but at weekends there was nothing to do, and taking the train down to the fleshpots of London tended to be very bad for the health. I rented a little cottage in Tarporley, Cheshire, about twenty miles from Manchester. I had many guests in that cottage, and I found the most lovely, plump and practical Northern lady as a housekeeper. Joan Lewis was to look after me for many many years. She went with me to London, to Kent, and even out to Hollywood. She was that old-fashioned thing, a loyal servant. We became the greatest of friends, but she always called me 'Mr Clark'.* I redecorated the cottage with the help of a young friend called Tony Warren, who was working in the promotions department at Granada. Tony was from London, and he wrote those little voice-over inserts between programmes – 'Don't forget to watch *The Jackie Ray Show* at 10.30 tonight' – which everyone assumes just write themselves, and was very frustrated. He was also as camp as coffee, and would roam round the pubs of Salford, absorbing local colour. In 1959 he invented *Coronation Street*, and I was able to watch its progress, and even help in a modest way, from the vantage point of Denis Forman's office. What Tony did not realise was that any work done while on the staff of a TV company is automatically the property of that company. After the success of the first six episodes, Granada had to remind him that they owned the show. Tony got more money as a script writer than he had as a promotions writer, but he also got very disillusioned, and often very drunk. Soon he left the company to go off on his own.

Forman put in a new team to do the *Coronation Street* scripts, and a new producer and director. Once Tony's format was in place, all they had to do was follow it. It is worth remembering that for nearly four decades *Coronation Street* has been at the top of the TV ratings, and its popularity has paid for all of Granada's great cultural programmes. *Coronation Street* has enabled Granada to become Britain's most successful independent television station, and even to expand into a conglomerate. As far as I know, Tony Warren

---

* Twenty-seven years later I got a call from a hospital in Cheshire. 'We have a Miss Joan Lewis here who is dying, I'm afraid. She is often delirious, and she keeps asking for you. Could you come up?' 'I'm on my way,' I said, and got straight in the car. It was the most enormous hospital I have ever seen. Joan was lying in bed, looking dreadfully ill. 'Now, Joan,' I said, 'it's Mr Clark. What's the matter?' 'Oh, Mr Clark,' she said, sitting up, 'I'm sorry to bother you, but now you've come, I'm sure everything will be all right.' We sat and chatted for hours about the past, Joan getting stronger every minute. 'I'll be back tomorrow,' I promised. That evening the nurse rang again. Joan was so much better, she said, that they were thinking of sending her home in the morning. Perhaps I could drive her back to Tarporley. 'Of course,' I said. She died during the night, but at least she didn't die in despair.

never received a penny in royalties. All he got, and still gets, is a credit line on that rapidly moving roller at the end of each show: 'From an original idea by Tony Warren.' That's showbusiness.

Denis Forman was supreme boss of the studios, and life as his assistant was exciting, but it didn't last long. A new design department was being planned, and for some reason it would not fit into the space allotted for it in a new building next to the studios. I was sent over to investigate the problem. SLB was marching about, snorting and snuffling through that wonderful broken Jewish nose, and glaring at the plans. Mr Pook, the office manager, was clearly on the verge of a nervous breakdown. Television production was expanding weekly in 1960 but the site was not, which meant a continual struggle for space. The studios were virtually run on plans, and I had got in the habit of carrying a little scale rule in my pocket, just in case. I put the rule against a spare set of drawings which were lying on the desk.

'Excuse me,' I piped. It was very, very dangerous to make direct communication when SLB was present. As in the army, a subordinate was really meant to go through the next-highest rank if he had anything to say.

'Yes.' They all glared impatiently.

'This plan is marked 1/20 scale, but drawn to 1/25.' Pandemonium. Mr Pook had not brought a scale rule, so he had to grab mine. SLB snorted and glared. I fled. The messenger of news like that can be pretty unpopular. But the next day, without any explanation, I was made deputy head of the design department.

It turned out that the head of the design department, who was an American, had refused to do something SLB had personally told him, and been pretty offhand into the bargain (I discovered later that he had just inherited $10 million). This was tantamount to suicide; a month earlier one of the programme directors had grown a beard. 'I don't like beards,' SLB had said. The next day he shaved it off. 'I don't like sycophants,' said SLB, and the director had been fired anyway.

The easiest way to get rid of someone, if you don't want to actually sack them, is to appoint another employee to do their job as well as them, and not explain why. When they angrily demand to know what is going on, you graciously accept their resignation. This is what happened to the head of the design department. After two weeks he had gone, and I was left in control, at least until another head was appointed.

I had already discovered that there was a major war going on between the design department and the construction department. The latter was run by two brothers, George and Cyril Speller, who were very much of the old school. They thought the designers were arty-farty egotists, wasting money in order to see their fancy scenery on the telly. The Spellers couldn't bear to see the sets they had built being thrown away after every show, so they had devised a scheme of unitary construction. This meant that the designers would have to design all their scenery using only pre-made units – standard-size 'flats', reveals, doors and so on – which could be fitted together in different patterns, repainted for each show, and then taken to pieces again. Naturally the designers resisted this like crazy. They could see that I knew nothing about design whatsoever, and assumed I would support them (I was 'arty' too, after all).

Sorry, fellas. After much secret consultation with the Speller brothers, and many phone calls, I marched into Cecil Bernstein's office with my plan. Cecil was Sydney's little brother, and his power was really only nominal, but I guessed that if I told him my plan rather than Denis Forman, who was away, he might be flattered, and support me. I explained the situation in dire terms, and then offered my solution: sack all the designers. And who would replace them? New, brilliant, innovative designers who were waiting in the wings. I had found two excellent British designers working for CBC TV in Canada who wanted to come back home, and who were perfectly willing to accept the unitary construction plan.

Poor Cecil was very nervous. He conferred with the Speller brothers, and eventually he agreed. A week later I was still temporary acting head of design, but with designers whom I had hired (or promoted), and with a very happy construction department to back me up. I had also acquired a reputation for ruthlessness which SLB and Forman greatly appreciated, but actually it was just the rapid application of common sense.

Every studio programme has to have a designer, so for a year I got a wonderful overview of all the different shows that Granada produced. Then another crisis occurred. When ITV was created in 1954, the great bogeyman had been American sponsored television, in which advertisers rather than TV companies dictated the contents of the programmes. The Independent Television Association (ITA) had been given a charter especially designed to prevent this happening in the UK, but as so often with watertight legislation, there had been a loophole. This one allowed for the existence of a ghastly thing called an 'advertising magazine'. The sales department would get a hotchpotch of clients to buy into these – Buxted Chickens, Anadin, Bex Bissell Carpet Shampoo, etc. – and the programme department would then be given the job of putting the sales pitches of all these products into a twenty-minute show which people might conceivably want to watch.

It was a completely impossible task. After many people had failed, Forman asked me to have a try. I sensed that no one except a comedian could reconcile continuous hard-sell sales messages with entertainment, but the job meant being posted to London, and that, after two years in Manchester, was hard to resist. I loved the North, but I am never completely at ease living in the country. I only feel half alive.

I moved into a house in Cheyne Walk with my old Oxford friend Reginald Bosanquet, who had recently separated from his incredibly seductive wife. Reggie was reading the *News at Ten* on ITN, and was a much-loved public figure. The trouble was that he was also a serious boozer. He used to judge his intake of alcohol very carefully, so that he was just sober enough to read the nightly news bulletins, and would then get plastered immediately afterwards. One Sunday we went on a picnic, and I brought along a bottle of gin, two bottles of white wine and two bottles of champagne. Reggie polished them all off without turning a hair. He then went and bought a bottle of port and a bottle of brandy from a pub, both of which he emptied before passing out, peacefully, on the grass.

Living with Reggie meant that I too was drinking more than I ought to. I was also having a predictably dreadful time with the 'ad-mags', which I had completely failed to improve. There was nothing for it but a complete break. I found a home of my own, stumbled into marriage, and soon found myself forced to leave Granada and move to New York.

I arrived in America at exactly the right moment. For years the television industry there had been controlled by three commercial companies, ABC, NBC and CBS, and they were permanently locked in a ratings war for the vast audience. Only very occasionally (as a sop to the intellectuals) did they put on anything remotely 'cultural', and when they did they always regretted it immediately, since they saw their viewing figures drop like a stone.

Then as now, the safest thing to do was to go for the lowest common denominator, and this meant a diet of inane quiz shows and situation comedies.

America is full of clever, well-informed people, and there had to be a reaction. It came in the form of so-called 'public television'. In the late 1950s, public television stations sprang up all over the country. They put out educational programmes for young children all day and cultural programmes for adults in the evenings. They did not carry any advertisements, so the only financial support they had was from the public – hence the name. By 1960 most large towns in America, with the notable exception of New York, had public broadcasting in operation. Some PBS stations even received corporate support in return for modest announcements: 'This programme has been made possible by a grant from Xerox', or whatever.

There was an obvious need for such a station in New York City, but the commercial networks had resisted all attempts to establish one. I suppose they felt threatened by the number of opinion-makers who might watch a cultural channel, even if the mass audience ignored it. In the end, after many battles, a station was set up just outside New York State, with a powerful enough transmitter to reach the city and get round the skyscrapers. Just after my arrival in New York, Channel 13, 'WNDT New Jersey', was born (all American television and radio stations' call signs start with 'W'. 'NDT' stood for 'New Dimensions in Television'), with its transmitter across the Hudson River, but its offices and studios in Manhattan.

I applied for a job there as soon as I heard about it, even though I had not got my immigration papers, and had only been allowed into the USA on a tourist visa. A month later I was hired, and joined a group of earnest young idealists in the task of creating a television station out of thin air. It was rather like being back at the Royal Court. We were all professionals, but we were revolutionaries too. We had set our teeth against the impersonal, money-grabbing attitude of the network television executives, and we were determined to create something really worthwhile.

The commercial stations were ruled by the Neilsen Ratings, which purported to tell the advertisers exactly how many people were watching each minute of each programme. Producers treated the ratings as if they were gospel truth, and sacked actors and scriptwriters if even a blip in the figures seemed to go against them. The Neilsen Corporation was based in Chicago. I once went to stay with an executive of the company for a weekend, and he took me to dinner with old Mr Neilsen. What a horror story. Neilsen's cronies struck me as a bunch of elderly, reactionary teetotallers. They appeared to be anti-black and anti-homosexual, and I can't help feeling that their views strongly influenced the sort of television that was being made by the commercial networks at that time.

Luckily, Channel 13 did not have to worry about ratings. We were thrilled if we got a rating of one (out of 100). Reviews in the *New York Times* and the *New York Herald Tribune* were what mattered to us, and because the television critics were bored stiff with the network rubbish, we got a lot of attention. Soon our programmes became a centre of debate in that highly intellectual city.

Obviously it was not possible for the small staff at Channel 13 to make enough programmes to fill a fifteen-hour day, and so a great deal of our material had to be bought in. The BBC was then the undisputed king of cultural TV, and a great many of our programmes came from them. As I walked past a preview theatre, I often used to hear my father's voice coming out of the darkness as he talked away in his pre-*Civilisation* films, on great temples, royal palaces and so on. (He had always spoken to me in exactly the same tone that he used on television, so this could be quite unnerving.) We also started some of the series which made Channel

13 famous. *Sesame Street* was an instant success. Julia Child was the first person to do a cooking show on television at lunchtime. *Masterpiece Theater* was presented by the incomparable Alistair Cooke, and became a legend.

Naturally the three networks were furious about this new and lively presence on New York's television screens. They stirred up trouble with the unions, and even forced our technicians to go on strike on our opening day. But the production staff stepped in, and we got through (the head of accounts became a cameraman, and I operated a sound boom). The networks also seduced away any of our executives who were too successful (but not me!). They would offer them wonderful jobs in California on huge salaries. When it was too late for them to come back to us, they would 'let them go'. The producers would be left stranded in California with nothing to do, while we had to search for replacements.

Channel 13 struggled on, always on the edge of extinction, but gradually it built up a core audience of loyal supporters. I was lucky enough to team up with a writer named Ray Sipherd, and together we made a series of arts documentaries. As we had no money at all, we had to be very inventive. Ray discovered that a huge archive of photographs of the Depression commissioned by the Works Project Administration, or WPA, in the 1930s was sitting in New York Public Library. It had been hidden there by a zealous librarian from a government which wanted to eliminate the evidence of what a disaster the Depression had really been. Ray sifted through literally thousands of incredibly moving black and white images, and wrote a script to go with them. We found that one of the original photographers, Ben Shahn, who had become a famous graphic designer, was still alive. We drove down to Pennsylvania with a tape recorder, and persuaded him to read Ray's script into a microphone. When he reached a quotation from John Steinbeck's *The Grapes of Wrath*, he began to weep, and the resulting commentary in this old, shaky Jewish immigrant's voice was very moving. The film won the station many awards, but it didn't help with the money.

Eventually I was allowed to make my own series, which I called *Art: New York*. By 1961, the centre of the art world had indisputably moved from Paris to New York – from the Old World to the New, and I set out to make a record of all the major artists who lived and worked in the New York area. I was given a budget of $2600 to make twenty-six half-hour programmes – $100 per film. I found a young man who knew much more about the art world than I did, and paid him $20 a week to be my assistant. I spent $40 each week on 16mm black and white negative, and I put $5-worth of petrol into the Channel 13 Chevrolet station wagon. The remaining $35 paid for the processing of the film I had shot.

I stuffed a 16mm Bolex movie camera into my pocket, and set off with my assistant to record anything we could find. We could not afford lights, so everything had to be filmed out of doors, and we had no sound equipment either – just like Hollywood in the 1920s, in both cases. We would persuade the artists to let us film them at work, and then they would come into the studio at a later date and record a commentary. The important thing was to get a half-hour of usable silent film for the artists to watch. With the exception of Willem de Kooning and Jasper Johns (both of whose work, coincidentally, I did not admire), all the artists we approached responded with courtesy and warmth. Very few of them had been filmed before, and they were often fascinated to see themselves in action.

Once we got them in the studio, I would point a TV camera at their faces and then intercut, on videotape, between the film of them working and their reactions to what they saw. It was an extremely humble, not to say amateur, way of making a programme, but such was the genius of many of the artists that it often made fascinating viewing. Jackson Pollock was dead, but I made a film with his widow Lee Krasner Pollock, who was herself an abstract painter, and a great personality. Mark Rothko, Robert Motherwell and the sculptor David Smith were among the abstract expressionists who allowed me to film them. Andy Warhol and Roy Lichtenstein represented the new 'Pop' art. Andrew Wyeth was the great traditional figurative painter, very much out of favour at that time, but I went down to Chad's Ford in Pennsylvania to film him too. Alexander Calder had invented the 'mobile', made up of brightly-coloured pieces of metal dancing delicately on wires, and he took us round his exhibition at the Guggenheim Museum. We visited the great collector Joseph Hirshhorn at his mansion in Connecticut, and the architect Philip Johnson in his 'glass house', which he had designed without any walls. Altogether we managed to make twenty-three films before the money ran out. Some of them got pretty horrendous reviews, but at least they were seen and discussed.

After *Art: New York* I still had no budget and no studio, so I began to record live programmes in the courtyard of the New School, on 13th Street. There were readings by the greatest living American poets, like Marianne Moore, and wonderfully noisy jazz concerts with musicians like Thelonious Monk and Sonny Rollins. We could record all this on videotape, although we were not allowed to edit it (too expensive), so the result was often full of mistakes, but, in our poverty and innocence we were oblivious to criticism.

In 1962 Ray Sipherd and I were joined by a theatre producer called Jack Landau, who looked like a penguin, and for three glorious years we three were the arts programming department of Channel 13. We could do almost anything we dreamed up, providing we stayed within budget. It was a golden age, and like all golden ages, it provoked a reaction. Eventually the bureaucrats took over, and all the senior producers who had allowed us so much freedom were sacked. (Poor Jack Landau went to Boston, where he was murdered, it was never discovered by whom.) New steely-eyed ex-CBS executives moved in, determined to stop all this dangerous experimentation and innovation. We were told that the station must revert to pure education, and the consequent drop in the number of our viewers was, I am sure, very welcome to the networks.

The videotapes on which my programmes had been stored were all wiped – 'degaussed', it is called – by a big magnet. The laboratories which held my original films were told to destroy them, and not a single record of them remains. Three years of work, and a visual record of the most exciting period in art since 1910, went down the drain. Only *Years Without Harvest*, Ray's film of the Depression photographs, remained, because it won so many awards.

We all knew that real television – commercial television – was run by a bunch of cut-throats whose only interest was to enhance their power. At Channel 13 we were meant to be different. We were a band of pioneers, united into a family by a common aim – like characters in a Mary McCarthy short story. Our only interest, we had claimed rather pompously, was to spread culture to the people of New York, to relieve their diet of rubbish. We did not have the sense to realise that commercial forces will always take over in the end, or the honesty to admit that we had all enjoyed a fabulous three years doing precisely what we wanted to do at someone else's expense.

It was clearly time for us all to find new jobs, and I decided to return to England.

VIII

ROMANTIC REBELLIONS

ROBERT HELLER WAS HEAD of features and documentary pro-grammes at the Midlands ITV station, Associated Television, or ATV. When I first met him in 1965 he was in a condition which is quite common among television executives: he had so many knives in his back that there simply wasn't room for any more. This meant, among other things, that he always sat with his back to the wall, he never left his office even to go out for lunch, and he had his own private toilet. He had originally been brought over to England from America to be head of programming at Granada, but after a while he had fallen out of favour with Sydney Bernstein. One day when he returned to the Manchester studios from lunch, he was stopped by the commissionaire.

'I'm sorry, sir, you can't go in.'

'Don't be a fool! I'm Robert Heller, Head of Programming.'

'My orders are to prevent you entering the building.'

'And what about my office, and all my personal things?'

The commissionaire pointed to a pile of plastic bags in the corner of the lobby.

'Everything is there, sir, I believe.'

Bob was a very experienced programme-maker, and he was soon hired by Lew Grade of ATV. He was one of those very short, stout bald men who don't seem to change height when they get up from their desk, a little like Lew Grade himself. But while Lew exuded energy and confidence, Bob had acquired a furtive, hunted look behind his horn-rimmed glasses. Lew liked to come straight to the point, but Bob would talk for ten minutes in a hoarse whisper before you could understand what he was getting at.

Bob was fascinated by English privilege and the Establishment, and in 1965 he commissioned me to make a one-hour documentary film on Harley Street. I rushed up and down interviewing grand doctors and consultants, and marvelling at how old-fashioned it all was. The resulting film was not very good (again), but at least it had a message: if you are rich, and there is nothing particularly wrong with you, then a smooth bedside manner and a private room can be very comforting. But if you are seriously ill, the best place in the world to be is a large London teaching hospital. (I always remembered this, and thirty years later when I found I had cancer I went to the Charing Cross Hospital in Hammersmith.)

For the next five years I made many films with Bob Heller. He particularly liked to find 'highbrow' intellectual interviewers and pitch them against distinguished men who were specialists in other fields. We did two series in the studio with the writer Angus Wilson, and his gentle probing manner was surprisingly effective.

Bob also admired Bernard Levin, and in 1975 he sent Bernard, with me, to interview Herman Kahn, the great futurologist, at the Hudson Institute in New York. Kahn was the original of Dr Strangelove in the Stanley Kubrick film. He was amazingly clever, and amazingly fat – at least the size of two normally fat men. He had originally been at the Rand Corporation, and now he had set up his own think-tank to advise governments and corporations about what to expect. He was actually a warm-hearted man, but he was detached, and if you are detached enough, you get very unpopular indeed. He told us about the time in 1972 when President Nixon had asked him how to get the remaining US troops out of Vietnam.

'That's so easy that I won't charge you,' said Kahn. 'You just send over a lot of airplanes and fly them out. I think that what you are really asking me is: "Do I need to get the troops out of Vietnam if I want to win the next election?" That question will take longer to answer.'

A month later Kahn had worked it out. 'Take no notice of the protesters,' he told Nixon, 'Stay in Vietnam. You will lose the next election if you don't.' Nixon followed this advice, and it had proved correct, but by the time I knew Kahn he was doubtful. 'I can't help being detached,' he said, 'and I'm a Republican, but now I wish we had got out of Vietnam and Nixon had lost the election.' The problem was that Kahn was incapable of giving an incorrect answer.

Bernard Levin did a wonderful interview with him, but when we got it back to England we realised that it was useless. Herman Kahn was an impatient man. He spoke so quickly, mostly without moving his lips, that no one could understand a single word he said. Bob Heller was not the least bit worried. He had the soundtrack of the film professionally transcribed, and distributed a copy to the appropriate journalists and television critics. Since they found it much easier to skim through a transcript than to sit down for half an hour in a viewing theatre, the programme received excellent reviews, but I imagine it got very low ratings.

The most successful film I made for Bob was called *Man of the Decade*, and was shown in 1970 (we had not got round to thinking it should be 'Person of the Decade' then). I didn't like the idea of an hour-long film on just one man, so I decided to split the programme into three segments, and asked three eminent people to nominate different candidates as man of the decade. Each of them put up a very convincing case for their choice. Alistair Cooke chose President Kennedy, as the champion of the free world; the American writer Mary McCarthy — her only venture into television ever — chose Ho Chi Minh of North Vietnam, who had so successfully demonstrated that a small country can stand up to a superpower if it is struggling for independence; and Desmond Morris chose John Lennon. 'My candidate,' as he pointed out, 'has no tanks at his disposal; he is responsible for the death of no one. He is only a gentle musician, but he has had half the world singing "Give Peace a Chance".'

Alistair Cooke gave the standard Kennedy valediction, and I must admit that the mixture of the two voices was most impressive: Kennedy with that rasping Irish-American accent — '*Ich bin ein Berliner*' — and Alistair with his mellifluous transatlantic tones. I was with Mary McCarthy as she watched Alistair rehearse on a preview monitor in her dressing room. 'Phooey,' she said tersely, and turned off the set.

Desmond and I went down to film John Lennon and his wife Yoko Ono at their house in Ascot, and they were inscrutable and hairy, as gurus tend to be. Lennon loved the programme, however, and soon afterwards he asked me to make a film for him. He had an assistant called Tony Fawcett, known as 'Superchicken', who was meant to make all the arrangements. There was the usual period of total silence, then one night, at about 11.30, Tony called me at home.

'John wants to see you right away, to discuss the film project.'

'But it's nearly midnight,' I complained. 'I'm going to bed.'

At that moment the doorbell rang. Outside in the street was Lennon's chauffeur, with a huge white Mercedes 600 Pullman limousine.

'Right away, Colin,' said Tony on the phone.

I pulled on some clothes and climbed into the car, which shot round to Apple, the Beatles' headquarters in Savile Row.

'Sorry, Colin,' said Tony when I got there. 'John and Yoko have already left for Ascot. The car will take you down there now.'

Half an hour later, I arrived at the house in Ascot.

'Sorry, Colin,' said the staff. 'John and Yoko have gone to bed.'

'Well, I'll just have to take the car back to London,' I said, cursing my lost night.

'Sorry, Colin,' they said. 'The chauffeur sleeps here, and he's gone off duty now. Shall we call you a taxi?'

The next morning I rang Tony and told him exactly where John Lennon could stuff his film project, but I don't expect Lennon ever got the message. I never met him again.

By this time Bob Heller was far from well. His craftiness had gradually turned to craziness, and it was clear that dark clouds were gathering over his brain. When he found out that I was going to make a film about a mental institution, he decided that I was plotting against him. Actually it was a wonderful subject for a documentary film.

At Winsom Green, outside Birmingham, our Victorian ancestors had erected two large brick buildings, one a prison and the other a 'loony bin'. They were only about twenty feet apart, and the inmates of one would often spend a pleasant hour watching the inmates of the other try to escape – without, of course, informing the authorities.

In 1969, a brilliant young specialist doctor had been put in charge of the asylum, and he set about transforming it into a mental hospital. His first action had been to take the locks off all the doors. To everyone's surprise, no one had walked out. Little groups of inmates would wander down to the gates, but after peering at the traffic roaring by, and the gaunt faces of the pedestrians, they would scurry back to the safety of their wards. (The mentally ill usually prefer to be in hospital if possible, just as do the physically ill.)

The doctor gradually weaned his patients off the drugs which had made them zombies, and set up a factory where they could work and earn money. At the end of each week they would be taken to the local open-air market, where they could buy themselves little treats. The experiment was a huge success, a forerunner to our present attitude to mental health.

By the time I visited Winsom Green the factory was in full production, with managers, supervisors and secretaries as well as a busy shopfloor. I asked the doctor how many of his staff it took to run it.

'None,' he replied, with justifiable pride. 'They are all patients.'

Even so, a mental hospital, like any hospital, is not an easy place for healthy people to make a film. It takes a few days to get used to the total absence of normal conventions, and to realise that this freedom is not necessarily a threat. I decided that my production assistant and I should spend a couple of days living in Winsom Green before the camera crew arrived. This caused Bob Heller – already in an excitable condition – to accuse us of having an affair. My PA was a very pretty girl with long legs and a tendency to wear mini-skirts. Bob had correctly read my mind, but not hers, and nothing untoward was going on between us. Nevertheless, he cancelled the project, and the film of the doctor's achievements was never made.

Soon after that, Bob's mind went completely. When I advertised my little house in Pimlico for sale, he rang up in a rage. Why hadn't I offered it to him? I had no idea that he was even looking for a house. He quickly moved in, but he hardly ever emerged again, and within a short time he was dead.

By this time, my father had fallen out of love with the BBC. He had enjoyed making the *Civilisation* series, and he was too much of a realist to expect to be paid a lot of money for doing something which he enjoyed, but he still felt that the BBC had swizzed him. In his original 1966 contract, the BBC had agreed to pay him £12,000 for a year's work. When the filming went on into a second year, he was given a further £6000. The contract said that for each overseas sale of the series, he would receive a tenth of his first year's salary. In effect this meant that every time the BBC sold the thirteen films to a foreign country my father got about £300 after tax. When the series was sold to the USA for over a million dollars, he received his payment with resignation, but when he got a further £300 for the sale to Australia and New Zealand, he exploded. 'Australia and New Zealand are not the same country. They are a thousand miles apart, with completely different television systems.'

'I think you will see,' replied the BBC icily, 'that for the purposes of your contract, Australia and New Zealand are classed as one country.' Although it seemed insulting to both the countries involved, this was, and for all I know still is, a standard clause in all BBC contracts.

Pointing out nasty passages in the small print long after a contract has been signed is never the way to be popular. It was not hard for Lew Grade to persuade my father to make his next series for ATV.

I received this news with mixed emotions. I had spent most of my life trying to escape the influence of my parents. I had lived in America, in Portugal and in Manchester, and I had thought that I was pretty well camouflaged in ATV's studio at Elstree. All of a sudden, it was made clear to me that directing my father in a documentary art series was now a condition of my employment.

To my surprise, it went very well. We started by making five films, under the title *Pioneers of Modern Painting*, about Cézanne, Monet, Seurat, Manet and Edvard Munch. Although they were really only filmed lectures, we found a delightful location for each artist. For Cézanne we went to the quarries of Bibemus and his studio in Aix; Monet's water garden was still intact, so were the cliffs at Étretat; for Seurat we went to the Grande Jatte on the Seine, and also to the Cirque d'Hiver, the beautiful little round indoor circus in Paris which had hardly changed since Seurat painted it (there was even a little girl riding on a white horse). Manet was harder, but we filmed in the Tuileries in Paris and the cafés nearby. For the film on Munch we went to Aastgerstrand, the little town in Norway where he painted the beach and the jetty so many times.

No locations, however carefully chosen, can actually recreate the artist's work on camera, but to the naked eye the Norwegian countryside did look exactly like Munch's paintings. The stillness, the claustrophobia, the feeling that those long black winters are always only just around the corner, make for a very sinister beauty indeed. Scandinavian people seem to be haunted by spirits and ghosts and hobgoblins. No wonder they drink such a lot. At our farewell dinner in the Munch museum in Oslo, when the grim pleasantries and the speeches were over, dozens of bottles of whisky were lined up on the table. Within five minutes, every single person there, including the seventy-year-old lady director, was completely drunk. My father and mother and myself, the honoured guests, only just managed to escape before being submerged by intoxicated government officials.

The filming with my father went so well that in 1976 I decided to leave ATV and set up my own company. An American oil millionaire, who professed to be a great admirer of art, said that he wanted to put up the money to ensure that every single one of my father's lectures was recorded on film. He offered me $500,000 to do this, and then, after I had left my job and organised a production office, he changed his mind. He sent me to his London solicitors, who were unbelievably rude and treated me like a blackmailer. In the end I did find the money to set up my film company, from a pair of very courteous young men who were just beginning to go into film distribution: Sandy Lieberson, who later became head of production at Universal Studios in Hollywood, and David (now Sir David) Puttnam. I have been grateful to them ever since.

My father had hundreds of lectures in his files, and he took fourteen of them, on nineteenth-century artists, and grouped them together under the title *The Romantic Rebellion*. The classicism of

Ingres and Degas was contrasted with the romanticism of Turner and Delacroix, and the series could have been exciting. But by this time my mother had had a stroke, and my father refused to leave her. Instead of going to France, we had to film the lectures in his study at Saltwood, and illustrate them later with photographs of the paintings. Even so, the series had a modest success, and like *Civilisation* it was made into a book. My company had paid my father a reasonable wage, unlike the BBC, but when I offered him a bonus after the series was sold in America, he irritably refused to accept it. I suppose he didn't want our roles reversed that much.

After that series was finished, I asked my father to do one more film. I had always wondered where civilisation had sprung from. I knew my father had given a great deal of thought to the art of ancient Egypt, and I wanted him to tell me and his audience about the first appearance of 'civilised man' six thousand years ago. He was getting tired of travelling at last, and I am afraid I rather tricked him into it. I arranged for a meeting between him, the director Michael Gill and myself, and I secretly planted a tape recorder in a briefcase at my feet. I transcribed the conversation that followed, and from it I produced a prospectus for a film. I sold the idea to the *Reader's Digest* in America, and presented it to my father more or less as a *fait accompli*.

In a way, he was delighted. He had never visited Egypt, and longed to do so, even if it meant he would have to leave my mother at home alone. Normally, as soon as he went in front of a camera, my father's private concerns would disappear, but on this occasion he did look a little anxious. Even so, the film was stunning. The truth is that if you take a good cameraman to Egypt, you can hardly fail. The ancient Egyptians were just as sympathetic as their modern counterparts. They saw a beauty and a harmony in nature as well as in art, and their colossal monuments are always counterbalanced by tender little artefacts on a human scale.

By the time the film was finished, some palace revolution or other had taken place at the *Reader's Digest*. Although the film had cost them a lot of money, no one seemed to know what to do with it. The company now denies all knowledge of its existence, and the film has vanished without trace.

It was, however, extremely popular with the Egyptians, and there may even still be a copy hidden in a government office in Cairo. When President Sadat paid an official visit to London in the late seventies, I was invited to have lunch at Buckingham Palace to meet him. I assumed that the invitation was connected with the film, but just as with the *Reader's Digest*, no one present had heard of it, let alone seen it. I suppose that the suggestion to invite me had been made so long before, by someone so far removed from the actual event, that as in the Russian army, the reason for the original order had long been forgotten.

There is no denying that one feels incredibly grand when one goes to lunch at Buckingham Palace; that drive across the great courtyard, the guardsmen all presenting arms, the inner courtyard with its flunkies and red-carpeted stairs, and those unctuous courtiers who treat you like an old and trusted friend. You are never allowed a moment of discomfort. If you are the first to arrive at a party for sixteen, you will find exactly fifteen beautiful people waiting for you. Then, as each new guest walks in, one of the beautiful stooges will silently vanish, until the real party is assembled. Hundreds of years of practice have made it an uncannily smooth performance. I felt as if I was in that old Hollywood film *The Invasion of the Body Snatchers*. You were never quite sure who was genuine and who was a 'fake'. I managed to be both. For some reason 'The Hon.', which I am, takes precedence over a 'Sir' in Royal protocol, and that put me ahead of Field Marshal Sir Michael Carver. This greatly, and rightly, annoyed Lady Carver, but there was nothing I could do about it. The laws of protocol are as immutable as stone.

Things had not gone smoothly for President Sadat's party. He and his family had just flown in from New York on an Egyptian Airlines plane, and although they had been the only passengers on board, the airline had managed to lose all their luggage. I found that rather sympathetic (and very Egyptian – I mean it is quite hard to do), but the President was not amused, and nor was his wife. It meant that she and her pretty daughters were still wearing the same scruffy travelling clothes for a Buckingham Palace lunch party which they had worn on the transatlantic flight. Furthermore, I do not think that the surroundings of Buckingham Palace exactly made the Egyptian party feel at home. All this, combined with five-hour jet lag, gave them an extremely glazed appearance, and the meal was a strained affair. I was seated next to Sadat's eldest daughter. Someone had told her I made Hammer horror films, and she was very indignant when she found out that I did not. And then there was that dreadful royal food, not at all what one's tummy wants when it is nervous and is expecting breakfast.

But it was incredibly grand.

Quite by coincidence, my next film was made with Prince Charles himself. He had said that he wanted to make a programme on the subject of his great-great-great-great-great-great-grandfather King George III, who, while my similar number of greats grandfather was inventing the cotton reel, was busy losing the colonies. Charles felt that his ancestor had been badly treated by history, and to put the record straight he agreed to be interviewed by Alistair Cooke.

We set up our cameras in the White Drawing Room at Windsor Castle under the beautiful Romney portraits of King George's many children, but things did not go well. 'Can't record here,' said the sound man. 'Sort of strange buzzing noise coming from all directions.' Soon a large ormolu clock on the mantelpiece was identified as the culprit.

But you cannot just stop a clock in Windsor Castle. There is a special man, permanently on duty, whose only job it is to attend to the royal clocks, and no one else is allowed to touch them. It took some time to find this man and persuade him to put blotting paper in the royal works. He then pointed out that, blending perfectly with their ornate surroundings, there were eleven more clocks still ticking away in the room. It was an hour before they were all quiet and our sound man's 'strange buzzing' had gone.

By this time Prince Charles had arrived, and was getting very impatient. Perhaps he sensed, even then, that television interviews were dangerous things. He was extremely cautious about committing himself to anything at all, even when discussing the achievements of his ancestor two hundred years ago. As the whole purpose of the film – Prince Charles's purpose indeed – was to set out the facts, it was left to Alistair Cooke to put both sides of the argument.

'Do you think that King George III was very upset at the thought of losing the colonies in 1776?'

'Well ... er ... um ... er ... I think I read somewhere ... someone said ... er ... it was really that ... er ... if he hadn't been careful, he would have ... er ... upset his ministers.'

'So you think that perhaps Lord North was more to blame?'

'Gulp, gulp. Er, the King was a great family man, you know.' Et cetera.

He was right to be cautious. After the programme went out on television, I met the Duke of Grafton at a cocktail party. He took me on one side and told me that Charles had been very unfair to *his* ancestor, that it had all been King George's fault, and that he, the Duke, was very upset. Feelings still run high about the past in the rarefied atmosphere of the aristocracy.

In the middle of our awkward interview, Prince Charles invited Alistair and myself to lunch, and we set off for the dining room accompanied by liveried footmen. 'I'm afraid we can't have anything from the kitchen unless my mother is here,' said Charles (I had had exactly the same problem at Saltwood). 'I've brought some cold chicken sandwiches from London, and we can share those. I won't be able to have my own staff until I get married.'

'You must get married at once,' said Alistair.

'Yes, well, it's not that easy,' said Charles. 'You see, every time a girl tells me that she loves me [!], I have to ask myself whether she really loves me or just wants to be Queen. And whoever I choose is going to have a jolly hard job, always in my shadow, having to walk a few steps behind me, all that sort of thing.' Poor Charles. A clairvoyant he was not. He produced a large plastic container of sandwiches, which a footman handed round. I would guess that elsewhere in Windsor Castle over a thousand people were enjoying a nice hot meal at that very moment – including my film crew.

Like my father, Alistair Cooke had had a love/hate relationship with the BBC. His *Letter from America* radio programme, first broadcast in 1946, was universally adored (including, he told me, by the Queen. 'I listen to it in the bath,' she had confided to him roguishly), and is the longest-running radio programme ever.

Alistair made a marvellous television series called *America*, also directed by Michael Gill, which had been sponsored by the Xerox Corporation on the PBS network in the USA. Xerox had been so delighted by its success that in 1976 they asked him to make some more films, just for them. Alistair has two real passions, Mark Twain and golf, and he agreed to do films on those subjects, providing he could direct them himself. The BBC were wise enough to disagree with this proposal, but I was not, and I persuaded Alistair and Xerox to give the job to my production company.

Major difficulties quickly arose. Directing a film for television is a skill which you have to learn. Someone like Michael Gill makes it look easy, but there is a lot more to it than simply pointing a camera at what is going on. Alistair could not grasp this. He was determined, for the film on golf, to show the world that he could sink a very long putt. This was very much not just a matter of placing Alistair on the edge of the green and waiting for him to hit the ball into the hole. Firstly, it is very hard to sink a long putt, especially if the camera is running. You miss the hole many times, and waste a lot of valuable film. Secondly, if the shot is wide enough to include the whole green, the hole will be almost invisible. If you wanted to film a sequence of Alistair sinking a long putt, the shot list would run something like this:

Establishing shot of golf course.

Wide shot – Alistair walking onto the green, with the flag on the opposite side. Alistair takes out his putter.

Close-up – Alistair squinting into the distance.

Wide shot – from behind Alistair to the hole miles away and the caddy taking out the flag.

Medium shot – Alistair hunched over his putter.

Cut to close-up of the hole.

Cut to Alistair's eyes, peering at the hole.

Cut to Alistair's ball as the club strikes it.

Cut to the hole.

Cut to the ball rolling across the grass.

Cut to Alistair waving desperate encouragement.

Cut to the ball rolling.

Cut to Alistair about to leap in the air.

Cut to the hole as the ball drops into the cup.

Cut to jubilant Alistair, waving his putter in the air.

It may sound complicated, but that is how films are made. With the right soundtrack, that little ten-second clip could have the audience on the edge of their seats, and the ball would only have to be putted about two feet. But this was a technique that Alistair never understood, and the film was a disaster.

I quickly arranged for Tim Slessor, one of Alistair's favourite directors on the *America* series, to take over the Mark Twain film. But now another problem arose. Alistair was so passionately involved with Twain that he found it impossible to stand back. His script seemed to be in a sort of shorthand which it had taken him years to learn. For once his air of amused detachment seemed to desert him completely. In desperation I hired almost all his original BBC crew, including their top film editor, but nothing could be done.

The programmes were a failure, and I had to fly over to New York to explain this to Xerox. Xerox are a very rich company, and they didn't mind that much. Like *Reader's Digest* before them, they denied all knowledge of the film after a few months, and still do. But who was going to break the bad news to Alistair? In the end they decided that we should all tell him together, so a meeting was set up in Alistair's apartment on Fifth Avenue. Alistair was in high good spirits, swishing a 7 iron around and waiting for us to come to the point. No one dared to speak.

'Well, well, what is it? What are we here to discuss?'

Two million-dollar Xerox executives and several million-dollar Park Avenue lawyers sat gawping like schoolboys.

'The films don't work,' I said. 'Neither of them. They can't be transmitted.'

Alistair went pale, but he took it on the chin. 'I see. Well, it was fun making them, anyway. Thank you for telling me, Colin. And now I mustn't keep you. See you soon, I hope.'

Jane, Alistair's wife, showed me out. I had hated doing it, but it had had to be done, and I always think if you delay bad news, it only gets worse. Alistair was an extremely proud man who was not used to failure, and I felt that he had deserved to have the truth straight out.

As I walked into my hotel room, the phone was ringing. It was Alistair. Would I like to come to stay for the weekend with him and Jane at his little house on the tip of Long Island? Now that did take guts.

We had a lovely two days by the sea – we even played golf – and we never mentioned the films again. Alistair was the perfect host, but the wound must have been very deep. He has never wanted to see me since, and I can't say that I blame him.

By 1977 it had become the fashion for large American corporations to underwrite the cost of putting film series onto what had become the National Educational Television Network. IBM, Exxon, Mobil and Xerox had all enhanced their images by sponsoring intellectual programmes, most of which they bought from the BBC. As it usually cost less to put a whole series on public broadcasting than one advertisement on the commercial networks, it was a good deal all round.

My *Romantic Rebellion* series was certainly not up to BBC standards. I had neither the time nor the budget to make a 'blockbuster' series like *Civilisation*, and my father had, to some extent, run out of steam. Nevertheless, fashion is fashion. The American Can Company, a giant conglomerate which makes everything from tin cans to toilet paper, heard the magic name of Kenneth Clark and stepped forward with a cheque. The whole thing was really just an exercise in public relations. Nobody knew or cared if anyone actually watched the films when they went out on PBS. The important thing was to make sure everyone knew who had footed the bill.

American Can employed a human dynamo of a PR lady called Connie Stone to do this, and we were off. I love Connie. She has so much energy that she carries all before her – rather like an American Mrs Thatcher. She organised a whirlwind tour, in the American Can corporate jet, around the five cities in which American Can's largest clients – 7-Up, Coca-Cola, Schlitz beer, etc. – were based. In each city there would be a grand reception for customers and local dignitaries in the local art gallery. I would make a speech of introduction and show a seven-minute promotional film made up of the best clips from the series. Bill May, the president of American Can, would then make a nice pompous statement about his company's worthy intentions and we would all applaud. The next day we would all go on somewhere new. Connie ran each reception like that lunch at Buckingham Palace. If Bill May or I lifted our hands up to our ties, that was the signal that we needed to be rescued from a guest who was talking too much.

But no one can plan for everything. When we were in Atlanta, Georgia, our hotel was so close to the art museum that it was decided we would dispense with the usual limousine and take a cab. Bill May and I and Connie's chief lieutenant, Marsh Lewis, climbed into the first taxi on the rank and shut the door. Immediately we realised our mistake. It was night time, and the cab was being driven by a young lady, with what was clearly her boyfriend sitting beside her. As we three men sat squeezed into the back, none of us having the courage to squeeze out again, the boyfriend announced belligerently: 'Ah'm giving ma girl a driving lesson. Any objections?'

'Gulp, gulp, gulp,' from us.

'Off you go, honey,' he said, and the big yellow Chevrolet rabbit-hopped slowly out into the street. 'Now put your lights on, honey. Pull that little knob there.' Click. At least we were now visible to the other traffic. The museum was only two hundred yards away, and we began to relax. But Honey had not yet mastered the art of stopping. Despite frantic yelps from Marsh, we hopped right past our destination before banging into the kerb.

'I think we will get out here,' said Bill May with dignity.

No such luck. 'Don't any of you three move, or I'll get very mad,' said the boyfriend, clearly already very mad indeed. 'You just drive into that little road across there, honey, and we'll turn round and go back.'

The car lurched into the 'little road', which turned out to be a concrete tunnel leading to a ramp.

'Stop now, honey, and find reverse.' But Honey couldn't stop. Down the ramp we went, slowly but inexorably towards a barrier. This must have been operated by a beam or something because it magically opened just before we hit it, then closed again behind us. It dawned on us that we were trapped in an underground car park in what was probably an unfriendly section of Atlanta (every section of Atlanta is unfriendly), with two unstable and excitable young people who were not too well disposed towards their fellow man. Somewhere above us was a calm and well-lit art museum, filled with polite guests who were waiting for polite speeches. But down in the garage it was hard to know what to do.

The boyfriend took over the wheel, and set about doing a sixteen-point turn to point us back up the ramp again, although there didn't seem an obvious way of lifting the barrier. Bill May wasn't President of American Can for nothing. As soon as the car was still for a second, he jumped out and marched off up the tunnel. Marsh and I rushed after him. Honey shrieked, the boyfriend cursed, but at least they didn't actually pursue us into the night. By the time we reached the surface we were out of breath but very happy to be free.

'Next time we'll use a limousine,' said Bill May as we trudged back to the museum and our guests, 'however near.'

When I got back to London, Connie Stone asked me to join her company in Los Angeles. Her most prestigious client in those days was IBM. IBM executives had seen the huge worldwide success of the Tutankhamun exhibition in 1978, and had decided they wanted to sponsor *art*.

In England, when a commercial company sponsors an art exhibition, they do it purely for the prestige of their board of directors. They have grand black-tie receptions for their favourite clients and publish little self-congratulatory notes in their annual report. Their 'outreach' is limited to the traffic driving down Piccadilly. 'The Art of Claude Gelée, sponsored by the Megalomania Group of Companies' or some such nonsense is written on a banner outside the Royal Academy, and that is it. How the shareholders let them get away with it is a mystery. I suppose the majority of them are the banks and insurance companies whose directors get invited to the parties.

In the USA, large companies have to be more accountable. They have discovered that if they spend a little more money to make a film of the exhibition, and then distribute this film widely enough, they can extend their 'outreach' to a very large audience indeed.

I directed two films for IBM, one on the work of Picasso and the other on the treasures of Dresden, and in each case we made four versions: a one-hour television programme for the Public Broadcasting System; a half-hour version for foreign TV stations (each with a typed translation of the script, and a separate music and effects track so that a new commentary could easily be added in the right language;); a 16mm-film version which was sent, free, to every college and university library in the USA; and a twenty-minute film for showing in the museum where the exhibition was installed. That is 'outreach', American style. Total audience in London perhaps two hundred thousand, total audience in the USA about forty million, and all for an additional outlay of about $100,000.

To be fair, working for IBM wasn't always easy. Before I started making the Picasso film I was summoned to a high-level conference at their headquarters. Since every executive at IBM is a clean-shaven fifty-ish man in a dark-grey suit, with a white shirt and a dark tie, it is hard to tell who is in charge. On this occasion ten executives had got together to pass down a momentous decision. 'For the first time, Colin, the board has decided that in your film you may use pictures of nudes. Only in the paintings, of course, and not in close-up, but in general, nudity will be permitted.'

For once I was completely at a loss for words.

But when the finished film was shown to them, there were howls of pain. 'Colin, how could you?'

How could I what?

'You've used a painting full of nude women at the very beginning, and then you have even gone into details.'

'But that's the *Demoiselles d'Avignon*. It's a surrealist picture, made up of cubist shapes and African primitive masks. And besides, it's one of Picasso's great masterpieces. It will be the star of the show. You'll see.'

'Oh, Colin,' they wailed, fearful of some great IBM axe in the sky. 'Oh dear, oh dear.' *Avant-garde* they were not. I'm glad they never realised that the *demoiselles* in question were actually girls in a brothel.

I worked on all sorts of programmes with Connie – commercials, soap operas, dramas – and in the end I got the reputation of being the man who could be trusted to work with art. In Hollywood, any reputation at all is very valuable (with the possible exception of 'scrounging-bum-trying-to-peddle-useless-ideas', which applies to most of the people there).

Americans have a much more reverential attitude to art than Europeans, so I was treated with great respect, rather like a doctor or a priest. Best of all, I did not have to struggle for survival with the main Hollywood crowd. There is no group more ruthless than that – with the exception of the courtiers at Buckingham Palace.

I had a beautiful old house on the beach in Playa del Rey, and could afford to wait to be summoned whenever any prestige art event was planned. I made three films for the Getty Museum – now the richest museum in the world – and was invited to all their functions. They were the best client imaginable. They simply said, 'Here's the money. Make us a film on Leonardo (or Holbein, or whatever), and let us know when it is finished.' I used to come back to England and spend a peaceful week in the library at Windsor Castle, where again I was left completely alone, working with the original drawings. I would then make my film in London, using British technicians, who are cheaper and more skilful than those in Hollywood, and return to California with a thoroughly professional product.

Finally the Getty Museum asked me to make a film about its own history. It turned out that the museum had been built by the late John Paul Getty, the son of the founder of the Getty Oil Company, because someone had told him it was a good way to avoid paying tax. He had summoned his architect to Sutton Place, his house in Sussex, and produced plans of the Villa dei Papiri in Herculaneum. This was a two-thousand-year-old Roman building which had been buried by volcanic ash when Vesuvius erupted, partially unearthed in the eighteenth century, and then buried again when it was found to be of no interest. Drawings had been made, however, of how it might have looked if it had all been uncovered. Clutching these very obscure plans, Mr Getty announced that he wanted the villa exactly reproduced on his property at Malibu.

As the land was composed of a narrow valley, and the Roman villa had been wide and flat, this posed a bit of a problem. Then the architect had the brilliant idea of building the villa across the middle of the 'V' of the land, and putting a car park in the empty space underneath. Gardens, galleries, fountains and courtyards were all suspended in mid-air, and in the end a perfect replica of a marble Roman villa was created. They had a little difficulty in finding the craftsmen to do the tiling and mosaics and so on, but Hollywood was just down the road, and there is nothing they cannot build there. Craftsmen from the Walt Disney company were called in, and the job was done.

John Paul Getty had always had an eye for a bargain. He could never resist a cheap Michelangelo, or a Raphael for $10,000, that sort of thing. My father said that if you lowered a net into the capital cities of the world and asked the art dealers to throw in all the rubbish they most wanted to get rid of, you would still have come up with a better collection than Getty's. But for a tax dodge that didn't matter, and as Getty lived in England and would never fly in a plane, he wasn't going to visit the place anyway.

When Getty died in 1976, everything changed dramatically. It turned out that he had left most of his fortune to the museum – not to a foundation, just to the museum – and suddenly the staff there were free to do whatever they liked. Not only that, by US law they were required to spend all of their multi-million dollar annual income on art works, or lose their tax-exempt status. The junk was put in the cellar, masterpieces of all kinds were acquired, and endless parties were given to celebrate them. It was three years before the professional money men moved in. They doubled the value of the Getty shares, but transferred everything to a foundation which they knew how to control, and generally spoiled the fun. Everything is now highly efficient, and totally boring. As soon as Californians take something seriously, they ruin it. California is not a serious place.

By 1987, it was clear that the golden age of arts documentaries was over. I still had one loyal client in New York, but apart from him, it was time to retire. I had had a wonderful run for my money.

IX

ANOTHER LANGUAGE

ART IS A LANGUAGE. You can learn it, just like Portuguese or 'computer-speak'. If you take the trouble to learn the language of art, you will understand and enjoy it far more than if you do not. This is not a very popular view. Learning any language is hard work. It is so much easier just to open our eyes, the way a child does, and like what we like. But if you try this on a child, the problems become obvious immediately. The only 'art' that children like is what they have just done themselves. They do not even appreciate the work of a friend the same age (this is also sometimes true of artists).

When, at the beginning of the century, painters began to switch from representation to abstraction – from painting what they saw with their eyes to expressing what they felt – life should have got much easier for the viewer. In theory, art history became irrelevant, and did not need to be studied any more. The fine line between, for instance, the Renaissance and the early Baroque, was academic compared to the excitement of the immediate sensations inspired by the abstract canvas in front of you. But in fact it did not work out like that at all. The early abstract artists, Kandinsky, Malevitch and others, began inventing a new language which was just as complicated as the old one. They wrote about 'pure sensation' and 'concrete images'. They wanted their painting to be as non-representational as music, and it was, but music has more rules and conventions than painting ever had.

And there was another very important aspect, often politely ignored by critics and social historians – professionalism. A professional artist is someone who makes their living from their art.

They may be good or great, bad or dreadful, but if their life is dedicated solely to producing art, then, by definition, they are an artist. However creative and unworldly they may seem on the surface, professional artists do not want the general public getting in on their act. Some artists like to talk about their vocation, but most painters and sculptors are proud of their craftsmanship as well. They may, like William Blake, rely on 'inspiration entering their left foot, like a star', but first they must learn their trade. They must learn how to draw and how to paint.

The most damning criticism one artist can make of another is to accuse them of not being professional. I once said to Victor Pasmore, a lovely, gentle painter of the most obscure abstract canvases imaginable, that I found Francis Bacon's pictures of screaming cardinals, or popes, very exciting and dramatic. Pasmore replied, 'Yes, but he doesn't really know how to draw. That is why he blurs the details. Look at the Pope's knee, or his elbow. Bacon has had to rub them out.'

It would be absurd to think that anyone could just sit down and compose music. If nothing else, they would have to learn to read the notes and to know the classic scale, even if they wanted to avoid using it. The same is true of all the arts, abstract or not. A painter has to know how to prepare a canvas, or the paint will soon fall off. The many painters and sculptors I have known have all taken immense pains to get the right materials, and to apply them in the most economical way. And language remains an essential part of the ritual, just as it does in medicine or haberdashery or any other profession. An amateur is an outsider, to be kept in his place.

Occasionally artists have told me that they have lost their way, and that they no longer have faith in what they are doing. 'Go back to the past,' I tell them, 'back to the rules. Get back to what you know. Look at the Giotto frescoes in the Scrovegni Chapel in Padua. Hitch-hike if necessary. Go to the Biblioteca Ambrosiana in Milan and spend a whole week looking at the great Raphael cartoon for *The School of Athens*. Fly over to The Hague and study the Rembrandt self-portraits. You don't have to copy these great masterpieces, but if you look at them for long enough your faith in art will be restored, if nothing else. Waiting for sudden inspiration is a doubtful business. You might wait all your life.'

My father learned the language of the history of art while he was still at school, and when he married my mother, at the age of twenty-three, he made it quite clear to her that she had to learn it too. We still have her little notebooks for 1927. What is the difference between Giotto and Giorgione? How can you tell Monet from Manet, Picasso from Braque? (Very difficult sometimes, in both cases.)

We children were expected to learn the language of art as soon as we could talk. All through our youth, my father never passed a museum or an art gallery, an antique shop or even an old church, without taking us in and giving us a little lecture. This usually meant telling us how bad things were. 'That's a nineteenth-century copy,' he would say loudly, pointing to the curator's, or the shop owner's, pride and joy. 'This is all rubbish.' And of course he was usually right.

He had been Curator of the Ashmolean Museum in Oxford, and he modelled his home on that wonderful example. A Titian, a Bellini and an Andrea del Sarto hung next to large oils by Renoir, Degas and Cézanne, as well as endless drawings. He loved English painting, and Turner, Constable and Samuel Palmer were soon joined by Graham Sutherland, John Piper and Henry Moore.

When the war began in 1939, my father was Director of the National Gallery in London. There was an urgent need to get the country's art treasures out of reach of the German bombs. One of the gallery's curators was a lover of caves, and he mentioned the vast slate quarries he had seen in North Wales. These were huge hollowed-out caverns, reached by a long tunnel. The miners had laid rails along the tunnel and cut a tall slit in the roof, exactly parallel with the lines, so that the tall pieces of slate could be wedged vertically into the centre of a cart and taken out of the mine unbroken. The pictures in the National Gallery were tall and thin too. They could be taken into the mountain just as the slate had been taken out. If the Germans invaded Britain, as everyone in 1940 thought they would, the tunnel could be collapsed, leaving the paintings undiscovered, like some Egyptian pharaoh's tomb, until the danger had passed.

So all the great paintings of England went down to Wales. In a mountain called the Manod, special long huts were built with temperature and humidity control. (One famous oil painting was left outside the huts by mistake. After five years propped up against the cave wall, it was none the worse.) Two restorers were installed in special workrooms, and they set about cleaning the famous canvases and repainting them as they felt necessary. My father was constantly going down to advise them (restorers have a natural tendency to repaint the whole picture if they are left alone), and during school holidays we would be forced to go to Wales too.

We children liked the feeling that it was all a big secret. There was a group of apparently ruined houses at the tunnel entrance which really contained guards. The cave itself was dark and gloomy. It was easy, even for a child, to bump your head on the way in. Once inside, however, it was clear that we were really just a nuisance. We would be left for hours on end to wander about between serried ranks of masterpieces, trying desperately to find one we could like. I definitely preferred the nudes. It wasn't because they were sexy; nudes in great art seldom are. But if you own a human body, you can relate to other human bodies more easily than you can to, say, portraits of serious old men.

By far the greatest joy for us children was the company of the living artists my parents invited to join them on these trips. Someone – my father, I suppose – had come up with the idea that painters should be exempted from military service and given the task of painting different aspects of the war. From 1939 to 1941 my father was Controller of Home Publicity at the Ministry of Information, and he fought hard to have this idea put into practice. In the end all his painter friends were given the title 'Official War Artist', and were free, and even paid, to roam about wherever they wanted. They were not expected to paint for propaganda purposes, but simply to record whatever they saw. John Piper started by painting the Manod itself. Graham Sutherland painted many scenes of bomb-damaged buildings, including my parents' London flat, and Henry Moore went down into the tube station near our house in Hampstead, where he made his famous drawings of the thousands of people who took refuge there at night.

These sweet, kind, gentle artists were a complete contrast to our parents' usual circle of friends. None of those socially important people would ever have taken any notice of children. If they gave us expensive presents, it was simply in order to keep our parents happy, and not us. Once a grand lady called Lady Wimborne gave me a butterfly net, but when, in an effort to show her how much I appreciated it, I sneaked into the drawing room and popped it over her head, I got into frightful trouble. Old ladies in those days spent many hours making themselves up, and I remember that it took fifteen minutes to extricate Lady Wimborne from the net, rather like trying to get someone out of a car crash.

When my godmother, the American writer Edith Wharton, died in 1937, she left me her entire library, a portrait of herself as a young girl and her silver christening cup, but I was not even told about it until I was eighteen years old, and I was not allowed to take possession of my inheritance until my father had died.

The artists were completely different. They never gave us anything, except occasionally their paintings, but we loved them without exception, and it is true to say that from that time on I have found artists to be infinitely better company than anyone else. Perhaps it is because artists – except for society portrait painters – are not so bound up with the conventions that control most of our social behaviour. Artists appreciate, and even depend on, curiosity, spontaneity and enthusiasm, and this makes them wonderful companions, especially for children.

Collette's and my first love was the sculptor Henry Moore. My father was convinced that Henry was a genius, but that didn't affect him a bit, and he often seemed to enjoy our company more than that of the grown-ups. He must have had a powerful inner life to have produced all those masterpieces, but on the surface he was uncomplicated and simple. Like all children, we used to take advantage of this. We once got hold of an india-rubber chocolate which was part of a magic set. Sweets were rationed so strictly during the war that even this little brown squidgy object looked attractive, and we offered it to Henry as a joke.

'Thanks very much,' he said in his Yorkshire accent, and ate it.

'Stop! Stop!' we screamed. 'You aren't meant to swallow it! It was a fake! It was made of rubber!'

My father groaned. 'Now you children have killed one of the greatest artists of the century.'

'Actually,' said Henry, licking his lips, 'it was quite tasty.'

Henry survived. Like all great artists, he was quite aware of his talent. When I was nine, and was ill in bed, he did two lovely pencil studies of my head for my autograph book. Many years later I showed him the drawings, but with my thumb over the signature (just as I had shown my father his drawing of my mother).

'That's you as a little boy, isn't it?' said Henry. 'It's bloody good. Who did it?'

'You did, Henry,' I said, removing my thumb. Henry studied the drawing again. 'I told you it was bloody good.'

Someone asked Henry why he didn't paint like that American artist who specialised in pictures of children's faces with a luminous tear coming out of one eye. 'He makes a million dollars a year.'

Henry was still living in the farmhouse in Hertfordshire that my father had helped him to buy before the war. 'Oh, I could easily draw like that if I wanted to,' he said. 'But I make much more than a million dollars a year.'

In later life, I was actually responsible for a rise in Henry's income. One weekend in 1974 I took a friend of mine down to Henry's studio for a visit. Sam Dorsky had made a fortune in the rag trade. He was a great admirer of Henry's, but he was apprehensive about buying his work from the dealers in New York. Henry always responded to genuine enthusiasm, and the two men got on well. Sam asked if he could buy some of his work, and said he would write out a cheque for $100,000 there and then. Henry told him to make it out to his daughter Mary, and put a selection of his works on a carpet in the hall. The group included a large statue of a reclining figure, a medium-size carving, and several small bronzes and terracottas. Sam was thrilled, and it was arranged that everything would be shipped to New York by Henry's secretary later in the week.

It so happened that on the following Monday one of Henry's grand dealers came down to see him. 'What is all that sculpture doing in the hall?' he asked.

'Oh, I've just sold all that to an American friend of Colin's,' Henry said. 'I got $100,000.'

'What?' screamed the dealer, appalled. 'That collection is worth far more than $100,000. It's worth three times that. Why did you charge him so little?'

'I was going,' said Henry icily, 'by the prices you paid me for similar pieces last month.'

From then on, Henry would only accept money for a sculpture after he had seen a sales invoice from the gallery. He allowed the dealer a 20 per cent profit, and no more.

I like to think that this helped a little bit, but the dealers soon found a way round it. One, for example, sold each piece he got from Henry to 'a collector in Switzerland', who was actually the dealer himself. He would show Henry the invoice and take his 20 per cent. Then he would resell the work to another gallery in New York, also owned by himself, at a much higher price – leaving a nice profit safely tax-free in a Swiss bank – then show American customers the second invoice, and charge another 20 per cent on top of that. No wonder art dealers are so rich.

The most successful gallery in the 1960s and seventies was the Marlborough Gallery of London and New York. I asked Frank Lloyd, its owner, for the secret of his success. Frank was a supreme businessman, and he had a wonderful eye for a deal.

'I soon realised that there were not enough old masterpieces to go round,' he said. 'Rembrandts and Cézannes and all that. So I decided to make "masterpieces" today.'

'And how did you do that?' I asked.

'It was simple. I chose a few successful modern artists, offered to take all their work, and then charged the same price for them as I would for the Impressionists.'

'But why should collectors pay so much, especially when the artist is still working?'

'They're happy to,' he said. 'Collectors love to pay huge prices. It makes them feel secure.'

It was, quite literally, a confidence trick, in which everyone was happy to join.

Only occasionally did things get out of hand. I had got to know the American sculptor David Smith while I was making one of my films for the *Art: New York* television series. Smith was a wonderful abstract artist who did huge constructions out of scrap metal, some highly polished and very beautiful. He also liked to drink and to chase girls, and to drive too fast, all of which suited me fine. We spent a few riotous days and nights together in the spring of 1961 at his studio at Bolton's Landing, in upstate New York, and we became friends. Frank Lloyd knew I got on well with Smith, and invited me to the opening of his one-man show at Lloyd's sumptuous Manhattan gallery. After a couple of hours, Lloyd needed my help. 'Please, Colin, will you tell your friend that he has set his prices too high? I can't sell anything at all.'

I passed this on to David. 'Nonsense,' he said. 'Frank is just greedy. I will be killed in a car accident any day now, and these works will all be worth double what he is asking.' Smith proved to be right on both counts. He died in a car crash in 1965, and his prices went so high that only institutions could afford them.

Besides Henry Moore, the other great artist friend of our childhood was Graham Sutherland. Graham and his wife Kathy actually lived in our house in Gloucestershire for a short time in the early days of the war, as did my father's mother, and there was a running confusion between 'Gran' and 'Gram'. My father had helped Graham, like Moore, to buy a home, and although both artists paid him back many times with paintings and sculptures, neither of them ever forgot his early generosity. This meant that when we were young we had virtually free access to their studios at any time.

Graham and Kathy were wonderful hosts. They always made me feel welcome and important, even though I must often have interrupted Graham's work. In 1955 I turned up as he was putting the finishing touches to his portrait of Winston Churchill. 'Paint the bulldog,' Churchill had said, and Sutherland had done as he was told – but of course it was a bulldog in extreme old age. Little did I realise that this masterpiece would be seen by no one else, except from a distance at the Guildhall presentation at which its subject made his dislike of it clear. It was to be hidden away until Churchill's death, and then destroyed.

Graham Sutherland was perhaps the greatest portrait painter of the twentieth century, and it was natural that he should paint my father's portrait too. Both of them were nervous, because they were such old friends, and Graham was afraid he would not be able to see my father's face with a new eye. Despite this, no problems arose until after the picture had been finished. Graham told my father that it was Kathy who handled his accounts. My father had not expected to have the portrait for nothing, but he got an unpleasant shock when Kathy demanded Graham's standard fee. Graham's normal sitters were multi-millionaires – people like Somerset Maugham and Helena Rubenstein – and he considered my father to be a multi-millionaire too, partly I suppose because he was one. But my father did not see it like that at all. He thought of Graham Sutherland as earning much more than he did, and that was also true.

If Kathy could send the bills, then my mother could dispute them. My mother had definitely attracted Graham's eye in her youth, and she had always disliked Kathy underneath the surface. She now wrote to her in considerable rage, offering only half the sum which had been asked. Kathy, who probably did not like my mother much either, accepted, but made it clear that this would not include any of Graham's sketches for the portrait. She was well aware that these sketches, some of them in oils, were often the best part of the deal. Both ladies were very ferocious. It was many years before they made peace again, and in the meantime my father's relationship with Graham became pretty cool. Only the calm and sensible intervention of my brother led to everyone becoming friends again, and the sketches, which Graham had retained, were eventually handed over as well.

The fact that we had all these artists in our lives, that we lived in a house completely given over to paintings, and that whenever we went out with our parents we were forced to look at art, meant that we children learned the language of art whether we wanted to or not. In my case it was definitely 'not'. When I left school to join the Air Force in 1951, I felt that if I never saw another picture in my life it would be too soon.

I had a few prints and watercolours in my rooms at Oxford, which my father had personally hung for me, but that was enough. Then, in 1957, while on the *Titus Andronicus* tour, I found myself alone in Vienna with nothing to do. To my surprise, and out of sheer force of habit, I went into the Kunsthistorich Museum, just to have a look round. I could not speak a word of German, but at least I could speak art. In the first gallery I entered I had the surprise of my life. Breughel was the sort of painter my father didn't much like. He acknowledged his greatness, of course, but he really preferred painters who were more tender – Piero della Francesca, Giotto, Leonardo da Vinci and the like. But I was enchanted. For the first time, as I looked at a canvas I did not feel like a spectator. I could not resist being pulled right into the painting and joining in with the people. Each picture was like a time machine taking me back to the sixteenth century. One could taste the food, hear the laughter, feel the cold of the snow and the warmth of the fire. But it was not like being at Madame Tussaud's. These pictures were masterpieces of construction, of colour and light and shade. I spent many hours among that wonderful collection. I couldn't even tear myself away to eat. Everything my father had taught me came flooding back, and by the time the museum closed I was reconverted to art for good.

When I arrived in America in 1960, I realised how lucky I had been. New York had recently taken over from Paris as the centre of the art world. For the previous hundred years every painter had thought of France as the place where artists had to go to learn their trade and get their inspiration. All the artists of the Impressionist movement had lived in Paris at one time or another. Picasso had gone there from Spain as a young man. Edvard Munch felt he had to go to Paris from Oslo to learn how to paint. It was almost as if art was French, just as three hundred years earlier it had been Italian. But by the end of the war, in 1945, the painters in Paris seemed worn out. With the exception of Picasso, they devoted themselves to recreating what they had done before.

Then, in 1948, at the Venice Biennale, a new sort of art burst onto the scene. Jackson Pollock's huge paintings were exhibited in the American pavilion, and they caused a sensation. Pollock had put his canvases on the floor and dripped the paint on them with a brush or stick, apparently at random. In doing so, he achieved an abstraction which was disturbing, but also lyrical and very moving.

Pollock's freedom was immediately attractive to artists all over the world, but Abstract Expressionism, as it came to be called, was extremely unpopular with the public. The paintings seemed to have been done in a slapdash and haphazard manner. They could have been done by children, it was said, or by monkeys. This sort of criticism delighted the artists, who were trying to be as spontaneous as possible. They knew that nothing could have been further from the truth. They took immense pains to achieve that spontaneity, while at the same time retaining and using their professional skills. When I came to make a television programme about Pollock in 1960, I was amazed at the care he had taken to get his drips of paint in exactly the right places.

Pollock died in a car crash in 1956, but a photographer called Hans Namuth had once filmed him at work. In this film, Pollock starts off very slowly, skimming over the huge white canvas with the grace of a ballet dancer, dripping fine lines of paint in careful curves. He chooses his colours very precisely, and you feel that each application is the result of long and intense consideration. As Namuth's battery-operated camera started to run down, the film began to go more slowly. When it is now viewed at normal speed, it makes everything look as if it is happening very quickly. By the end of the sequence Pollock appears to be dashing all over the canvas like a madman, splashing paint in all directions, which gives a very false impression of how he actually worked.

One thing is obvious. Pollock was a deeply troubled man. It was a tremendous and painful struggle for him to get so directly in touch with his innermost emotions. What he did not realise – what none of the Abstract Expressionist painters seemed to realise – was that all the great artists of the past had faced a similar task, and had often felt the same despair. The painters of the New York School were convinced that Abstract Expressionism was a new and superior way of creating art. I suppose that they had to have this enormous sort of naive confidence in order to achieve what they did, but life soon became very hard for them. To rely solely on the contents of the subconscious mind for inspiration restricts creativity to one very small source.

Mark Rothko, the gentlest and most inspired of all the abstract painters, told me personally that one day soon he was going to commit suicide.

'Oh, really? Why?' I said. He had also just told me that he had once been Cary Grant's double in a movie, and he didn't seem to have a care in the world.

'The trouble is,' said Rothko, suddenly very serious, 'that each time I approach the canvas, I want to paint a completely different painting. I shut my eyes and do things that I have never done before. But when I open my eyes again, there is another Rothko.'

Since Rothko's pictures were incredibly beautiful, and were already selling for a small fortune, that didn't seem too much of a problem to me. What I did not have the sense to ask him was 'Why close your eyes? Why not try painting with them open for a change?' Rothko would have thought that to do this would have been a betrayal of everything that the new painting stood for, although it might have saved his life. As it was, he was as good as his word, and committed suicide in 1970, at the age of sixty-seven.

By 1960, the artists, the critics, the gallery owners and the cognos-centi of New York all knew that the language of Abstract Expressionism was here to stay. After five thousand years and many false starts, the rule of realism, of painters trying to reproduce what they saw, had finally been swept away for ever.

But art never stands still, and already another revolution had begun. It was a familiar situation – the old rebels, who had once shocked the world, now turned into the establishment, threatened by the young upstarts who followed them.

The abstract artists were all men – hairy, heterosexual giants, who boozed and womanised in the best traditions of conquerors and pioneers. The first reaction against them did not seem to be worth considering. 'Pop' artists were just a joke. They were nervous, hesitant, slim and, for the most part, homosexual. And what were they doing? They were taking simple, commonplace objects and reproducing them so faithfully that one could not tell the reproduction from the original. Some of them weren't using paintbrushes, or even canvases. They were using silk-screens of photographs that someone else had made. They were putting in the little dots you can see when you enlarge a printed photograph too much.

When I made a film in 1963 about the Pop artists Andy Warhol and Roy Lichtenstein, I was very nearly lynched. 'Tell me you were only kidding, Colin,' pleaded the critic of the *New York Herald Tribune*. (He had given the programme a 'joke' good review after it had been shown on television.) 'You did have your tongue in your cheek, didn't you?'

'No, I was deadly serious,' I replied. 'This is the new art.'

He roared with laughter, at my straight face and what he saw as my sense of humour.

Actually, anyone who talked to Warhol or Lichtenstein could tell at once how serious they were. They both took just as much trouble as Pollock had done ten years before, and indeed as every dedicated artist has done since the beginning of time. When I went to Warhol's studio, it was lined with aluminium foil and crammed with Mott's apple-sauce cartons and Brillo-pad boxes, like a supermarket store room. But Andy would get just as hysterical at the thought of anyone touching them as Leonardo would have got if you had leaned against the fresco of *The Last Supper*.

The Pop artists were not in any sense a 'school' of art, in the way that the Abstract Expressionists had been. They all thought of themselves as completely unique, despite the label. They were simply painters and sculptors who wanted to be allowed to use their eyes. The abstract artists and their circle still completely dominated the art world, but it was not possible to go back to representational painting. So the new young artists decided to make their work look like a joke. Then, if people laughed at it, it wouldn't matter. They took popular images like soup cans, or numbers, or the American flag, and produced works which were impossible not to recognise and very hard to ignore. The apparent lack of artistic input was deceptive. It was really just a trick to protect the Pop artists from the criticism which they, like their more conventional predecessors, feared.

In the midst of this battle, anyone who painted a 'normal'

representational picture was considered a charlatan and a fool. Despite this, in 1960 the most popular artist in America was probably Andrew Wyeth. He had painted a beautiful picture of a crippled girl on a hill, entitled *Christina's World*, which had been widely reproduced. Wyeth worked in an old-fashioned medium called egg tempera, which involved mixing an egg with the paint. This gave his paintings the hard, glossy look of an old master, and it masked the innovation of his style.

When I announced that I was going to include Wyeth in my series of films on modern American artists, I got the same reaction from my supporters as I had had from my critics after the Pop Art programme. I did not get any help from Wyeth either. The poor man had been vilified by the New York art establishment, and he had vowed never to talk to anyone who might represent it. I did, however, receive his permission to photograph the countryside near his house in Pennsylvania, so I set off with a film crew and started filming away. For two days we moved closer and closer, until we were right outside his studio. We were very short of film, so in the end we kept the camera empty, but ran around as if we were making *Gone with the Wind*. Finally, Wyeth's curiosity got the better of him and he came out to watch. We immediately swung the camera away. Every time he wandered in front of the lens, it was firmly pointed in the opposite direction. After an hour of this he was fed up. 'Listen,' he said. 'I'm Andrew Wyeth, and I want to be in your film after all.' We loaded the camera properly at last, and got everything we had hoped for. Wyeth was no exception to my rule about artists. He was a magical companion. As soon as he could see that we took him seriously, he was prepared to do everything he could to help.

Fifteen years later, his wife invited me back to film him again, and this time we spent hours together inside his studio.

'I never take anyone in here,' he said. 'Anyone at all.'

Where did he think the camera crew was, I wondered, as they filmed away behind me, while he and I talked about his paintings in detail.

'When I was a young boy,' he told me, 'we lived near here, opposite a farm owned by a man called Koerner. Koerner had an

One of Margot Fonteyn's many first-night parties in the Crush Bar at Covent Garden. *Left to right*: Colette; myself; Oliver Messel; Margot, in Panamanian national costume.

At Saltwood village church with the ushers for my first wedding, 29 April 1961.
Left to right: Reginald Bosanquet; Bruce Whineray; Lord Sainsbury of Preston Candover.

Violette and me with my father on our wedding day. Both of us already suspected that we were making a mistake.

Photographed at Saltwood in 1962 by Janet Stone, who was a great friend of my father's.

With my father in 1963.

My father on the battlements of Saltwood Castle in 1969. The tower was restored in the nineteenth century.

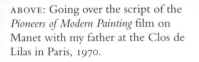

ABOVE: Going over the script of the *Pioneers of Modern Painting* film on Manet with my father at the Clos de Lilas in Paris, 1970.

RIGHT: Filming at Windsor Castle with Alistair Cooke and Prince Charles in 1976. I was right to look worried – HRH was very hard to interview, even though he himself had suggested the topic of his ancestor George III.

LEFT: A sketch by Graham Sutherland for his 1970 portrait of my father. The picture indirectly caused a cooling of relations between my mother and Sutherland's wife.

old German wife, and he also got himself a young black girl as a servant. Soon tongues began to wag, and as she was only fourteen, he was arrested. But the girl refused to talk, so Koerner was released, and the three of them – Koerner, his wife and the girl – went on living in the same house. Mrs Koerner went pretty crazy, and talked loudly to herself in German as she walked about the farm, while the girl and Koerner carried on their affair. Eventually the girl grew up, and when old Koerner died, she vanished.

'Imagine the effect that had on me, the little boy living opposite. And then I had a bit of luck.' Wyeth lowered his voice so his wife couldn't hear – although she was in the house, a mile away, and there was a microphone right in front of him. 'A couple of years ago, I met that girl again. She'd grown into a beautiful woman by now, of course, and I seduced her right where Koerner had seduced her, all those years ago. I must have been wanting to do that for thirty years.

'Look at this,' he said, and took a dust sheet off the canvas behind him to reveal a life-size portrait of the woman, lying naked on a bed. It was one of the greatest artistic *coups de théâtre* that I have ever witnessed, all the more so because it was completely unrehearsed. It was also one of my greatest failures. The cameraman had not fixed his lens properly to the camera, and light was getting onto the film. In the end I gave Mrs Wyeth what I had, but – to everyone's great relief, I suspect – the film was not good enough to be shown.

Another artist who loved to co-operate was Alexander Calder. In 1962 he had a one-man exhibition of his sculpture at the Guggenheim Museum on 5th Avenue in New York. A huge white mobile hung from the roof, almost meeting a black stabile standing on the floor below. The joy of Calder's sculpture is that however delicately balanced, it never stands still, and the planes and colours are forever finding new and unexpected relationships. All his work was very impressive, but unless it moved, I told Calder, it would not look like much on film.

'Well, it must move then,' he said. 'Everything must move.' The show had been laid out chronologically, starting at the top of the Guggenheim's great helical ramp and finishing at ground level. My plan was to put the camera on wheels and shoot the whole exhibit in one long shot, but the problem was to get Calder's delicate mobiles to move as well. I was limited, as always, by my budget of $100, so I got twenty children from the nearby Henry Street Settlement for Orphans, and simply let them loose. Calder was enchanted; he had never realised that his mobiles could move that fast. The staff of the Guggenheim Museum, though, were horrified. There is nothing a curator likes less than seeing one of his precious masterpieces revolving at forty miles an hour. But the director of the Guggenheim, Philip Messer, was a brave man. He always allowed me to film in the museum in any way I wished, and in the end nothing did get broken. It just had to be washed.

The architect of the Guggenheim had been Frank Lloyd Wright. Wright hated art, and he had done his utmost to make visitors to the museum feel uneasy. The long, sloping ramp of the main galley ensures that people can't stand still, and the wall around it is just too low to prevent them falling off if they lean over. It certainly hadn't been Wright's intention to build another solemn temple to conventional art, like the Metropolitan Museum a little further down 5th Avenue. Philip Messer understood this, and as a result the Guggenheim became one of the most active and exciting museums in America in the 1960s. By contrast, the Metropolitan remained like a great, dark, dusty relic of the past, as if trying to ignore the frantic activity which was going on outside its doors.

I went to the Metropolitan with my father on one of his rare visits to New York, in 1961. As we went through the doors, he put his collar up and pulled his hat over his eyes.

'I don't want the director to know I'm here,' he said. 'He is a horrible little man. He only wants to argue with me. I'm only here to see one picture [by a follower of Michelangelo], and then I'm off.' We had some difficulty finding the picture in the long, dark rooms. There were no visitors, and the guards seemed to be asleep.

But the 'horrible' director had his spies. Soon a young man appeared, and came up to us. 'Sir Kenneth Clark? The director has sent me to invite you up to his office. He wishes to ask your advice.'

My father grumbled loudly, but he could hardly refuse. In the director's office was a long painted sketch, obviously done by Goya for his fresco in the church of San Antonia de la Florida, outside Madrid.

'I've been offered this for sale, and I can't decide if it's genuine or not,' said the director, very humbly it seemed to me. 'What do you think?'

My father looked at it very carefully. 'It's too pretty,' he announced. 'It's a fake.' And he marched out. I never did work out if he was flattered to have been asked (he didn't like being flattered), or angry at having to do the director's job for him.

Of course, the Metropolitan Museum did have many brilliant young experts on its staff. One of them was Thomas Hoving, who had been put in charge of The Cloisters, an annexe of the museum near Columbia University, where its medieval collection was housed. Hoving discovered that the inspiration behind an ivory cross made in Bury St Edmunds in the twelfth century was basically anti-Semitism, and this caused a significant ripple in the mainly Jewish art world of New York. I made a film about this cross with him, just to show that my *Art: New York* series wasn't exclusively about modernism. Eventually Tom Hoving replaced the man my father didn't like as head of the whole museum, and brought it up to date.

As the great heterosexual champions of Abstract Expressionism began to self-destruct or fade away, the rising young art intelligentsia wanted something new. Another curator at the Metropolitan was Henry Geldzahler, and it was he who became the link between Pop Art and the establishment. Geldzahler was a homosexual, as were many of the Pop artists, notably Andy Warhol. Despite appearances, Warhol was a serious artist, and he craved approval just as much as he wanted to shock. From the very beginning Warhol and Geldzahler were friends, and Warhol was much in debt to Geldzahler for his support, and for the academic seal of approval which it conferred on him.

Warhol had found a dealer, Leo Castelli, who was prepared to sell his work. Castelli decided to charge enormously high prices for Warhols immediately, just as the Marlborough Gallery had done for Henry Moore and David Smith. I felt that we pioneers should stick together, and asked Andy if I could buy the beautiful silkscreen picture of Elizabeth Taylor which he had brought to the television studio for my film on Pop Art.

'Sure, Colin,' he whispered. '$4000.'

That was the price of a brand new Cadillac limousine at the time, and while it may seem facetious to compare a work of art to a car, it serves to show how far a painting like that was already out of my reach. Also, none of us – except for Andy – was exactly sure that his picture was a work of art. To have suggested that it would later change hands for many millions of dollars would have been considered absurd.

Despite these huge prices, in the early 1960s Warhol never seemed to have very much money himself, partly because he was determined to make films. As soon as the fashion began to swing back from abstraction to realism, many of Warhol's contemporaries decided that they should abandon the constraints of a flat, two-dimensional canvas altogether. Claes Oldenburg was beginning to create his huge outdoor sculptures. Robert Rauschenberg was putting car tyres and stuffed goats onto his paintings. Christo was trying to erect a white fence right across California. Warhol wanted to go further still.

One of the most popular art events at the time was a 'happening'. An artist would lead a group of his or her friends in an apparently random activity, and pronounce it art. Andy Warhol's precise mind did not like this idea, but he wanted to do something on a performance scale, so he started his career as a maker of films. His technique was very simple: set up a camera with a lens that could zoom in and out, fix it to the floor on a tripod, and load it with the largest roll of film he could find, which ran for half an hour. He would then point the camera at the action, zooming in and out and panning from right to left whenever he felt like it. The action, such as it was, appeared to be as random as the direction, but actually it had been carefully scripted and rehearsed. Andy's plots were interminably long, and although his technique meant that he did not have to spend any money on editing, the static camera-work got very monotonous indeed. When the thirty-minute film ran out it would be replaced by another, and eventually all the rolls would be spliced together. The only moment of visual excitement for the audience was when one of these splices went through the projector, and a series of mad hieroglyphs chased themselves across a blindingly white screen.

The first film which Warhol showed me focused on President Castro of Cuba and his relatives. For an hour and a half (three rolls) a dozen or so actors of Latino appearance screamed and argued at the tops of their voices in Spanish and broken English. The plot was made even more confusing by the fact that Castro, of whom the others were obviously in awe, was played by a young woman. But it all made perfect sense to Andy, and he was most concerned, after the screening, to know whether we had enjoyed it. The truth was that by the end of the film one did have a very good impression of what life in a large, argumentative Cuban family must be like.

Andy's next film was about two men, both intelligent and middle-aged, lying on a beach on Long Island discussing the relative merits of heterosexual and homosexual love. Behind them, sitting on the sand, were a young man and a young woman, both beautiful, and obviously flirting with each other. Nothing actually happened, but in the course of the debate the viewer was gradually drawn into agreeing with one or other of the men. In the end, and very subtly, both came down on the side of homosexuality, and decided to see who could seduce the young man first. The fact that the young man was obviously attracted to the girl did not come into it.

That film ran for two hours, but Warhol's next film ran for eight. *Sleep* was incredibly boring, but then it was intended to be. Warhol had decided that since most of us live our waking lives vicariously, that is to say watching television and films, why shouldn't we sleep vicariously as well? There is no need to chase villains with a gun. You go to the movies for that. So if you can't sleep at night, come to watch *Sleep*, and Warhol's actor will do that for you too.

A camera was set up over a bed, and the actor climbed in. For eight hours – Warhol had chosen a very good sleeper – the camera ground away while the actor slept peacefully beneath it. Then the whole thing was put on a special projector in a cinema near Times

Square, where people are notoriously nocturnal, and the public was invited in. It must be admitted that very few people managed to stick it out for the full eight hours. Many of the 'in' crowd went to have a look, but once they had sat there for half an hour and it had dawned on them that nothing, absolutely nothing, was going to happen for another seven and a half hours, they got up and left.

Warhol would go along to the cinema late at night to see if anyone he knew was there. It became a great test of loyalty for all his friends. I found that the only answer was to have a lot of wine with dinner, then go in and fall asleep myself. One night Andy found me sleeping peacefully in the stalls, and was absolutely delighted. It must have been one of the few times in history that an artist felt he had received an enormous compliment when he discovered someone unconscious in front of his work.

As Warhol became more famous he became more of a recluse, although, like all the artists I have known, he was wonderful company even when he said nothing at all. Many of the people in his circle became obsessed with him and went crazy, just like the people around Marilyn Monroe. Like Marilyn, he was so talented that he could not help attracting publicity whatever he did, and like her he was destroyed by it. No wonder the three New York artists from that time who outlived the rest of them – Jasper Johns, Robert Rauschenberg and Willem de Kooning – would have nothing to do with me at all.

For six glorious years I lived at the very centre of the New York art world. The sexual revolution arrived, but we took that in our stride. What we cared about was creativity of a different kind. We spoke art and lived art twenty-four hours a day. Many nights I would go to sleep with my 16mm camera on the bed beside me, ready to jump up and start filming anything 'artistic' at a moment's notice.

By 1965 the excitement in the visual arts had reached fever pitch. Pop artists were treated like pop stars, and their work began to suffer as a result. The Abstract Expressionists who had survived were revered as old masters, and they wisely withdrew from the public gaze. My role as chronicler was taken over by PR companies and advertising executives who knew how to cope with the publicity machine. I was thirty-two years old, and found myself out of my depth. Although I continued my friendship with many of the artists, I decided to concentrate my camera exclusively on the great arts of the past.

X

MONSTERS

WE ALL HAVE OUR FAVOURITE EPITHETS, words we choose again and again to describe those whom we admire or despise. My parents, secure in the knowledge that they were always right, did not hesitate to use the strongest terms they could think of when something or someone incurred their disapproval. Not for them 'I'm sure he is very nice, dear, but . . .'. 'How awfully common!' they would cry, or 'She is so dreadfully bourgeois!' or, in extreme cases, 'So-and-so is a monster!'

To be fair, they didn't call someone a monster at random, just because they happened to cross swords with them. A monster had to be pretty special. They had to fulfil some basic requirements before they could qualify. Monsters had to appear to be totally selfish. They had to be egocentric, only interested in their own importance, or plotting for their own gain. Monsters were completely unscrupulous, lacking in any modesty or restraint. They were often noisy, shouting down cleverer people than themselves – like my father for example – and eating and drinking with abandon. Monsters ignored all the rules of good behaviour and good taste.

This definition gave rise to two problems. The first was that people like that are often very good company indeed. In small doses, they can be funny and refreshing, and their energy can result in their becoming famous in their own right. The second problem was that it was a perfect description of my grandfather, Kenneth Clark Senior. Both my parents absolutely revelled in telling us children what a monster he had been, so much so in fact that, in my father's case, it was quite clear that he had adored him.

As a result of this, my father was attracted to monsters all his life.

He loved to tell stories of their hideous exploits, but the stories almost always ended up with roars of laughter and what looked to us very much like approval, and even envy. My mother would freeze with horror. '*Pas devant les enfants*,' she would hiss, and clench her fists.

But monsters don't get very far if they just behave badly. The key to their success is often their enormous charm. They smile and flirt, where someone with more taste would remain reserved, and they make very good dinner party guests indeed. Despite herself, and against her better judgement, my mother would often fall under their spell.

My first experience of a genuine monster was in 1938, when I was six years old. Robert Boothby MP was funny and witty, and he was a protégé of Winston Churchill. On this occasion he had been invited to stay the weekend with Sir Philip Sassoon, a multi-millionaire and probably a monster himself, who lived at Port Lympne in Kent, a house now owned by John Aspinall the gambler. My parents were great friends of Sassoon, and had bought a house at the end of his drive with the doubtful name of Bellevue. Bob Boothby was also a frequent guest, and one afternoon he suggested that the whole party go over to Folkestone races.

When we arrived – for the children were invited too; it must have been the nanny's day off – Boothby took us off for a closer look at the horses. I don't think he liked children, but he was desperate to have a bet on the big race, and we were the only excuse he could find to get away from all the millionaires in the box.

'You choose which horse you think is going to win,' he explained, 'and then you go over to one of those men yelling and waving and you put your money on your horse's nose.'

This seemed a jolly funny place to put it, but we pleaded with our mother to let us join in, and she gave us each a ten-shilling note. Ten shillings was a lot of money then – the equivalent of about £20 today. I remember a special gleam coming into Bob Boothby's eye (children always notice something 'special').

Bob had charm to spare, even for us. 'All right, boys and girls,' he said. 'Let's go back to the paddock and make our choice.'

'We like the jockey with the black and white colours,' we said. (The horse must have belonged to Lord Derby. Those are still his racing colours.) 'We want to put our money on his horse. How do we get close enough to put it on its nose?'

'Oh, that horse won't win,' said Bob. 'The one in the pink and green is the favourite. Let's bet it all on him.'

'No, no!' we cried. 'The black and white. Please, Mr Boothby. Can you put our money on the black and white?'

'Oh, very well,' said Bob, and he went over to the bookies and put it on the pink and green.

Needless to say, the pink and green horse did not win the race, and the black and white one did, and at quite good odds too, but did Bob apologise, or pay us our winnings out of his own pocket? It never even crossed his mind.

'Never give a sucker an even break' was Bob's motto, and he stuck to it all his life. At the end of the war he got caught out in a particularly scandalous piece of trickery, and Churchill disowned him for good. Even so he got a knighthood, and he ended his days doing quiz shows on television. With his pipe and his bow tie, he was immensely popular. No one could resist his gruff chuckle. He was the one politician everybody felt they could trust.

The next 'monster' to amuse my parents was a film producer called Gabriel Pascal. 'Gaby' was a Hungarian, and he told us wonderful stories about how, as a cavalryman mounted on a dashing white steed, he had accepted the surrender of the entire Austrian army. He had been armed only with a sword, he said (the Austrian army must have looked pretty foolish), and even showed us the weapon in question. It was hanging over the mantelpiece in his rented house, near the film studios in Denham, and it looked suspiciously shiny, like a sword in a film, but such were Gaby's powers of persuasion that we believed him absolutely.

The fact that he was very short and stout did not put us off at all. Nor did it stop George Bernard Shaw from giving Gaby the film rights to all his plays. This was a real coup. GBS had received many lucrative offers over the years, and turned them all down. Gaby never had any money of his own (just like Bob Boothby), but he was very good at persuading other people to part with theirs.

Alexander Korda, boss of London Films, gave him a free hand to adapt Shaw's work for the cinema, and so long as Gaby was the producer all went well. His first film, *Pygmalion*, in 1938, was a great success, as was *Major Barbara* two years later. Gaby had discovered Deborah Kerr – 'My little Deborah' he called her, although she was actually quite large – and she became a star after *Major Barbara*, just as he had forecast she would.

When Gaby started to direct his films, the result was not so good. His Baron Münchhausen character made him imitate Eric von Stroheim, the great Hollywood director of the 1920s, complete with megaphone and white cap. In 1945 he offered me the part of Ptolemy in the film of Shaw's *Caesar and Cleopatra*, with Vivien Leigh, but my parents wisely turned him down on my behalf.

Nevertheless, Gaby invited me to visit him on the set, and I spent hours crawling around inside the great hollow plaster sphinxes as the Roman troops marched into Alexandria again and again. It gave me my first taste of filming, and I loved it. Most people do not take any interest in how a film is made, and why should they? A film is an illusion. The audience only want to enjoy the result. They may be interested in the actors' private lives, but they don't want to know how they act. Actors just put on costumes and make-up and walk about pretending to be someone else.

Watching from inside the sets of Gaby's films, I began to realise just how complicated a process it all was. Films are not shot in sequence. The first scene in the film might easily be the last one to be acted in front of the camera, and so on. Actors and actresses have to be prepared to do a scene – even a love scene – all alone, knowing that their partner will do the other half at a later date and the whole thing will be edited together in a cutting room far away. Acting in a film and acting in the theatre are two totally different disciplines. Gaby was no more able to grasp this than was Laurence Olivier, and his films now look artificial. At that time *Caesar and Cleopatra* was the most expensive film ever made in Britain, but it was not a success. But Gaby himself was irresistible. He always had the best ideas.

In 1947 Colette and I joined him in Venice for the film festival, and he was a sensation. He had brought Jean Simmons with him, the star of Powell and Pressburger's *Black Narcissus*. Jean was engaged to marry the actor Stewart Grainger, and I gave her my usual youthful, uncalled-for piece of advice. 'Don't marry him,' I said. 'He is a cad.' But she did, and he was.

Then, to our amazement, Gaby suddenly and miraculously married a lovely young Hungarian girl called Valerie. He would lie on the beach at the Venice Lido trying to do a deal with Roberto Rossellini, and these two fat, brown and, to our eyes, extremely ugly men would argue as to which of their wives was the more beautiful, while Valerie and the young Ingrid Bergman splashed about together in the sea with us.

Gaby's only problem was money. He never had quite enough. Towards the end of his life he wrote to my father to ask for help. He had conceived the idea of turning his first successful Shaw film, *Pygmalion*, into a Broadway musical. Would my father like to invest? I wish he had. *My Fair Lady* became one of the longest-running musicals ever, and eventually a very successful film. The show opened on Broadway in 1955, but poor Gaby had died, broke, a few months before.

My father loved people like Gabriel Pascal. Perhaps he was frightened of turning into his mother, who had been so disapproving and so prim, and every now and then he needed an injection of his boisterous and badly-behaved father. As a result our house was often filled with artistic characters who were as extrovert as they were talented.

If my mother had had a choice, she would definitely have preferred aristocrats to artists. Although all my father's friends were very charming to her, they were not afraid of making a lot of noise. My mother hated noise. When my father sneezed, which he did quite a lot, she would say, 'K!' quite sharply to him, and he got in the habit of mumbling, 'I'm so sorry. Atishoo! I'm so sorry,' into his handkerchief, even if she wasn't there.

One Christmas Maurice Bowra, an old friend and later Vice-Chancellor of Oxford University, noticed this and decided to put a stop to it. Maurice was short and stout and had a very loud voice. He came up quietly behind my mother and let out a sneeze like a wounded bull elephant. My mother nearly fainted, but she could not quite award Maurice monster status. He was a wonderfully warm-hearted and wise man. So my mother stopped saying 'K!' whenever my father sneezed, but he did not stop saying 'I'm so sorry,' each time, and in the end this became more annoying than the sneeze.

Gradually we came to accept that monsters were just as likely to be invited to my parents' dinner parties as anyone else. The dancer Robert Helpmann, the conductor Malcolm Sargent, the general administrator of the Royal Opera House David Webster and many others would come to amuse us children before the dinner, to which we were not of course invited, began.

My brother Alan also became a little more independent and noisy than my mother would have liked ('Klaxon' Clark, Maurice Bowra called him), and he sometimes got called a monster too. Colette was a model daughter, beautifully serious and wise, but I suppose that all mothers get jealous as their daughters begin to flower. When mother/daughter riots begin even the CRS, the notorious French riot police, do not dare to intercede, and there were times when my mother became a bit of a monster herself. I am more like my Scottish grandmother. I hate fierce arguments – what we called 'rows' – more than anything else in the world. I had to go out to look for monsters of my own.

Dominic Elwes was one of the most amusing and talented young men of his generation. His father, Simon, was a famous portrait painter, who had given all his sons a good home and a good education. But 'Dommy' decided very early on that there were easier ways to get a good life than to work for it. In 1957 he and I shared a flat on the corner of Berkeley Square in Mayfair. I had just finished six months working on *The Prince and the Showgirl* with Marilyn Monroe, and ordinary life was looking a bit dull. Dommy soon changed that.

Like all monsters, he had tremendous energy, and the fact that he never had any money at all did not slow him down a bit. To watch Dommy give a really grand dinner party was an education. He would invite say fifteen people, those whom he most wanted to impress, to the most expensive restaurant available. He would be a wonderful host throughout, as if he did not have a care in the world. Then, just as the meal was ending, he would order something a little bit unusual – angels on horseback (bacon and kidneys on fried bread), perhaps, or a devilled oyster, and everyone would laugh as he gulped it down.

CRASH! Dommy would fall full-length on the floor, or sometimes, for extra effect, on the table. He would clutch his throat, go purple in the face, and foam would appear on his lips.

'I've been poisoned,' he would gasp, writhing in pain. 'I'm going to die. Call an ambulance.'

Consternation would take hold of all those grand guests. 'Poor Dommy. And after he had bought us all that wonderful dinner.'

'You should sue the restaurant,' they would call out as Dommy's inert form was carried away on a stretcher to have his stomach pumped out at the nearest hospital. No one, not even the nervous restaurant owner, could be so indelicate as to mention the bill. Not while there was a life at stake.

And you can't pump someone's stomach out without their permission. Half an hour later Dommy would be back in our flat drinking a bottle of (my) lager and happily talking of what a success his dinner party had been.

On one occasion, someone had read that if you drank half a bottle of iced gin in one go, you would die, and he bet Dommy £50 that he couldn't do it. This time Dommy's death throes lasted for nearly an hour. No wonder his son Cary is such an excellent actor.

But that sort of life is hard to sustain. Dommy was saved for a while by a beautiful heiress, and they lived together in Paris for several years. Then Dommy discovered that, like his father, he could paint portraits, and he got one of them into the Royal Academy Summer Exhibition. This success caused him to assume that his finances were now assured, and he told the Paris heiress that he had really loathed her all along, and moved back to London. Portrait painting is very hard work – something that Dommy had overlooked. Soon he was relying on his friends again, and his charm began to wear very thin. One night, after dinner with John Aspinall and his wife, I went back with them to their house in Belgravia.

'Don't move your head,' said Aspinall as we got out of the taxi. 'Just glance up at the window.'

Sure enough, there was Dommy's face, peeping out between the curtains. He had been living there as a house guest for many weeks.

'I wonder what he's up to now,' said Jane Aspinall as we went upstairs. We opened the door to find Dommy spreadeagled on the carpet, pale as death. His breath was coming in short rasps; a half-empty bottle of pills was in his outstretched hand.

'Well,' said Aspinall to his guests. 'Sit down, sit down. Who would like a nightcap?'

We carefully stepped over Dommy's corpse and arranged ourselves on the sofa.

'I'll just go and powder my nose,' said Jane.

Dommy could bear it no longer. 'You see what you've driven me to by your meanness!' he shouted, jumping to his feet in a rage (Aspinall had stopped giving him any cash). 'Even when I pretend to commit suicide, you don't have any pity for me.'

In the end, Dommy ran out of jokes. He wasn't stupid, and when he saw that the game was up he took his life, for real. As with so many monsters, one could only feel sad to see such a waste.

John Aspinall was quite the opposite. He was the great survivor, always larger than life. He was a genuine monster of the old school. Aspinall never pretended not to be tempting you to almost certain disaster. Oh, but what fun it was going to be on the way there, how important you would feel. Beautiful girls and aristocratic men would make a fuss of you. Champagne, jewels, discreet servants always at your elbow, it was enough to make any (rich) young man's head spin. Aspinall was like the coachman in Walt Disney's film of *Pinocchio*. 'All aboard for Pleasure Island, where you can do anything you like.' The little boys in the story who fell for this temptation had a wonderful time, all right. Then they gradually turned into donkeys, got slung out and had to work hard for a living.

'What's your name, little man?' the coachman would roar, picking one up by the tail.

'Colin Clark, sir.'

'Oh, you can still talk, can you? And you've still got some money, in a trust fund somewhere! Throw him back! We're not finished with him yet!'

Aspinall loved taking risks. He would set up the most wonderful salons where the rich could gamble for huge stakes. He was the banker, taking a percentage of each bet, so he could only lose money if one of the players went bankrupt; and when they did, Aspinall would sometimes pay their debts and make them work for him.

Aspinall was responsible for changing the gambling laws in Britain. Until he came along, gambling with cards had been restricted to places like Monte Carlo, where most people never went. The only place that an Englishman could have a flutter was at the racecourse. Aspinall decided to challenge this, and to make himself a millionaire in the process. He set up a gambling saloon in his house, and in 1957 one of his parties was raided by the police. I was present when they burst in, and it was amusing to watch them get almost everything wrong.

First a policewoman, in a long evening dress, came to the door and asked, 'Is Johnny there?' This was a silly mistake, since everyone called Aspinall 'Aspers', but the butler opened the door anyway. 'Aspers' certainly wasn't trying to hide. When the boys in blue poured in after the decoy and arrested us all, they got a marquis, two earls and two Greek millionaires as well as a few assorted hangers-on like me. We had been playing *chemin de fer*, and there were huge piles of gambling chips everywhere. What the police did not know was that the box under the table, which also contained a lot of chips, was Aspinall's cut. At his trial Aspinall defended himself by saying that he was just giving a private party for his friends (which was true), and he was acquitted.

In the end Aspinall and I fell out. We had never really been friends, and I could not afford to invest in his club, but I did lend him a large sum of money, really all the money I had, to put down as a deposit on the building in Berkeley Square in which he wanted to start his gambling club. In return, he gave me a post-dated cheque which he said he would honour after several of his bigger debtors had paid up. While I was waiting for this to happen, flushed with the feeling that I was now an important member of Aspinall's circle,

I gambled far more recklessly than usual. I stopped when I thought I had lost about a quarter of my capital (we all gambled on credit, of course, and not with actual cash), but when I turned up to settle with Aspinall the following day, he told me that I had lost it all.

He may have been right; I had certainly been pretty drunk by the end of the evening. I had already deposited Aspinall's post-dated cheque in my bank, but now he told me he would bounce it by keeping his account empty, so I was totally broke.

In desperation I rang my bank manager, Mr Brown of the Clydesdale, a cautious Scot if ever there was one. Yes, funnily enough, he thought he could help. Like many solid citizens, Mr Brown did not approve of Aspinall. It so happened that the manager of Aspinall's bank was a personal friend of his. He could ask his friend not to present my cheque until there were sufficient funds to meet it. That way it would not bounce. But Mr Brown would only do this if I swore, absolutely swore, that I would never gamble again.

God bless you, Mr Brown. I don't know if there are still any bank managers like that. I got my money back. I never did gamble again, except by investing in stocks and shares, where I have invariably lost. But I had reneged on a gambling debt, and for that I have felt guilty ever since. Aspinall has gone on to become extremely wealthy. He had single-handedly redistributed the wealth of Britain's aristocracy, and you get very rich doing that.

Aspinall is the supreme example of someone who believes in the survival of the fittest. He is often said to be redeemed by his love of animals, and he genuinely admires the fierce beasts who chew up the meek and spit them out. (I know a couple whose son was killed by one of the tigers in his zoo, and I'm not sure if they would agree.) The way Aspinall goes into the cages with his tigers and wolves and gorillas is certainly amazing. If one of them eats him one day, I do not think he will mind.

Having said all this, I must admit that Aspinall comes into the category of 'great men', as well as 'monsters' (the two are by no means mutually exclusive). The power of his personality is extraordinary, and it is even, in the end, something you have to admire.

As soon as I was banned by Aspinall, I looked round for another monster to take his place. Thanks to Mr Brown, I still had a little of the money which my grandfather had left me, and I seemed to be determined to throw it away as quickly as possible, goodness knows why.

Lord Timothy Willoughby D'Eresby was everything that I was not. He was strikingly handsome and extremely rich. His father was the Earl of Ancaster and his grandmother was Nancy Astor, the first woman to sit as a Member of Parliament. The Earl was a silent aristocrat of the old school. When I met him in Timmy's house he asked me where I lived.

'In Margaretta Terrace,' I replied.

'Good heavens,' he said, 'what a long way away.'

'It's just down the Kings Road,' I said, 'the other side of Sloane Square.'

'Oh, I know where it is,' replied the Earl. To him, anything outside Belgravia or Mayfair was a long way away.

Timmy was very dangerous. He ran his life entirely according to his whims. When you were with him you never knew what you would end up doing or where you would be doing it. Timmy loved the bizarre, and eccentric people were attracted to him like paperclips to a magnet. I was the only normal paperclip there. Timmy collected talented lost souls who would stay up drinking with him all night, then dash off with him to his house in the South of France without going home to pack.

Timmy never took his eyes off you while he was talking to you. He spoke quietly, even gently, but he expected to be obeyed. I had met him through his beautiful sister Jane, and he had invited me to his birthday party at his London house in Wilton Row. As I walked there I realised that I had not got a present for him, so I went up to the flower-seller who had (and whose family still has) a barrow on the corner of Belgrave Square.

I can't just buy a bunch of flowers, I thought. He's bound to have flowers already.

'How much for the whole lot?' I asked.

'The whole lot?' said the man. 'There's over fifty bunches of flowers here.'

'How much?'

He named a sum.

'Will you take a cheque?'

'Oh, well, seeing as you're a toff, sir, all right – but how are you going to carry them all away?'

'You're going to help me,' I said, and together we struggled across the square to Timmy's home. I defy anyone to turn up at a party with fifty bunches of fresh flowers and not be popular. Timmy simply loved gestures like this, and we became friends for life.

A few years later, he repaid the compliment. I had married my French ballerina by then, and this had upset Timmy greatly. He and I were never lovers – Timmy loved the ladies even more than I did – but he still saw it as a sort of betrayal. I was living in New York, and Timmy was in London, where he had opened his own nightclub called Whips. Before I had left for America I had had that lovely, fragile mistress called Shelagh. Parting with her had been as hard as parting with Timmy, but I had known that it was time for me to start a new life.

After an absence of a year, I came back to London for a holiday. I telephoned Timmy and he told me to meet him that evening in the Ritz bar. I agreed, although I had great misgivings about seeing Timmy again, which he must have sensed. It was as if I was going back to an addiction that I had already shed.

When I got to the Ritz, Timmy wasn't there. Instead, waiting in the corner was Shelagh. Somehow Timmy had found her and told her to be there without telling either of us about his plan. It was a beautiful surprise.

Then the barman came over. 'From Lord Willoughby, sir,' he said, and handed me an envelope. It contained the keys to Timmy's house in Wilton Row, and a simple note: 'The champagne is in the fridge.' That was it. Shelagh and I spent a glorious night together, before finally parting for ever.

Quite soon after this, Timmy began to self-destruct in earnest. He was not really a gambler, but on one of his visits to Monte Carlo he had won a huge amount on the tables, and he had used the money to buy the speedboat of an Italian playboy called Gianni Agnelli (later Chairman of Fiat). He became obsessed with the idea of going across the Mediterranean in this boat from Monte Carlo to Corsica, a hundred miles away. The boat could do twenty knots with ease, so the journey should only take five hours. He wrote to me about this plan, and said he was having quite a lot of difficulty in finding a passenger. Would I go with him?

I would not. The Mediterranean is famous for its sudden squalls. Just because the water is like glass in Monte Carlo, it does not mean that it will remain like that all the way to Corsica. Speedboats are very unreliable in rough water, and this one had no proper safety equipment, not even a radio. Added to this, I have always been deeply suspicious of boats. My grandfather had loved to race ocean-going yachts, but none of his enthusiasm had rubbed off on me. As soon as I see a boat I am tempted to get on it, but as soon as I am on it I want to get off. I had once gone on a friend's boat, intending to cruise up the coast of France. The moment we were out of sight of the land, we had run into heavy weather. For ten hours we battled with the wind and the rain, and we were very relieved indeed when we saw the lights of a little port in front of us. Funnily enough, we even seemed to recognise it. It turned out to be the same one we had left that morning. We had not taken the local currents into account, and had spent the whole day cruising in exactly the same spot.

I declined Timmy's offer, and begged him to reconsider, but in the end he did find a companion, and they both vanished without trace.

There are not many immutable truths in life, but there is one on which you can depend absolutely: if you are down to your last few thousand pounds, and are looking round desperately for a way to make it increase, you will soon find some charming person who will make the whole lot vanish completely. It won't look like a gamble, of course. Your new friend will be doing you an enormous favour, letting you in on secret information, giving you that very special tip. So great will be their charm that you will not even question why, when they are such a recent acquaintance, they should be doing you such a kindness.

The first of many people I found in my life who was willing to do me this service was called Ronnie Cornwell. Ronnie was the best con-man ever. I had never seen anyone who looked so trustworthy in my life. He was your favourite uncle, your family doctor, Bob Boothby and Father Christmas all rolled into one. He was stout and beaming, with white hair and bushy white eyebrows. He wore a black jacket and a waistcoat, and striped trousers like a faithful old family retainer, or Lord Reith. Ronnie knew how to fix anything – tickets for the Cup Final, a box at Ascot, dinner at the most exclusive restaurant in town. He had an attractive wife, who hardly spoke but who obviously worshipped him. His account-ant was perpetually on call to substantiate his claims to wealth and inside knowledge.

Ronnie could turn up at any hotel in the world, the grander the better, and stay for two weeks without paying a penny. He would take over the most expensive suite and fill it with flowers and champagne (on credit of course). Then he would summon the manager and tell him, in the strictest confidence, about the huge deal he was going to pull off, even promising to give him a little share. In return the manager would ensure that Ronnie received the very best services that the hotel could provide. The manager wasn't hard to persuade. Any guest in that suite would receive the hotel's best services anyway. He was flattered to be taken into the great man's confidence and, fortified by champagne, he gave the necessary orders.

The poor man had not learned the famous dictum that when you sit down to play cards with the big boys, if you can't tell which of the players is the sucker, then it's you. So Ronnie would live like a king, and the bill would soar to prodigious heights while he charged everything to it, including meals, hired cars and even air tickets.

When Ronnie judged that the manager was about to bring up the subject of payment, Ronnie's wife would arrive, and would call the man in for a quiet chat. Ronnie was exhausted, she would explain. As soon as he was better she would bring the bill to his attention, but he couldn't be disturbed at the moment. More charm, more champagne. The whole thing would be put off for another three or four days.

Then Ronnie would summon the manager again. 'I hear that my bill hasn't been paid, and I am simply furious. I am going to telephone my accountant right now, in front of you, and demand to know what is going on.'

A long explanation by the accountant would be cut short abruptly by Ronnie. 'A cheque in another four days is no good. Why should I ask my good friend the manager to accept a cheque, which will take days to clear? I want you here, in the hotel, with x pounds' – he would name an enormous sum, at least double the size of the bill – 'IN CASH. Be here by Friday, without fail. I have friends here whom I need to reward for their patience.' (Big jovial wink at the manager.)

Sure enough, on Friday the little accountant would turn up with a briefcase, and Ronnie and his wife would go down to the lobby to meet him. 'You see,' Ronnie would beam at the manager, 'I told you I'm a man of my word. Well?' turning to the accountant. 'Give me the money.'

'Oh, I don't have all that cash with me. That would be too dangerous.'

'What?' Ronnie would roar, with terrible rage.

'It's all right,' cried the accountant. 'I have a certified cheque from the bank. There's a branch round the corner who will cash it for me without question.'

'Very well,' Ronnie would say. 'We'd better go there right away.' And Ronnie and his wife would march purposefully out of the hotel, with the accountant following behind.

It would be some hours before the manager realised that they were not coming back. A search of their room would reveal only the remnants of what they had ordered on room service. So great was the manager's shame and confusion that very often the police would not even be called. And so confident was Ronnie of his powers that a year later he would turn up and stay at the hotel again, in the same suite. 'You never received the money? I can't believe it. My poor wife was taken ill in the bank, but I told them to send you the money at once. Let me call the bank. Oh, it's Saturday. Well, on Monday then. Perhaps I should call the police. In the meantime, send up my usual champagne, etc. etc.'

In the face of this blast of confidence, flattery and bluff, I was as helpless as a baby. Ronnie invited me to Royal Ascot and gave me a few good dinners. Then he showed me a piece of derelict property, which he did not own, promised to double my money in three months, and took the lot. What was difficult to comprehend about Ronnie was that *everything* was fake. His office, his car, his chauffeur, his 'regular' box at Ascot, were all just hired for the occasion, and never paid for. His wife was not his wife, and his accountant was just an accomplice. Only his powers of invention were real. Happily, he passed those on to his son David, the writer John le Carré.

On one of my trips to Monte Carlo with Timmy Willoughby I had fallen under the spell of a Panamanian lawyer called Tito Arias. Until then, all the monsters I had known were loud, pushy and dominant. Tito was a monster of a quite different type. His voice was quiet to the point of being incomprehensible. He never raised his voice or made any effort to be the centre of attention. He had the lazy charm of a baby who is so spoiled that he absolutely knows that he is going to get what he wants, and that he can toss it out of the pram again the moment he is bored with it.

I had first met Tito when he came down to Saltwood as the new husband of Margot Fonteyn. Margot had been a friend of my parents since the Sadlers Wells Ballet Company had been reinstated at the Royal Opera House, Covent Garden after the war. My father was on the board of the Trustees of the Opera House, and Margot had become their most important new star. It was immediately obvious that she was a dancer of incredible talent, as well as being an enchanting person. Meat was rationed in England during the war, and my sister and I had been happy to give up our ration cards every now and then so that Margot could have a good steak.

Margot wasn't exactly beautiful, but she was extraordinarily attractive. She was also a very bad judge of men. First she fell in love with her partner on stage, Robert Helpmann, who was a genuine monster in his own right. Bobby was a malicious Australian homosexual who never even pretended to return her affection until his own career started to slide. Anyone seemed better than that.

Tito Arias came from one of the leading families in Panama. He obviously thought the world of Margot, but his situation was precarious. He was endlessly involved in plotting to overthrow the Panamanian government, which was in the hands of a rival branch of the family. (No nonsense about consulting the electorate in Panama.) Margot just giggled and refused to take it seriously, but Tito was obsessed. On his visits to Saltwood he would walk round the grounds telling me all about his problems in a series of almost incomprehensible grunts and mumbles. I suppose I was the only person who would listen.

'It's so expensive,' he would complain. 'No one realises how much a revolution costs. The telephone bills from London alone are incredible. Margot never makes a fuss' – guess who was paying – 'but one day they will bankrupt us. I swear that this will be my last revolution. As soon as my uncle is back in power I'm going to stop plotting against him, and get him to give me a job.'

'How many revolutions have you had?' I asked.

'This will be my seventh,' said Tito in an absent sort of way. 'But I've promised Margot it will be my last.'

Tito was always said to be the lawyer of Aristotle Onassis, the Greek shipping magnate. This was possible, because the Onassis fleet was registered under the Panamanian flag, but I think Tito was really more of a 'fixer', someone who could smooth things over with government officials. When he married Margot his prestige with Onassis increased dramatically. Onassis was having an affair with the opera singer Maria Callas, and suddenly the two men had something in common.

None of this seemed to have the least effect on Tito. When Tim Willoughby and I were invited by Onassis to a lunch party at Monte Carlo's Sporting Club – I suppose because Timmy was the grandest young English milord available – Tito and Margot were there, and so was Callas, but Tito was taking no part in the conversation.

'Come and see what I can do, Colin,' he said, beckoning me to sit beside him. He took an orange from the table, got a little penknife out of his pocket and started to carve. After a few deft strokes, he turned it inside out and converted it into a huge phallus. I was so convulsed with laughter that the whole table stopped talking.

'What are you doing, Tito darling?' called Margot. 'Show us what you've got.'

Tito gave a sly grin, and held it up for everyone to see. The ladies gasped. The men gulped. Onassis's eyes popped out. Poor Margot was really very prim and conventional. 'Oh, Tito,' she sighed.

There is no doubt that Tito thought about sex a bit too much. When his uncle did win the revolution, and Tito was made Panamanian Ambassador to London, he became a seducer on an international scale. Margot would give wonderful first-night parties after each new ballet, never knowing if Tito would turn up or not. On one occasion I met him in her dressing room before the performance, and later he phoned to say he couldn't join us for dinner because he was in Paris.

In the end he was shot at a lunch party in Panama. It was said to be by a political rival, but I was told that it was because he had had his hand up a married lady's skirt under the table. The tabletop was glass, and the jealous husband had ripped away the tablecloth and drawn a gun. Tito was paralysed from the neck down, and Margot devoted the rest of her life to looking after him, but he never really changed. He had been incoherent before, but his speech had been badly affected by the shooting, and now Margot was the only person who could understand him.

'What did he say?' I asked after he gulped something to me with great urgency.

'Oh, just some silly vulgar joke about that girl's legs,' said Margot wearily.

Tito hired a pretty secretary, and even eloped with her to Spain. Since he was totally confined to a wheelchair, and could hardly even breathe, it was an incredible triumph of the will. Margot really didn't know whether to be sad or proud. Finally she took him back to Panama, the prisoner of her endless patience and love. After a few years, Tito was dead, and so was Margot. Tito Arias was the sort of monster for whom you gave your life.

Although Margot had been a wonderfully devoted wife to the unfaithful Tito, she did make one more disastrous attempt to find love before she retired to Panama, once again with a ballet partner. It is actually very rare that female stars fall in love with the men who act opposite them. Marilyn Monroe certainly had not fallen for Olivier, and Vivien Leigh usually loathed her leading men. But it was something that Margot seemed unable to resist.

Rudolph Nureyev was as unsuitable as Robert Helpmann had been, and for very much the same reasons. I first met him in Paris immediately after he had defected to the West in 1961. He had done one of his famous leaps, over the barrier at Orly airport, to escape going back to Russia with the Kirov Ballet. My first wife, Violette, and I were living in Paris at the time, after our disastrous honeymoon in Italy, and Violette was very much part of the French ballet community in which Nureyev first took refuge. We all knew that he was going to be a great star, and so did he, but in those early days he was quiet and polite and anxious to make friends.

One really should not use the word monster to describe people who have incredible talent and become famous for it. They can not all be expected to remain as sweet and modest as Margot Fonteyn. There is a natural tendency for great stars to attract sycophants and to become spoilt. They face continual demands on their time, and they have the right to insist on getting their slightest wish granted in return. Not unnaturally, they can become self-centred and autocratic. But Nureyev never forgot our early friendship.

'Colin,' he would say when I went round to his dressing room after some incredible performance, 'why do you never come to see me dance?' (As if he did not have a big enough audience already.)

'I do come, Jazz,' I said.

'*Rudi*,' he would say imperiously. (Jazz was a nickname which we had given him when he first came to London, to disguise his identity.)

'I do come, Rudi, whenever I can. But you have so many admirers.'

'Nonsense,' he replied. 'If you were in the audience I would know it. I would feel it.'

I once gave him a lift to a party in my car, and he gave me a long dissertation on why sex with boys was so much better than sex with girls.

'I'm sure you're right, Rudi,' I said. 'But I am looking for love.'

Rudi laughed. He may have become a bit of a monster, but he was irresistible all the same. 'Oh, I fall in love every time.'

When we were children, my sister and I had often been alarmed by our parents' homosexual friends. Of course they had been 'stars' – our parents' friends all seemed to be stars – but unlike the artists and their wives, the unmarried men obviously did not appreciate children. The three who alarmed us most were Somerset Maugham, Noël Coward and Cecil Beaton.

Maugham was as dry as dust, but he seemed to have a calming effect on my mother, and she loved him. In 1954 she took me out to stay with him in the Villa Mauresque at Cap Ferrat, in the South of France, and I changed my mind about him completely. He could clearly be ruthless and cruel, but when he set out to seduce someone, he was irresistible. Like many very clever people, he could listen as well as he could talk, and this made him seem extremely sympathetic.

Noël Coward was different. Whenever he came to our house, I would simply curl up with embarrassment. He was so different from my father, I suppose. He would show off shamelessly, all the time. Didn't he know that there was one thing which one must never do? 'Colin's showing off again' was the nastiest – and most frequent – insult that my brother could think of. But Coward didn't seem to mind. He wanted to make everyone laugh, and he was brilliantly witty – too witty, really, for a child to understand – so he got away with it.

Many years later, I went to pick up Irene Worth for dinner after she had been appearing on stage with Coward in London. 'I'm not ready yet,' she said. 'Go and talk to Noël. He's a bit gloomy.'

I knocked on Noël's dressing room door with some apprehension. There was no earthly reason why he should remember me.

'I'm Colin Clark,' I said. 'K and Jane's younger son.'

'Oh, of course, so you are.' He was clearly exhausted after the performance, but if he was disappointed not to have a grander guest, he never showed it. For half an hour he chatted to me as if I were an old friend. He was frank and modest and wise, and as with Maugham I was completely won over. It was as if all that 'monstrous' behaviour had been an act, kept in place to cover a brilliantly intelligent but rather private person. What was one to think? The cat, after killing so many mice, had finally retired to her basket and purred. Can she really have once been the terror of the house?

Most monsters have some redeeming features, but not all. An example of this is Ian Paisley, leader of the Democratic Unionist Party of Northern Ireland. He had the aggressive egomania common to most politicians, but he also behaved like a bully. He is a heavy man, with a head shaped like a battering ram. I invited him to ATV television studios in 1975 to talk about his philosophy of life, not to make a party political statement. This did not stop him trying to cow everyone into submission – the interviewer and me included. Soon the make-up girls were close to tears; floor managers did not dare to give instructions; everyone stood to one side as Paisley rushed headlong into a diatribe about the wickedness of other people. None of us could believe that such an intelligent man could be so stupid. We were a team of people employed to do nothing else but to make him look his best. It was like shooting the messenger before he has even given you the message.

Unlike some monsters, Ian Paisley does not seem to have changed. Convinced that it is impossible for him to be wrong, he has gone on giving exactly the same performance which, as someone once said of the actor Anthony Quinn, has so consistently failed to win him an Oscar.

Many monsters become famous. They have a sort of iron-clad egotism which we envy, and secretly admire. Occasionally, like Princess Margaret, they are born in the public eye, but most of them have pushed and shoved their way to the front of the queue, and stand there inviting our criticism and shrugging off our abuse. But there are monsters on a more modest scale, monsters who try to avoid the spotlight as much as possible, and it is from the ranks of these that you can get a monster of your very own.

When I first came across Adrian, he was having a pee in front of my house in St Peter's Square in London. I was staring absently out of a first-floor window when I saw a tall young man walk in through the front gate, unzip his trousers and start to relieve himself on the flowerbed.

'Oy!' I yelled. 'Cut that out!' But the triple glazing muffled the sound, and the young man clearly could not hear me. He sauntered round the lawn, and then peed again. I huffed and puffed, but I could not open the bedroom window more than an inch.

'Cut that out!' I shrieked through the slit, but to no avail. Slowly and deliberately he peed for a third time, gazing round all the while. I now realise that this is a trick thieves use to see if anyone is watching. If no one yells 'Oy! Cut that out!' they can be sure that they haven't been seen. But at the time I was completely mystified. No one needs three pees in such quick succession.

Then the young man went out through the gate and up to a BMW parked nearby. He didn't seem to move his hands, but the front window of the car simply vanished. He leant in and took out a briefcase. Then, and only then, did he look up and see me in the window. Our eyes met and we gazed at each other in mutual amazement for about five seconds, before he went loping off around the corner. It was a long time before the police turned up, and there was nothing they could do. I gave them a very accurate description of the culprit, and that was that – as common an occurrence in London today as it must have been three hundred years ago.

Ten days later I saw him again. This time I did not try to open the window, I just picked up the phone. The police arrived in about forty-five seconds, and he was nabbed. I felt rather guilty, as I do when I have caught a mouse in a trap, but the young man didn't seem to mind a bit. I could see him laughing and cracking jokes as he was bundled into a Black Maria and driven away.

'Mind you, you haven't exactly made a friend, Mr Clark,' said one policeman. 'And he'll be out of our hands in a couple of hours. He's only sixteen, so we can't hold him. Are you sure you want to press charges?'

'If I don't,' I said, 'he'll have a licence to rob all the cars around here to his heart's content.'

'Just thought I'd mention it,' said the policeman with a sigh.

Sure enough, a week later, there he was again. This time I happened to be sitting outside the house in my car, fiddling with the radio, when I saw him creep up beside the car in front. I hooted and glared, and the young man, recognising me, glared back. Fight or flight? Luckily he decided on flight, but my blood was up. I started the car and set off in pursuit. As he ran along the footpath by the church two hundred yards away, I drove on to the pavement and scrunched to a stop, squeezing him between the passenger door and the railings.

Now what? Quite suddenly our faces were almost touching. Neither of us could move, but there didn't seem a formula for what to say or do next. We were both just embarrassed. I rolled down the window.

'What's your name?' I asked sharply.

'Adrian,' came the sullen reply.

'Where do you live, Adrian?'

He gave me the address of what I knew to be a local authority hostel.

'I will come and see you tomorrow morning,' I said. 'We can't have you robbing every car in my square.' I reversed away, and Adrian ran off, as surprised, I think, as I was.

The next morning at 10 a.m. I turned up at the address he had given me. Yes, they had an Adrian. The social worker was deeply suspicious. What did I want?

'I want to talk to him, that's all,' I said. 'You can be present if you want. Now fetch him at once.'

Adrian came downstairs in his pyjamas, very far from pleased to see who was there.

'You're the one what got me nicked last week. Mind you, they can't do nothing to me. I'm only sixteen.'

'Well I'm not having you rob my square any more,' I said. 'You can go and rob somewhere else. Tell me about yourself.'

When he wasn't 'in care', Adrian lived with his Mum in Hammersmith. His father had returned to Grenada soon after he was born. He had left school now, and spent his time hanging around, bored, just pinching anything that wasn't actually nailed down. For once I did not know what to say. What an incredibly different world from my own. But Adrian was a teenage boy, and I have a son of my own. They couldn't be that different. And he had a lot of charm. He didn't do drugs, he said. He never used violence, or attacked people. He'd always been a good pupil at school, and indeed he did seem remarkably bright.

'I'll try to help you find a job,' I said, 'if you promise to leave my square alone. Come and see me next week, and this time ring the bell.'

So Adrian came. He sat on my front step, played with my son, who was then aged five, and said he would like to work in the music industry. I got him an interview with Island Records, but he never turned up. He couldn't resist the joys of a life of crime, even though he left my square alone from then on, as he had promised. The police used to arrest him about once a month. They knew perfectly well what he was up to, but their hands were tied because of his age. On one occasion they arrested him just because he was wearing a pair of Ray-Ban sunglasses. How could he possibly afford those on what the government gave him? Sure enough, they found stolen property in his room.

Just before his eighteenth birthday, the police persuaded him to own up to everything he could remember doing, while he was still a juvenile. He pleaded guilty to twenty-three burglaries and five thousand thefts from cars. The police were thrilled, so thrilled that they didn't bother to produce all the evidence, and the result was that the magistrate gave the police a ticking-off and let Adrian go free. But they got him a week later, and he was given six months in a young offenders' instittion.

He wrote me beautiful letters, and even seemed quite happy where he was, as if he'd found a family. I had become like an uncle to him by this time, but I still didn't know how to help. If I gave him a lecture about good behaviour, it made no impression at all: he got about twenty of those a day from his Mum. The next time he got caught he was given two and a half years. He said he learned a lot in prison – mainly how to thieve. By this time I had met his Mum, and she was charming. I talked to his probation officer, and she liked Adrian too. All we could do was try to help him with his life. There were plenty of people who would knock him about. We all felt, and still feel, that if Adrian thought he was abandoned completely, he could become very dangerous indeed. Three months after he had finished his second sentence he was caught burgling a factory. Now he has come out of Wormwood Scrubs again, and is absolutely determined to go straight.

In his last letter to me he wrote: 'People are always telling me that life is like one long straight road with lots of side roads and turnings. Well to be honest with you, for the past seven years I've been stuck on a roundabout going round in circles while everybody has been passing me by waving! Maybe it's about time to take a detour and try to get back on the road before it's too late.'

It is quite easy for a dominant personality to consider himself as outside the rules of conventional morality. Many of the monsters I have known have broken the law in one way or another, and all of them have skated on some pretty thin ice. If Adrian is the only one who has actually been to prison for any length of time, he is certainly not the only one for whom the shadow of the Scrubs was more than just a bad dream. The fact that the others escaped incarceration was due to their charm, and their ingenuity, and their education. Poor Adrian had the first two in abundance, but he missed out completely on the third, so I suppose he never really stood a chance.

ABOVE: The Lola T70 Mark III B. Our official time of 0–60 mph in 3.1 seconds has never been beaten.

RIGHT: My father at Saltwood in 1978. I find myself unconsciously adopting exactly the same posture when I write.

Alan and me posing at Saltwood, 1984.

With Alan at the Sotheby's sale of our father's estate in 1984.

LEFT: Alan at Saltwood with his Rolls-Royce Silver Ghost.

BELOW: In the house in Hammersmith.

LEFT: Helena and our son Christopher, 1988.

BELOW: In Portugal with Helena, 1990.

XI

CARS

'DON'T GIVE THE BOYS ANY MONEY,' my mother used to say to my father. 'They will only spend it on cars and petrol.'

For many years this was true. Alan and I collected cars, swapped cars, raced cars and crashed cars with complete abandon. I couldn't say that cars had priority over pretty girls, but they certainly ran them a very close second. After all, if you had the former, it was much easier to attract the latter. Cars represented freedom, and they also represented power. A big eight-cylinder engine has a lot of power. For a schoolboy to be able to accelerate himself from zero to sixty miles an hour in less than ten seconds is very exhilarating, as well as very dangerous.

Alan had started me off while I was still at Eton, with that V8 Allard two-seater sports car which I later crashed into a bus. The Royal Air Force then made matters worse by giving me a jet fighter plane whose two engines produced 12,500 horsepower each. As soon as I reached university, I started to look for the most powerful car I could buy. My brother had bought a Jaguar XK120 in 1950, and I naturally wanted something even newer and quicker. The answer seemed to be a brand new creation called the Austin-Healey 100. Donald Healey had been building sports cars for some time, of dubious reliability it must be said. In 1950 he had teamed up with Austin, who made family cars, and put Austin's 2500 cc engine in a very pretty little two-seater body, with which I immediately fell in love.

It so happened that a friend of my parents knew Donald Healey and persuaded him to let me have the eleventh car, out of an original pre-production run of twelve, to be made at his factory near Warwick. After a month they told me it was ready, and I went down on the train to collect it. I took a taxi to the factory and proudly handed over the cheque. Sure enough, there was my car, silver and blue and as cute as a button, sitting with its hood down in the corner of the shed. I couldn't wait to drive it onto the open road.

'Oh, no, you can't take it now,' they said, looking at me as if I was mad. 'You need to tax it. You need numberplates. You need insurance.'

For the first time, but not the last, I was forced to recognise that where cars are involved, officialdom comes first. Back I went on the train, to return a week later when all the paperwork was complete. But the Austin-Healey was worth it. The MG TD which I had in the Air Force was dreadfully old-fashioned and slow by comparison (0–60 mph in 23.9 seconds!). The only problem with the Healey was that the designer did not seem to have put in a fire wall between the engine and the cockpit. I certainly never needed to put on the heater, even with the top down on a frosty day, and in the summer, one simply cooked.

A year later, in 1954, I was introduced to the Bristol. Bristol cars were then still made by the Bristol Aircraft Company, and their design was similar to a plane, with a streamlined aluminium body and long wires running throughout the car to control its functions. After the Healey, the Bristol 401 seemed the epitome of sophistication, an image I was now anxious to acquire. My wind-in-the-hair sports-car-driving technique had been quite successful while I was in the Air Force, but it didn't cut much ice with the more sophisticated young ladies of Oxford. The Bristol had leather seats, and wind-up windows, and the two-litre engine was relatively quiet. Cruising up to a nightclub in Mayfair in the early hours of the morning, the Bristol gave exactly the impression of suave sophistication which I now thought suited me best. I owned three second-hand Bristols in succession, a red 400 coupé, a dark green 401 (the best) and a pale blue 402 convertible, which I had driven out to Portugal. I was fond of them all, but after another year it was time to move on again.

I suppose that, as with the ladies, I wanted to try as many different models as I possibly could. A car showroom in Bond Street, with a persuasive salesman called Major Brown, then showed me a convertible Lagonda. This was smooth and fast but it was also big, and I returned to Oxford with it in triumph. The Lagonda did not last very long either. One evening a friend of mine and I went to dinner in it with a professor called Raymond Carr. It was a jovial affair, and we all got extremely drunk. I remember driving all the way back to my college at about ten miles an hour, and having some difficulty in sticking to the road even at that speed.

Oxford colleges used to close their gates at midnight in those days, so my friend had to help me climb in over the wall. I passed out as soon as I got on my bed, but a few minutes later I was woken by my friend who, very resourcefully, had climbed in after me, and found my room. It was raining, he said. (I dimly remembered that. Perhaps it was the reason why I was wet.) Could he borrow the Lagonda to drive home? He was at another college, quite a long walk away. I gave him the keys and returned to sleep. Alas, he could not resist taking the Lagonda for a test drive. On the first fast corner outside the town, the car went into a spin, left the road and turned over several times. My friend was rushed to hospital, and the Lagonda was a total wreck.

When Raymond Carr was contacted, he told the authorities that I had also been in the car, and there was a frantic search for my body. (Carr told a friend of mine that he had driven in to work that day by a different route than usual, in case he came across my body in the road. Thanks, Raymond.) Eventually, of course, they found my body in my bed, with a hangover, and they were none too pleased about it. I lost my driving licence for a year (for allowing my car to be driven uninsured), and when I got it back I certainly didn't buy another Lagonda.

During my first year at university I used to go up to London almost every night. The road was wide but twisty (there was no motorway), and the challenge was to get from Piccadilly Circus to Oxford town centre inside the hour – impossible, except in the early hours of the morning. My wallet had been severely dented by the Lagonda affair, so as soon as I got my licence back, I embarked on a collection of 'bangers' – old sports cars in the last years of their working lives. After 'bangers' go bang they usually stop going for good. The need to keep them running was so urgent that I learned a great deal about how cars work – probably more than I did about political history from Lord Blake, and this knowledge has proved more useful, too.

Often a simple solution was the best. My 1937 Straight Eight Railton convertible caught fire while I was actually driving it. It was one of those rare cars, like a Morgan, built largely of wood, and it burned quite well. I was near my parents' house in Hampstead at the time, and I just kept going, through traffic lights and stop signs, belching flame and smoke. When I arrived home I dashed inside, grabbed a bucket of water and threw it all over the car. After the hissing had subsided and the seats dried out, I restarted the engine and it went perfectly, but I never quite trusted that car again.

It was not until I started to work on *The Prince and the Showgirl* in 1956 that I could afford a good car again. This time I bought a new Gran Turismo Lancia Aurelia coupé, and so for the first time in my life I owned a smart, modern car that worked. It had a quick, light engine and fantastic brakes, and it cornered as if on rails. It also had the most seductive cloth seats, including a little bench seat in the rear.

I persuaded many people to ride in that car, mainly young ladies, but my most reluctant passenger was the world champion racing driver Mike Hawthorne. Someone had dropped him off at my house in Cheshire one weekend, and had gone away, although Hawthorne needed to be at Oulton Park motor-racing track for practice. When I offered to drive him there, he wept. He had an absolute horror of being a passenger in a car, but the Lancia was not insured for anyone but me to drive, and after the Lagonda incident I didn't want to lose my licence again. In the end, the world champion lay down on the back seat, wrapped a scarf around his eyes, and we set off. I never went over 30 mph, but for the whole ten miles or so, although he could see nothing at all, Hawthorne pleaded with me to slow down. He was to die in a road crash a few years later, but at least he was driving himself at the time.

Quick though it was, the Lancia was a little low on power.

Jaguars were not nearly as sophisticated as Lancias, but they did have bigger engines and a lot more shove. I had got bored with leaky canvas tops by this time, so I next went through a series of Jaguar saloons, but, with the exception of the C-type, Jaguars are not cars you can love.

The amazing thing is that once a car has been designed, it is very hard to change. Handling characteristics, gearbox and engine problems, and even styling details continue down the years, no matter how many generations of engineers try to alter them. A brand new 1997 Jaguar XJ6 has exactly the same 'feel' as a 1958 Mark VII, even though it has been redesigned many times. A Porsche is still a Porsche, and a Rolls-Royce is a Rolls-Royce, no matter what. Only occasionally does a manufacturer start with a clean sheet — I suppose it is an incredibly expensive process — and come up with a brand new car.

The Mini and the Volkswagen Golf were two examples, and I must have had as much pleasure from my Austin Cooper S and my Golf GTI as from any car I have ever owned. Another brand new concept was the 'pony' car from the USA. The idea behind it was to take the chassis of a small family car, insert the engine from a big family car, and put a new sporty body on it. The result was actually rather dangerous. The suspension, steering and brakes, which were carried over from the small, cheap car, were concealed by the new sporty body, and they had not been designed for power. It did not really matter in America, where cars do not need good suspension, steering or brakes, but in Europe you need these things very badly.

I brought a 6.6 litre Pontiac GTO convertible over to England in 1966, and although its acceleration in a straight line was almost unbeatable, I had to plan ahead when I wanted to stop. If I drove too fast my brakes would simply fade away, and when I came to some obstruction in the road the apprehension was so great that I could actually feel my heart shrink within my body. It was like being in a jet fighter all over again.

In 1967 I sold a little house that I had built in Italy to an American opera singer for an absurdly large sum, and my serious car-buying began. I was determined to acquire the best car made, and I set out to try them all. The first test that I insisted on was acceleration. If a car couldn't 'outdrag' the Pontiac, it did not qualify. I would turn up at each grand car showroom, with the GTO parked round the corner, and ask for a drive. If anything even came close to the initial rush of the American car, I would challenge the salesman to a brief test. None of the cars could keep up. The Jaguar, the Porsche 911, the Aston Martin, the Alfa Romeo and the Maserati all faded into dots in the Pontiac's rear-view mirror.

Then I saw the 275 Ferrari GTB4. What a beautiful car! Once again, it was love at first sight. The whole feel was absolutely right, and it ran rings round the Pontiac. I ordered one immediately, and drove down to Maranello in northern Italy to collect it from the factory. There was my car, metallic silver with blue leather upholstery, the most exquisite thing I had ever seen.

'Oh, no, you can't take it now,' the Italians said, looking at me as if I was mad. 'You need to tax it. You need numberplates. You need insurance.'

But this time I was ready for them.

'Do you have relatives in Warwick?' I asked, took a spare set of numberplates out of my briefcase, and fixed them on the car.

'That's not legal!' they howled as I drove off into the dark, with my friend in the Pontiac trying in vain to keep up.

The Ferrari was very fast, but there are faster. I have never liked driving on racetracks, but the idea did come into my mind that if I could put a racing car on the road I would probably go faster than anyone else. In 1972 I spotted an advertisement for a Lola T70 Mark III B which had been built for racing in the USA. The Canada-American series, or 'Can-Am', was a series of races for sports car prototypes of unlimited engine size, and the seven-litre Lolas had done very well, until McLaren had brought out an eight-litre model and swept the board.

The car offered for sale had been built for a Swiss racing driver called Joachim Bonnier, but he had been killed in a crash, driving something else, and his Lola had never been used. It was sitting in the workshop of an eccentric specialist Swiss car builder, who was planning to prepare it for the road. I went out to Switzerland to see it, and I fell in love again.

A few weeks later I flew out to Geneva to drive it back to the UK. There was no problem with numberplates this time – the owner was only too glad to see the car go. His mechanics had got it to start, but they had fitted the wrong belts in the engine, which meant that the cooling fan did not work and the battery would not charge. I had brought my film editor, a very brave man called Michael D. Cummings, as a co-pilot, and we had a seriously bad drive back through France. We went through twelve expensive batteries and goodness knows how many gallons of water, as well as petrol, before we arrived at Calais. There, on the tarmac in front of the hovercraft, the Lola stopped for good. Everyone got in a bit of a panic over this strange immovable apparition, but the captain of the hovercraft put me at ease. 'Mine's broken down too,' he said, indicating the vast bulk of the *Princess Margaret*. 'I'll have you hauled on board while we're waiting.'

'And hauled off too, I'm afraid,' I said, but at least I got the car onto English soil.

It took two years to get the Lola sorted, and the seven-litre engine up to full power. It always ran pretty hot. The paint on that part of the body over the engine – which was in the middle, of course, just behind your back – would blister up into a huge bubble if the car stood still for twenty seconds or more. But its acceleration was not in doubt. Tony Dron, of *Motor Magazine*, and I determined to set a record for the 60 mph dash by a street-legal car (our official time of 3.1 seconds has never been broken). To do this it needed a three-plate metal to metal clutch, racing tyres (the tread on a racing 'rain' tyre looks like a normal street tyre) about eighteen inches across, and about 600 brake horsepower at the rear wheels. None of this is ideal for London traffic, but I managed to bribe a friendly garage into giving me an MOT, and in 1974 I drove the car up to the Motor Institute Research Association in Leicestershire for the trial.

It so happened that there was a petrol crisis at the time, and a 50 mph limit had been imposed on all roads, even motorways. The Lola did 65 mph in first gear, and eighty-five in second. Even in fourth gear (out of five) it would have stalled at fifty. I had to go at a minimum of eighty to get more than five miles to the gallon, and as it was only just after dawn, I decided to forget about the speed limit and press on. I didn't see the police trap until I was in it, and then it was too late to lift my foot from the accelerator. Suddenly I was going under a motorway bridge which was covered with gesticulating policemen and flashing lights. I knew I was in serious trouble, so I didn't touch the brakes. I simply knocked the car out of gear, turned off the engine, and rolled peacefully to a stop about a mile down the road. Sure enough, after a few minutes I saw two police cars giving chase. I hunched down, waiting for the inevitable, but to my intense surprise they just went flashing past. Hardly daring to believe my luck, I waited for a full five minutes, then started the car again and set off, this time at a gentle 70 mph. Many miles later I caught up with the police, and their faces, when they saw me in their rear-view mirror, were a study to behold. They pulled me over at once.

'Oh, you shouldn't stop me,' I said. 'You should have stopped that other fellow. He had a car just like mine, and he shot past me at terrific speed, just before I reached your bridge.'

Even a British bobby could not quite imagine two T70 MK III B Lolas on the same stretch of road at the same time, but they took it in very good heart. They climbed all over the car in genuine admiration, and told me that I had gone through their radar at a speed of 171 mph, a record they thought would be difficult to beat.

After the excitement of the Lola, I began to settle down. I still loved V8 engines, but in more comfortable cars. I had a 1976 8.2 litre Cadillac Eldorado convertible, and you could not get a bigger V8 or more comfort than that. It had front-wheel drive, and would haul round the steep corners of the Hollywood hills at a very impressive rate, but it did use a great deal of petrol – anything over four miles per gallon was considered good.

When I got back to England, the obvious choice was a Rolls-Royce. Since 1964, Rolls-Royces have had Chevrolet engines and General Motors automatic transmissions, and a Rolls is basically just a well-screwed-together American car. They are delightful to drive, slowly, and I have owned five of them at one time or another, including a 1937 Phantom III Sedanca de Ville formerly owned by the Maharajah of Jaipur. But I now think Rolls-Royces are too expensive. I can no longer see the point in driving around in something which costs as much as a nice suburban house.

Nor can I see the point of a supercar either. The last time I wanted to go fast, I bought a second-hand twin-turbo 4 x 4 Ford Sierra for £3500, and it would see off just about anything, especially in the wet. Why pay more? If you want luxury and power, you can buy a Mercedes 450 SEL 6.9 for about £5000 which will go as quickly and quietly and reliably as any car made. And for daily use I have a 3.0 V6 Chrysler Voyager multi-purpose vehicle (MPV) which I bought new in 1990. Despite a total lack of 'service' it has never let me down (I change the oil every three thousand miles, of course). It holds all the luggage my wife thinks is necessary for a holiday abroad, and it can seat up to seven of my son's friends on the trip to school. It has the best possible view from the driver's seat, and yet it is still quite quick if need be.

Anyway, the roads are too crowded now for speed – wouldn't you agree?

XII

LOVE

I SUPPOSE THAT SOME READERS of this book might have got the impression that I went through life forever trying to seduce the next lady who came along. Nothing could be further from the truth. I was simply making my way along life's path, trying to find a mutually loving and rewarding relationship. I always tried to be considerate and attentive. I was very rarely pushy or forceful — indeed, I have often felt that I was not forceful enough.

Several times in my life I have had to point out to a beautiful lady who wanted to stay in my home that, alas, I would not be physically strong enough to sleep alone if she was also in the house. I just could not do it. The first time this happened was in 1959, when I bought my house in Chelsea. I had no idea about conveyancing and all that stuff, but I knew that I had to live somewhere, so when I met a very polite man who wanted to sell his house in Margaretta Terrace, I agreed to buy it. I handed over the money, he handed over the keys, and we parted.

I went round to the house the following day and let myself in. His furniture had not yet been removed, and nor, to my surprise, had his wife. She was a beautiful pale creature with long red hair, and she was sitting in the living room, refusing to move or even to speak. (I eventually learned that they were getting a divorce, and I suppose he had sold me the house in order to get rid of her.)

I tried to explain to her that I must move in that night, and that I didn't think there was enough room for both of us to lead separate lives. There was only one bed, for a start. But she just gazed at me and said nothing. That evening, when I returned from dinner, the living room was empty. I was a little bit disappointed, but when I went upstairs to the bedroom, there she was. We lived together very happily for six weeks. Then one day I came home and she had gone. She had hardly ever spoken, but apart from that, or perhaps because of it, she had been a perfect companion. It never ceases to amaze me how easily ladies can adapt themselves to any situation, once their mind is made up.

I have a tendency to pamper people I am fond of, and this has often led to the lady becoming spoilt. Whenever I have been brave enough to take a firm line, to resolve the situation one way or another, I have had a better, if shorter, relationship.

Penny was a researcher on a documentary film series I was making. She was married, but her husband never seemed to be around. Penny was small and vivacious. Her pert and bouncy bosom was usually concealed by nothing but a shirt. She knew that we all had difficulty keeping our eyes off her figure, and she did not seem to mind at all.

I had my own cottage in the country by this time, and I used to go down there on weekends to work on my scripts. One Friday evening the doorbell rang, and to my great surprise and delight it was Penny.

'You forgot your notes,' she said, 'and as it was a lovely evening, I thought I'd bring them down.'

'Oh, how kind of you, Penny,' I said. 'And how gorgeous to see you, too. Come in and see my hide-out. Have a drink. Stay for dinner.' Full of enthusiasm, Penny came in. Now I was immediately convinced that she had come down to seduce me. She was wearing jeans and one of those little T-shirts that are cut off about two inches below the bust and leave the tummy bare. Across her bosom was written the word 'Piglet'. The whole effect was devastating and had me weak at the knees, but I said nothing, and tried to focus my eyes on something else. Over dinner Penny was great fun, but she didn't really flirt, so it surprised me when she announced that she was going to spend the night.

'Oh, that's wonderful news. I hoped you were going to do that,' I said.

'Not with you,' she said, twinkling. 'I'll spend it down here, on the sofa.'

'No,' I said. 'I'm sorry, you will not. If you want to spend the night at my house, you've got to spend it in my bed, or not at all.'

'But it's too late to drive back to London now, and I'm sleepy.'

'Perhaps you are,' I said sternly, 'but I am simply not strong enough to resist your charms. I would pester you all night, and neither of us would get a wink of sleep. If you won't come to bed – which I'm sure would be simply wonderful for both of us – and you are determined to sleep here, then I will get into my car and drive back to London. I know my limits.'

'But I might get scared.'

'What of? I'd be in London. I think we should go to bed right now.'

'Well, we'll see,' said Penny. She gossiped and laughed and chatted for another hour, and then she took my hand and led me upstairs.

Throughout our affair, Penny never mentioned her husband, although I knew that he did exist, and was somewhere in Essex. When we were parted by a change of film production we ceased to be lovers, but remained the best of friends.

On another occasion, a most beautiful friend of mine simply telephoned and told me that she was coming to live with me for a while.

'But Mary,' I said, 'you know what that means.'

She was well aware that I had adored her for years. 'Of course I know what that means, Colin darling,' she said, and in she moved. I knew that she was rich enough to go and stay at Claridge's if she had wanted to, so I was hardly putting her under any pressure. I was just immensely flattered that she had chosen me to move in with. There was no question that we were in love. We were just two devoted friends, having the most loving possible relationship.

After two months Mary announced that she intended to get married to someone else. Her fiancé, who was abroad, was returning soon, so she must move out of my house and prepare for his arrival. There were no tears, no recriminations, just many thanks for an interlude of joy that caused no one any harm at all. If that isn't rare, I'd like to know what is.

I do not think that, up to the end of my second marriage, I had anything to be ashamed of at all. I could not pretend to have the rectitude of a Trappist monk, but I had not behaved like a South American playboy either. However, when, in 1980, I found myself a bachelor again, I did go a little mad. The male menopause, I suppose. I was still making films in Los Angeles, and I soon acquired three mistresses: one in Oakland, one in San Francisco (perilously close), and one in Los Angeles itself. Pat was American, but Swedish by birth; Ella was from the Philippines; and Olga's parents originally came from the Middle East. Each had incredible appeal, and I spent a glorious but exhausting two years going from one to the other.

Each summer I would return to my house in the mountains of north Portugal for a rest, and when I got there I needed someone to teach me Portuguese. Nadia was indeed a wonderful teacher, although she was only twenty-four. She came from Goa, a former Portuguese colony on the west coast of India, and her skin was as smooth and dark as Guinness. I would lie for hours with my head on her naked tummy, practising my irregular verbs. At last I was out of reach of Pat and Ella and Olga, but not, by any means, alone.

Then, in the spring of 1983, my father died. At the time I was working on a film for the Metropolitan Museum in New York, but I was living in Boston, and I had not bothered to tell my family my address. It was my ex-wife who found me – she knew me better than anyone, of course – and told me that my father was seriously ill. She had already found out the time of the next flight to London, and she kindly agreed to meet me when I arrived. We drove down to Saltwood together, to the considerable surprise of my brother Alan ('Colin is doing a Richard Burton'), but were too late to do anything but attend the funeral.

We went to the flat which my brother always made available to me in the village, and as I was clearly distressed, my ex-wife offered to stay the night, 'So you won't have to be alone.' There followed a scene which I can only compare to that of Laurence Olivier seducing Claire Bloom, as Lady Anne, over her husband's coffin in *Richard III*. We sat on opposite sides of the living room, hardly daring to speak. The pain of our divorce two years earlier was still fresh in our minds, and the tension was almost unbearable. We both began to tremble with anticipation at what might come next. Slowly, inexorably, we inched closer and closer together, until we could have held hands, and yet we did not dare. The room went dark – neither of us could have moved to turn on a light – and then suddenly we were wrapped in each other's arms again, and that is how we spent the night. It was probably the most dramatic night of my life – all the pent-up emotion of ten years of marriage expressed in a single desperate embrace. The old rivalries and bitterness had gone, the recriminations were forgotten and the hang-ups were a thing of the past. We had always enjoyed each other's company, and with no obligations to weigh us down, we could afford to be completely ourselves. If only it had been like that when we had first met, who knows how happy the marriage could have been?

But alas, and ever so sadly, one has to realise that 'you can't go home again'. You can't go backwards. The laws of nature simply don't allow it – even Burton and Taylor had had to admit that. We had changed. We were different people now. The bond that still existed between us was really that of old friends, who had been through some desperate times together and managed to retain their affection. Friends like that can live together, but they should never get married. Being deeply and passionately fond of your partner is not enough. At least not for me. I need to be in love. The marriage vow is meant to be for ever, and there are so many temptations along the way. Only love can keep me on the straight and narrow.

I will admit that I have sometimes been impulsive. Looking back, I can see where I have rushed in when a wiser man would have feared to tread – never mind an angel. Like my father, I have too often been captivated by a pretty face or an inviting glance. Due to my parents' generosity and my modest film career, I have never been short of money. I very much enjoy spoiling the object of my affections. I don't feel that I have the right to make demands on other people, but I am flattered when they make demands on me. On the other hand I can be stubborn, and have often clung to a love affair long after I should have walked away. By the age of fifty, I had often been in love physically; I had been in love emotionally and intellectually; and I had even been in love spiritually. But I felt I had never managed to combine all these forms of love at the same time.

And then I met Helena, and I knew at once, at once, that I had found the person I had been searching for all my life. I could not explain it in a million years – I don't think anyone could ('Sex, fear and death. The three great mysteries,' as my father had said) – so all I could do was to accept it as a fact.

I was at a party in London in the summer of 1983, on one of my rare visits from Los Angeles, when I saw her across – as in the musical *South Pacific* – a crowded room, and my heart nearly leapt out of my chest. I had never been particularly attracted to oriental ladies in the past. Of course there is something irresistible about a little Chinese figure combined with a demure and modest manner, but there were several other similar ladies at the party, and I did not even notice them. There was just something magical about Helena's face, her bearing, her expression, which knocked me sideways. Was it the curve of her cheekbone, or her lip? Was it her gentle, patient eyes? Or was it those freckles? Who had ever heard of a Chinese lady with freckles?

Like the actress Cheryl Ladd, Helena was used to having this effect on men, and she did not particularly welcome it. When I pushed myself forward and gurgled some sort of introduction, the reception I received was cool, to say the least. I was already smitten to the point of desperation, and her coolness soon made me hysterical. That was a mistake. Helena's coolness turned to ice. Who was this old fool, capering around in front of her? Away with him.

Then, suddenly, she seemed to have a change of heart. 'My name is Susan,' she said. 'My number is . . .' I scrabbled for a pen, and wrote it on the palm of my hand. 'Call me tomorrow evening, if you like.' And with a hint of a smile she was gone.

Naturally, I couldn't sleep. I spent the whole night trying, and failing, to conjure up every detail of our meeting, until my mind was spinning like a top.

At 6.30 the next evening, I called.

'Could I speak to Susan?'

'Speaking.'

The voice was more robust than I had remembered, and much more cheerful.

'My name is Colin,' I blurted out. 'Colin Clark.' (It sounded so banal. How I wished I was called the Marquis of Huntingdon!) 'We met at Steve's party last night. You told me that I could call you.'

'Oh, yes,' replied the voice doubtfully. 'Jolly good.'

Pause.

'Well, I thought you might like to have dinner tonight, or something,' I mumbled lamely.

'Jolly good. Where?'

'Say eight o'clock. Where would you like?'

'The New World restaurant, off Gerard Street. Ask for Susie Chan. You'll find me. See you then. Bye bye.'

I almost felt thrilled, but something puzzled me. Why the sudden friendliness? Somehow the voice, and the manner, did not quite fit the images racing through my brain.

The New World restaurant is in London's Chinatown, and it is always packed with Chinese people all speaking at once. I was nervous, but I need not have been. Susie was a cheerful, friendly girl, a little bit goofy, but attractive all the same. There was only one problem – she was not remotely the person I had expected. We had a nice dinner and laughed a lot, but how was I to tell her that?

I asked about all her friends one by one, but none of them seemed to fit. Is she slim? Has she got black hair? These questions always get a yes when you are describing Chinese ladies, but none of them sounded like the one I was thinking of. It didn't seem to bother Susie that she had no idea where she had met me. She hadn't got a boyfriend, and was quite happy to be wined and dined without the embarrassment of a forced romance. But she was my only link with my beloved. (I had already asked Steve, but he just roared with laughter and said 'Forget it,' and hung up.)

So I invited Susie out again the following night, and by then she had clearly been briefed. Luckily, ladies are curious. The mysterious object of my attention couldn't quite bear to hand me on a plate to Susie without finding out a little more about me. (I might have been the Marquis of Huntingdon, for all she knew.) I finally guessed this, and so, instead of asking Susie about her friends, I began to tell her about myself. I was single, I told her. I was wealthy (I exaggerated a bit). I lived in London (a lie). I had no girlfriend (double lie). And so on.

On our third date, as Susie and I were eating our lobster with ginger sauce, I looked up to find my beloved (I didn't even know her name) making her way across the room towards us. She didn't address me, of course, but started chatting to Susie in Cantonese.

I seized my chance. 'Please tell me your name,' I said, jumping to my feet and stretching out my hand with what was meant to be my most charming smile, but probably looked like a leer.

'I'm Helena.' Tiny smile, downcast eyes, very sweet, quiet voice.

'Well, Helena, I've been trying to contact you ever since we met at Steve's party. Please give me your telephone number again.'

She looked at Susie and giggled.

'Oh, all right,' she said, and at last she did. 'But don't call before noon.'

The following morning, a Saturday, I called her. I clearly woke her up, but I didn't care – I was a desperate man.

'I want to see you tonight and tomorrow night and I'm going away on Monday and I want you to come with me,' I said in a rush.

Ice again.

'You haven't asked me what *I* want.'

'Oh. Sorry. Yes. What do you want?'

'I want you to take me to dinner at the New World tonight at eight o'clock.' Click. That was it.

But I was totally elated. Now I knew I would win. I guessed that Susie had not given too bad a report of me. After all, I had been as charming as I possibly knew how, and I had not tried to seduce her on the first night – something that most girls hate, unless they decide to seduce you.

That evening it was Helena's turn to inspect me. She didn't listen to a word I said at dinner, but talked animatedly to Susie when she appeared, by coincidence, and sat at the next table. The following night we went to another restaurant, and the same scene was re-enacted. To the Chinese, these rituals, and how one reacts to them, are far more important than anything one might say. Chinese ladies have learned at their grandmother's knee that men always tell lies anyway. They know how to observe without listening and almost without seeing. This was just as well, as in my besotted condition I probably looked and sounded pretty idiotic. But I was not deterred. I was a man obsessed with a single idea – to make this lovely creature my partner for life.

My sister Colette, with whom I was staying, thought I had gone completely mad.

'A Chinese girl? Whom you don't even know? How old is she? What does she do? What about her family? You've gone potty!'

And Helena agreed with her. No, she would not come to stay in my romantic little palace in Portugal. She was going to Germany, to the christening of her brother's daughter, and would be staying there for a week.

Her upbringing had hardly been typical. Her late father had been a property developer in Hong Kong. He had had five wives, and sixteen children, of whom the four youngest were by Helena's mother – one daughter and three sons. The wives had all over-lapped, so half-brothers and half-sisters were often the same age. The girls were considered of no importance compared to the boys, and affection had been in short supply. In all her childhood, I later learned, Helena had never been hugged or kissed by either parent, and was hardly ever given a present or a toy. All of the children had been sent to England for part of their education (Helena was at Baston Independent School for Girls in Kent), and had acquired British passports.

For the moment, it was just as well that Helena could not come to Portugal. I had already invited two other lady friends, at separate times, and they would have been extremely hard to cancel, but I did make Helena promise that she would let me call her again when I got back. Just as we were saying goodbye she asked for my telephone number in Portugal, which she wrote down on a cigarette packet with her fingernail.

Thus encouraged, I went off the next day in high good spirits, and, I must admit, had a wonderful holiday in the sun. In the middle of it the telephone rang. It was Helena. She was in Heilbronn, in Germany, and was thoroughly bored. Fond though she was of her brother, she found his wife's relatives fantastically dull.

'I'm in love with you!' I bellowed down the phone.

The line between West Germany and Northern Portugal was predictably bad, and my declaration got no reaction at all.

'How can I prove it?' I yelled.

Helena suddenly got practical. 'I want a doll in Portuguese national costume. An embroidered jewellery box. A gold Rolex watch. Some fresh *marrons glacés* [I was driving back via Paris]. And a blue Dior vanity case for my mother.' Click.

These Chinese girls come straight to the point, I thought. The worst thing was that I knew she really wouldn't care much if I didn't get the things and she never saw me again. It was becoming like a fairy tale, in which the princess gives the prince some impossible tasks to complete before he can return to the castle. But what the heck? I was single. I had some money (just as well – have you any idea of the price of a gold Rolex?). And I was in love.

On the trip back to London, I made a detour. I am not a Catholic, but, on an impulse, I went to Lourdes.

Lourdes is the most incredible place you can imagine. After driving for hours in the direction of nowhere, you arrive in a hideous small French town, full of souvenir sellers and little hotels. You park, with great difficulty – they clamp cars there quicker than anywhere I know – and then you walk down to some huge gates leading into the shrine. Once inside, the cars and the souvenir shops vanish. You are in a huge garden, with six churches and as many chapels, and there are so many people there that you can hardly move – at least ten thousand. They are all organised into groups (thank goodness), and they walk purposefully around, carrying the sick, attending different masses and collecting holy water, for the most part in total silence. You just can't imagine how they all got there. They are not inspired by tourism or, like me, by curiosity. They are inspired by pure faith. It is very, very impressive.

I felt like a visitor from another planet. No one took the slightest notice of me. (Why should they?) They didn't even seem to see me. They were all there to ask the Almighty for help for one reason or another, mainly for loved ones who were ill, so I determined to ask for some advice for myself. I walked into the largest of the churches, and knelt down. There was only one thing I wanted to know.

'Should I marry Helena?'

'Yes.' The answer came back before I'd finished the question.

'I know nothing about her,' I went on. 'Let's say for the sake of argument that she's had an affair with that man over there, slept with both those men over there, is still secretly in love with that man over there and always will be. I mean, I know absolutely nothing about her. Should I marry her?'

'Yes.'

Well, you can't go to higher authority than that. I went back to my car, drove to Paris, bought the Rolex and the *marrons glacés* and returned to London. My mind was made up.

As soon as I got back to London, I rang Helena and asked her to come down to my flat in Saltwood village for the weekend. Quite frankly, I had done a lot of work (and spent a lot of money), and it now seemed time to get the object of all this passion into bed. (Here we go again.)

She would come, she said, on one condition. She must have her own bedroom, with a lock on the door, and the key on the inside. There were two bedrooms in the flat, but that didn't quite fit in with my plan. Nevertheless I agreed, and after I had presented all my trophies from Paris, we drove down to Kent.

Alan had lent me the flat because he doesn't like to have anyone except his wife and two sons staying the night at Saltwood. Even though it has fourteen bedrooms, he has been determined to keep the castle as private as possible ever since our father gave it to him in 1970. He even used to encourage his dogs to chase Lord Clark when the old man pottered over to get a book from the library. But Alan enjoyed going for a long walk with me on a Sunday morning, so he gave me somewhere to stay nearby. I had done my best to make the place comfortable and pretty, but I suppose I had created what Helena could see was a bit of a bachelor pad. As soon as we arrived, she retreated to her room and locked the door.

Now what?

Helena had a fresh set of demands. I must sit down and write a letter to every single one of my lady friends, past and present, telling them that I never wanted to see them again in my life. Then I must destroy all records of them: photos, letters, souvenirs – everything.

'What?!? When?'

'Now.'

Yes, now, or she was going straight back to London. I felt like a character in a Verdi opera. I tried roaring and shouting. I would even have sung an aria if I could have, but the door stayed locked.

And what if I wrote the letters?

If I wrote the letters to her satisfaction – she would read each one – I must put them in envelopes and stamp them, and post them in a letterbox in front of her eyes. Then she would stay with me. It was all or nothing.

I wrote the letters, five of them, and pushed them under the door for her to read. Then I went out and posted them in the village street, in full view of Helena's window. I hate to cause distress, and I'm not at all good at saying no. Writing those letters was extremely painful, and I was rather grim as I mounted the stairs again.

Now the bedroom door was unlocked, and Helena was delightful. She was flirtatious, but still demure. She laughed and held my hand, and was interested in everything. Suddenly she didn't seem to have a care in the world. And I felt marvellous. I realised that she had been quite right. All that dead wood, all those old skeletons (sweet, lovely and loving though they had been) had been despatched for ever, and I was free to start all over again with a clear conscience.

We spent a rapturous weekend together. To my great relief Helena, who looked twenty-five, turned out to be thirty-three. She ran our relationship completely at her own speed, and this too was a great luxury to an umming and aahing fool like me who had never quite learned how quickly or slowly he should go.

Once, when I got gruff, Helena just walked up very close to me and sat down. I was standing in the middle of her living room at the time, and I had to catch her to prevent her from falling. Now, who can be cross when they are standing with an adorable little Chinese person sitting quietly in their arms? Do oriental ladies have to learn this incredible skill of man-management, or does it just come naturally? I didn't care. I was supremely happy, and I knew that I had made the right decision. When, after a few weeks, I mentioned marriage – good God, how risky, I know, but You did keep saying 'yes' at Lourdes – Helena simply said that if we weren't married by the following April (it was then September), she would leave. No recriminations, no tears, just a clean break.

We were married in London on 3 April 1984, with Steve as the chief witness, and we have been blissfully happy ever since. I have never looked at another woman. On the contrary, I can gaze at Helena all day long, and still feel the joy of the first time we met. After a long and, for the most part, enjoyable search, I have found someone whom I can love completely. And as for sex, I can only say that when your heart and your mind and your soul are involved, as well as your body, sex moves onto a different plane altogether. Gone is all that grubby doubt and guilt. The awkwardness, the lack of confidence, the anxiety, the hang-ups all become irrelevant, and a thing of the past.

But let no one think that Helena is merely my handmaiden, a geisha keeping an old man happy with her tricks. What she has is the great gift, the essential gift of all successful wives, of being able to make a man feel strong without herself having to appear weak. Underneath her demure exterior, Helena is as strong as steel. She is a wonderful wife. She is the mother of our beautiful ten-year-old son. She has been my constant companion in good times and in bad. She is my best friend, and my partner for life. Once any human being has found that, everything else drops into place. No wonder we spend such a lot of time searching for it.

Epilogue

MY FATHER AND MY BROTHER were both older and cleverer than I. That was inescapable, and I could do nothing about it. What I did not like was to be told continually, even by my loving mother, that I must never contemplate being on the same level as them. To try to do so would somehow be futile, and against the natural order of life. So I must suppress my ego accordingly. If your father and brother achieve fame, my family said, it is because they naturally deserve it. If you get any attention at all, it is because you have been 'showing off'. Even if you find yourself in quicksand, you must never struggle. You will only make things worse and embarrass us all, and that would be in very bad taste. 'Oh dear! Colin is waving his arms around again. Don't whatever you do catch his eye. Why didn't he stay in California, where he belongs?'

This is the genuine cry of a younger brother, younger son, but what a lot of joy goes with it. The joy of not being expected to succeed makes any success seem doubly sweet. The joy of being able to observe, yourself unobserved, is a much underrated pleasure. There is a joy, too, in loving someone with all your heart and not expecting to be loved in return; and there is the supreme joy of going through life with no preconceived idea of how you should behave, of being able to question each convention as it comes along and decide for yourself whether to follow it or not.

More than anything else, a younger brother, younger son can be free.

Index

233